FERRIES ACROSS
THE HUMBER

This book is dedicated to all who worked on the Humber ferries.

On the bridge of *Wingfield Castle* in 1973. *Will Green (author's collection)*

FERRIES ACROSS THE HUMBER

*The Story of the Humber Ferries and
the Last Coal-Burning Paddle Steamers
in Regular Service in Britain*

Kirk Martin

PEN & SWORD
TRANSPORT

First published in Great Britain in 2014 by
Pen & Sword Transport
An imprint of
Pen & Sword Books Ltd
47 Church Street
Barnsley
South Yorkshire
S70 2AS

ISBN 978 1 78383 102 9

Typeset in 10pt Minion by Mac Style, Driffield, East Yorkshire
Printed and bound in India by Replika Press Pvt Ltd

Pen & Sword Books Ltd incorporates the imprints of Pen & Sword Archaeology, Atlas, Aviation,
Battleground, Discovery, Family History, History, Maritime, Military, Naval, Politics, Railways, Select,
Transport, True Crime, and Fiction, Frontline Books, Leo Cooper, Praetorian Press, Seaforth Publishing
and Wharncliffe.

For a complete list of Pen & Sword titles please contact
PEN & SWORD BOOKS LIMITED
47 Church Street, Barnsley, South Yorkshire, S70 2AS, England
E-mail: enquiries@pen-and-sword.co.uk
Website: www.pen-and-sword.co.uk

CONTENTS

An aerial view of New Holland showing the pier, dock and railway sidings. Across the Humber Estuary is the north, or Yorkshire, riverbank and Hull is to the right. Cars followed the road towards the pier, crossed the railway via a level crossing and used the left hand side of the pier to access the ferries. New Holland engine shed formerly stood alongside the triangle of railways south of New Holland Town station. *Brian Peeps collection*

ACKNOWLEDGMENTS

My warm thanks go to both Alf Ludlam, author of many articles and books on the railways of Lincolnshire, as well as a history of the railways of New Holland and the Humber ferries, and to Rodney Clapson, local historian of Barton-on-Humber, for their help with the ferry services and transport links in northeast Lincolnshire. I am grateful also to Maria McKenzie and Louise ffoulkes for reading my initial draft and making helpful suggestions; to Mike Mercer of Arts Magic Ltd for use of the DVD *Monarchs of the Humber,* created by Robin Walters and narrated by Rob Haywood; to Jamie Macaskill and Jim Mitchell of Mail News Media, for permission to use newspaper articles and arranging the use of photographs; and to my editor Helena Wojtczak for contributing an item on the life of John Ellerthorpe and for supplying many additional press cuttings. Thanks to Debbie Hall of Mail News Media, Phil Wright of Radio Humberside and Phil Haskins of Hull Civic Society for help in finding people with memories of the ferries. Myra Allen of the Paddle Steamer Preservation Society and *Steam Railway* magazine have also given valuable support.

I would like to thank the following people for providing photographs and other material, and for sharing their memories and knowledge: Grant Anderson, Martyn Ashworth, Tom Baxter, John Beasley, Chris Braithwaite, Sandie Braithwaite, Malcolm Brown, Dave Carrick, Beryl Chamberlain, Jack Close, Andy D'Agorne, Francis Daly, Janice Edmonds, Dave Enefer, owner of the website www.davesrailpics.co.uk, Michael Free, Ted Gaytor, Chris Hannard, Alan Harrod, Peter Hough, Ashley Howard, Dave Hunter, Henry Irving, Polly Irving, Ken Knox, John Leeman, Maurice Mawer, Tim Mickleburgh, John Miller, Dave Parry, Kathleen Parry, Brian Peeps, Geoff Plumb, Val Richardson, Jean Robertson, Ray Sargeson, Joan Savage, Stephen Sharpe, Jean-Philippe Stienne, Angie Stephenson, Gordon Stewart, Paul Thomas, Bertram Thorpe, Andrew Waddingham, Susan Watkin, Pat Watts, Kenny White, John Whitehead and Peter Wilde, owner of www.humberpacketboats.co.uk website.

This book could not have been written without the help of the staff at the following institutions, too numerous to name individually, who facilitated access to archive material, books, newspapers and journals: British Library, St Pancras; British Library Newspapers, Colindale; the *Dalesman;* East Riding Archives and Local Studies Service, Beverley; Ferens Art Gallery, Hull; Grimsby Reference Library; *Grimsby Telegraph;* Hartlepool Central Library; Hartlepool Maritime Experience; *Hull Daily Mail;* Hull History Centre; Hull Maritime Museum; Lloyd's Register Library; Mitchell Library, Glasgow; National Archives, Kew; National Maritime Museum, Greenwich (Caird Library); the Search Engine at the National Railway Museum, York; North East Lincolnshire Archives and Records Office, Grimsby; Passenger Focus (formerly Transport Users' Consultative Committee); Stena Line (UK); University of Glasgow Archives; the *Yorkshire Post* and the Waterways Museum, Goole.

An aerial view of Hull with *Lincoln Castle* tied up at Corporation Pier before the demolition of the upper promenade deck in 1965. Note shipping in Humber and Prince's Docks, the crane on Minerva Pier and the Marine Café on Corporation Pier. Paragon station is to the left in the distance and the mouth of the River Hull is on the right. *Grimsby Telegraph*

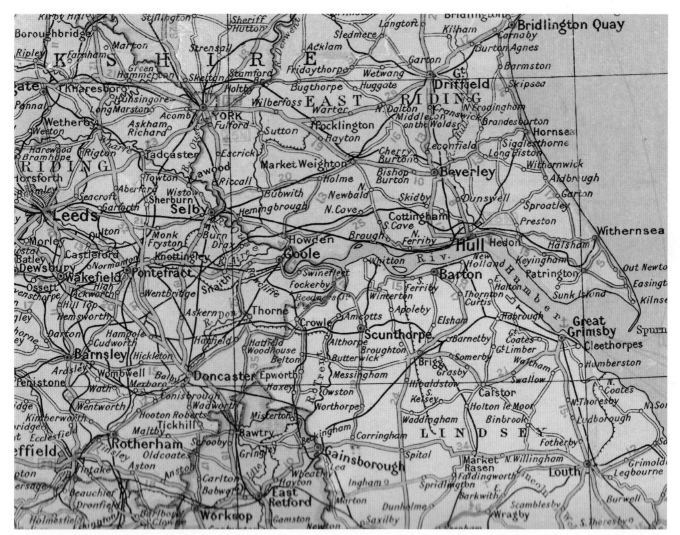

The Humber, shown on a pre-First World War map of Britain. The new docks at Immingham opened at this time and were situated to the north of Grimsby although not yet named on this map. *Author's collection*

The author and *Lincoln Castle* in 1976. *Katharine ffoulkes*

Chapter One

RARE SURVIVORS ON THE HUMBER

Arriving at Hull University in the autumn of 1972, it wasn't long before I started to explore the area of the city beyond Paragon station and the main shopping centre. I came across the town centre docks which, as paintings in the Ferens Art Gallery made clear, had once thronged with shipping. The oldest, dating from 1778, and simply called 'the Dock' before being renamed Queen's Dock in honour of a visit in 1854 by Queen Victoria and Prince Albert, was now filled in and laid out as Queen's Gardens. However, the other three – Humber Dock of 1809, Prince's Dock of 1829 (originally called Junction Dock and also renamed at the time of the royal visit) and Railway Dock of 1846 – were all still in water and surrounded by old warehouses, although there were no longer any ships moored alongside them.

Beyond these docks, which followed the line of the ancient town walls, was the Old Town itself, the medieval heart of the city, bounded to the east by the River Hull and the south by the Humber Estuary. At that time Humber keels and barges still moored alongside the wharves and eighteenth-century warehouses lining the River Hull, as they had done for hundreds of years, although modern ships by then used the larger docks out along the estuary – the Victoria Dock of 1850 (which had recently closed), the Alexandra Dock of 1885, the King George Dock of 1914 and the Queen Elizabeth Dock of 1969. The docks to the west – Albert Dock of 1869, William Wright Dock of 1873 and St Andrew's Dock of 1883 – were, by the early 1970s, largely associated with Hull's fishing industry.

Humber barges, tugs and keels on a busy day on the River Hull, looking south towards the Humber. *Kirk Martin*

Eighteenth century warehouses seen across the River Hull. *Kirk Martin*

Walking through the narrow streets of the Old Town – with their unusual names like Land of Green Ginger and Sewer Lane – I came to Corporation Pier, jutting out into the muddy water of the Humber Estuary. In those days trawlers still passed by on their way to and from the Icelandic fishing grounds. The coast of Lincolnshire appeared as a flat and distant shore, with few prominent features. Close by the pier was the Minerva, which had, and still has, fine views out to the Humber and also what must be the smallest snug in any pub in Britain.

It was at Corporation Pier that I discovered that the cream-coloured telephone boxes of Hull's independent telephone network were not the only unusual thing about this city. Looking out across the estuary – which is some two miles wide at this point – I could see the unmistakable shapes of two paddle steamers passing each other in mid-stream. One had a long plume of smoke trailing across the water and was approaching me; the other, with a faint haze of smoke above her funnel, was heading away towards the distant pier at New Holland, some three miles away, upriver to my right. Slowly, the details of the approaching ferry became clearer, with the paddles thrashing up the water and leaving a double wake astern.

The paddle steamer turned towards the pier and men came out onto the sponsons to take up the coiled ropes. People called out and there was conversation and laughter. I could see cars on the rear deck as people emerged from passageways and looked towards the pier. With much ringing of bells and churning of water, the steamer swung towards the pontoon.

The captain was leaning over the edge of the bridge and there was a heavy but subdued bump as she came alongside. Ropes were thrown by deck hands and bells rang out. Paddles churned, she moved backwards and then forwards and the ropes tightened. Finally she was secure and her doors were swung back, a ramp dropped down onto the aft deck and people and cars began to leave the ferry and make their way up the sloping bridge from the pontoon.

I had come across the last regular ferry service in Britain still being worked by coal-burning paddle steamers. At that time, there were three: the *Lincoln Castle* and the *Wingfield Castle,* which were operating the ferry service, and the *Tattershall Castle,* which was moored at New Holland Pier, having recently been withdrawn.

Buying a ticket for the ferry at the booking office – which was really a railway station without any platforms or trains – was to go back in time. Walking down the ramp, stepping on board and crossing the car deck, I entered one of the side passageways that led past the engine room, where the triple-expansion steam engine was fully open to view, and then on past a small door, where I had a glimpse of a stokehold with a pile of coal in front of a boiler, and into the buffet, in which passengers could buy a cup of tea or a bottle of beer and a cheese roll.

Soon the ferry was underway, with much heaving and swaying as she turned out into the tide. I discovered that the motion of a paddle steamer feels very different from that of

The author's first sight of *Lincoln Castle* as she passes the entrance to Humber Dock, Hull in 1972. *Kirk Martin*

a propeller-driven ship: more determined, urged on as she is by two large paddle wheels whose floats dig purposefully into the water to impel her forward. Having enjoyed a drink in the buffet, watched the fireman in the stokehold, and lingered by the engine room to witness the mesmeric rising and falling of the connecting rods as they turned the heavy shaft linking the two paddles, and noticing the engineer, in white overalls, deep in conversation with another man who was holding an oil can, I ventured up to the deck to be buffeted by the breeze that always seems to blow across this wide estuary.

Away from the warmth of the passageways below, I watched Hull and its Corporation Pier receding and leaned on the well-varnished wooden hand rail, which vibrated to the rhythmic pounding of the paddles. A faint haze of smoke trailed behind us and, in the distance, and some way upstream, the long pier at New Holland could be seen. The other steamer was approaching. Soon it was close enough to give a clear view of its paddles and the passengers leaning, like me, on its hand rail. There were also groups of people standing on the car deck; they seemed more concerned to reach their destination than to savour the atmosphere of travelling on a coal-burning paddle steamer. And why shouldn't they? Paddle steamers had been working on the Humber for generations and were a familiar sight to the regular commuters.

When not attending lectures at Hull University, I became a regular passenger on the ferries, taking photographs and even creating a cine film of both steamers in action. Making

frequent crossings, I became friendly with the deck hands on both the *Lincoln Castle* and *Wingfield Castle* and soon got to know the engine room crew and, in particular, the firemen, one of whom invited me to join him in the stokehold after I told him I had fired steam engines on the railways. Firing the *Wingfield Castle* took some getting used to because, although the centre of the three fires was at a similar height to that on a locomotive, the two outside, or wing, fires were at face height and it took special skill to lift a full shovel up that high and send the coal hurtling over the fire to reach the back of the long, barrel-shaped firebox. I got to know John very well and had several trips with him on the *Wingfield Castle*, even writing a short story about him in *Green Ginger*, the university literary magazine.

Throughout 1973 I was also taking trips with fellow students and at New Holland we would walk up the slope from the pontoon to the railway station situated on the end of the long pier. Here there would be several sixteen-ton wagons standing in a siding, loaded with coal for the steamers, and a diesel multiple unit train in the platform waiting for passengers coming off the ferry. We usually opted to walk the length of the pier for a pint or two in the Yarborough Arms before returning to the ferry for the trip back to Hull.

My girlfriend Katharine and I joined one of the popular 'Riverboat Shuffle' jazz cruises, organised for university students. The *Lincoln Castle* ran east down the Humber for several miles towards Spurn Head and later, when returning up the Humber at dusk with a jazz band in full swing on the rear deck, we were watched with bemusement by some sailors on a Russian merchant ship. This was the height of the Cold War – was this, they may have been wondering, the decadent West they had been warned about?

At the end of my second university year, in June 1974, I needed a summer job and went to see Mr Wise, the ferry manager, in his office opposite Corporation Pier. Explaining that I had fired steam engines on the railway, I asked if they needed a fireman for the summer. I was sent over on a trial run and, grateful for my unofficial sessions in the stokehold of the *Wingfield Castle* with John, I was offered a job as a temporary fireman on the *Lincoln Castle*, starting the next day, covering for firemen taking their summer leave.

I began on the early shift at 06.15 and worked on the *Lincoln Castle* for twenty-seven consecutive days of early and late turns, having my first day off in late July, and working the rest of the summer. I was glad of the extra money, and it was also good to be back in manual work, which made a real change from the academic life I was leading. On the last trip of the day I would stand on the deck watching New Holland Pier recede and the long trail of smoke rolling back behind us above our double wake. Then it was time to hand over to the night man and get on my bike to make it to our local pub for a drink. I was so hot and thirsty that the first pint turned to steam half way down, but I really enjoyed the second one.

By this time *Wingfield Castle* had been taken out of service and the diesel-electric paddle vessel *Farringford*, which had been brought up from the Isle of Wight as a replacement, was operating the ferry alongside *Lincoln Castle*. Usually, *Lincoln Castle* was based on the Hull side but occasionally she would be switched onto the New Holland side and I had to cross over on *Farringford* to reach her. As she ploughed through the water her progress felt very different from that of the paddle steamers – rather like travelling on a bus with a dislocated axle. At New Holland I was glad to leave her cold deck for the warmth of the *Lincoln*'s boiler room.

What was a day stoking a coal-burner like? Cycling down the ramp just before six in the morning I would clamber down the steps under the engine, dump my bag on a small table where we kept our tea things and duck under the edge of the boiler to enter the stokehold. Unlike *Wingfield Castle* with her three fire boxes, *Lincoln Castle* had four, two central ones a couple of feet above the floor and two 'wing fires' at about face height. I would find that two fires had usually been cleaned by the fireman on the night shift, leaving the other two to be cleaned by the morning and afternoon men respectively. The stokehold was relatively peaceful after the wheezing and moaning of the pumps and the sound of the slowly turning crankshaft in the engine room. With luck, the nightshift fireman would have left me a long pile of coal shovelled out from the bunkers and laid opposite the fires; this was known as 'trimming' the coal.

If there was time before the first crossing, I would get started on the fire that had been burnt down for me by the night man. The fireboxes were long and barrel-shaped and

Wingfield Castle at Hull Corporation Pier, ready to depart for New Holland. **Geoff Plumb**

were divided in the centre by the grate. Above the grate, with its cast-iron fire bars, was the fire itself, with a heavy, hinged fire door, and below was the ashpan with lighter double doors that acted as dampers. Cleaning a fire involved using heavy fire-irons, first to shift the burning coal down the box and then break the clinker at the near end, dragging it out to fall at my feet on the metal stokehold floor. I could then tackle the clinker at the far end of the firebox by pushing the live fire over to one side and breaking and dragging the clinker back. Dousing the pile of red hot clinker with buckets of water filled the stokehold with swirling ash and steam.

My next task was to spread the live fire over the grate and build it up with fresh coal, which was known as 'pitching'. I could then see a healthy glow in the ashpan, which had formerly been quite dark, through the now-clear fire-bars. I would then pitch the other three fires and, with all the fire doors shut and ashpan doors open, the steam pressure would start to come round towards the 200lbs per square inch mark. With luck I got all this done before the bells rang out from the engine room telegraph, which told me that the ferry was about to depart on the first crossing. Once underway the fires might need a bit more pitching, especially if we had to go the long way around because of low tides and sandbanks. About half

A two-car diesel multiple unit newly arrived at New Holland Pier station in the summer of 1973 with a tail lamp on and 'New Holland' destination on the blind. *Kirk Martin*

way over I would 'box-up' the ashpans by closing the doors, to bring the steam pressure back for the lay-over at New Holland.

On the way over I would also duck inside the bunkers and trim a good pile of coal until I had a long heap lying opposite the fires. At New Holland the deck hands would bring four-wheeled barrows down the side passageways and, winching them up by one end, tipped fresh coal into the bunkers through fillers in the middle of the floor, which were covered with a heavy, cast-iron lid. One of the empty coal barrows was left in the gangway above the stokehold door and, on the way to Hull, we would find time to lift the ash and clinker by using a bucket on a rope, me filling the old battered bucket and the leading fireman hauling it up and tipping it into the barrow. The routine during twenty-minute crossings was to pitch the fires heavily at New Holland and lightly at Hull, where the laws concerning the emission of smoke meant British Rail could be fined if we produced too much.

On one occasion Katharine joined me in the stokehold and offered to fire one round trip. It was not easy for her to swing the loaded shovel up to reach the wing fires, which were above the level of her face, and then hurl the coal down the length of the firebox, but she kept the steam level up sufficiently to complete both crossings. She seemed glad to hand the shovel back to me afterwards, though. I often wonder if she was the only woman to fire a Humber ferry.

Not all crossings were routine, twenty-minute ones. As the tide receded we started making the longer crossings necessary to avoid the sandbanks. This could take up to forty minutes, and meant a journey downstream to 'Dead Bod'. I wondered about these trips known as 'Dead Bods', until one day I was up on deck and a crewman pointed out some graffiti on a riverside warehouse. It was a picture of an upside down bird with an arrow through its head!

Coal wagons stand on the central siding at New Holland Pier with several four-wheeled barrows alongside. The barrows were used to transfer the coal to the ferries. The sign warns: 'All vehicles turn right'. *Kirk Martin*

With the tide turning, the captain might take a chance of the shorter crossing and save twenty minutes on the detour downstream. On more than one occasion there was a sudden jolt, all the ashpan doors flew open and there was a strange feeling of solidity – we were aground on a sandbank. I once went up on deck during such an incident and saw the paddles churning slowly. Soon we were underway again, with a deck hand on the sponson dropping a marked pole into the water and calling out the depth to the skipper up on the bridge.

It was fascinating to hear the other firemen, engineers and deck hands tell stories of their years on the ferries. Many of them could remember the paddle steamers used before the three 'Castles' arrived: the *Killingholme* and *Brocklesby* and even the older *Cleethorpes*. Others recalled taking livestock across and told me of a bullock that careered off towards the buffet and of a pig that managed to clamber into the engine room. My own experience of animals on the ferry was limited to a horse and cart which came over on one early morning crossing and one occasion when we carried a lot of tiny chicks in boxes. Some had escaped and I regretted helping to catch them when I realised they were probably destined for a factory farm.

I was occasionally booked to fire on a river cruise down to Grimsby or up to Goole. Passengers sometimes liked to help out: I even had a vicar down in the stokehold on one trip, perhaps dreaming up a sermon on the fires below as he stoked the fires on a paddle steamer. Once we had a one-way booking by the Midland and Great Northern Railway Society, from New Holland to Grimsby, where our passengers left us. We returned empty, making fast progress on the run back to Hull. The stokehold became hot in the fierce glare of the fires and the hand rails were almost too hot to touch as I climbed up on deck for some fresh air, my face smutted with coal dust. It reminded me of the older firemen telling me of their time firing large ships in the merchant navy, with sealed stokeholds and forced draughts, where the hand rails were too hot to hold without rags in their hands.

The cruises could end up late at night at New Holland and we were expected to lodge on board, sleeping where we could, for a bit extra in our pay-packets. However, one night I was taken off mid-stream by a pilot boat that had been sent out from Hull, as there was sufficient steam to get her to New Holland and a night man would be on board. Stepping onto the pilot boat over the black choppy water, the two boats rising and falling against each other a mile out from the shore, was an experience I shall never forget. One slip and I might not have been here to recall the experience.

I was once booked to fire on a cruise from Hull upriver to Goole, when *Lincoln Castle* was berthed overnight at New Holland. I crossed over on *Farringford* and boarded *Lincoln Castle* to discover three dead fires and only one showing any signs of life. George Coupland and Harry Holmes, the maintenance men at New Holland, told me they needed steam to turn the engines over. The pressure gauge, which had a red line for a working pressure of 200lbs per square inch, showed a sleepy 50lbs. I carefully added coal to the one live fire that was fighting a losing battle with the draught down the firebox. I then tackled the other three fires by literally emptying the boxes and filling them with fresh coal, in front of which I transferred some of the fire from the one good box so that flames were soon darting down the fireboxes. George helped me get the ashes up into the spare coal barrow. By ten o'clock we had sufficient steam for the engines to be turned over. Things were looking up as my leading fireman and the engineer finished their preparation and the deck hands made ready for departure. We moved down to the pontoon to get rid of the ash barrow and then set off across the Humber to Hull, where we were to pick up our passengers. Just then the engineer beckoned to me. 'Don't put too much on, and box them up quite early, I'm not going to push her hard on this trip'. I followed his advice and we were soon heading upstream, but with the tide, towards Goole. I was able to divide my time between pitching the fires and getting some fresh air up on deck. The Humber was changing from the wide estuary I was used to, to the much narrower River Ouse. I could clearly see the cattle in the fields on either side. Eventually, with the aid of the river pilot, we docked at Goole. While the passengers

The diesel multiple unit sets off down the pier towards New Holland Town and Grimsby while *Wingfield Castle* prepares to leave New Holland Pier with thick smoke drifting back from her funnel. *Tattershall Castle* is on the left. *Kirk Martin*

Tattershall Castle after withdrawal in 1972, moored on the west arm of New Holland Pier while a DMU crosses to the platform line. *Geoff Plumb*

Wingfield Castle alongside New Holland Pier, ready for departure. The smoke indicates that the fireman has started to build up the fires. *Kirk Martin*

Bringing the coal onto *Lincoln Castle* at New Holland in one of the four-wheeled barrows. Others are still on the pontoon, having been hauled by tractor. The barrows would then be wheeled by hand down the alleyways either side of the engine room to the bunker-filling holes, where they would be winched up using a pulley and chain which were attached with a shackle to the ceiling. *Kirk Martin*

explored the town, we 'mashed' our tea and ate our 'snap' on the rear deck in the sunshine.

As soon as the passengers began to return, I went down to the stokehold and started building up the fires. Opening the ashpan doors I heard the bells ringing out and felt the floor sway as we turned out into the tide. Before long, two men ducked under the boiler. They were wearing overalls and looked so much part of the crew I merely nodded to them, expecting them to start mending something. But they just looked at the shovel and I realised they were volunteers, keen to have a go.

'The engineer says it's OK by him if it's all right by you', one of them said, indicating the fires that I had just boxed up. I handed them a shovel each.

'Have you fired before?' I asked.

'We fired all the way to Goole last year', he replied.

'I'll just get some air, then', I said, and climbed the ladder, glad of the chance to lean on the hand rail and watch the world go by. They did a good job, but I was back in the stokehold for the crossing to New Holland and then it was back to Hull on the *Farringford*.

In September I returned to my tutorials and lectures and sessions in the library, knowing that firemen Joe Davies, Terry Hopper and Tom Marrison, deck hands Chris Braithwaite, Les Claxton and Alan Harrod, engineers Pete Moore, Jock Brown and Arthur Mount, captains Wright, Bolderson and Harvey, the mates, the buffet staff and all those in the office and on shore, would be doing what generations had done – keeping the service going all the year round.

In early January 1975, Katharine and I were sitting in the Marine Café on Corporation Pier when the chief clerk came over and asked if I was free that day and the next. He offered me two afternoon turns on *Lincoln Castle*, with George Hambley as leading fireman. When the university broke up for the summer, I was back on the ferry full time. It was good to be back in the stokehold again. My first trip was with Harry Baker as leading fireman, one of those who remembered the earlier paddle steamers in use before the Second World War. Most of the older firemen had worked at sea on coal burners during the war and could tell stories of frightful experiences, especially on Russian convoys. For those three summers I was witnessing a way of life and a part of our history that was sadly nearing its final chapter.

About this time I became involved in the Humber Paddle Steamer Group, which had been formed in 1973 with the aim of saving a paddle steamer for the Humber, the obvious candidate being *Lincoln Castle*. In April 1975 I wrote a short article called 'All Day and Every Day' for the HPSG magazine *Humber Packet*, describing a day firing the ferry. I also had articles published in *Ships Monthly* ('Stoking the Lincoln Castle', June 1975) and *Railway World* ('B.R. Firemen 1975', December 1975) which hopefully inspired some people to take a trip on *Lincoln Castle,* now that she was the last coal-burning paddle steamer in regular service in Britain.

The year 1976 was my last at university. Within four days of my final exams in early June I was back on the ferries. After three early turns, on Saturday 19th June I was booked

The classic lines of the fore end of *Wingfield Castle* alongside New Holland Pier, just prior to departure. *Kirk Martin*

on for a maintenance day. I crossed over to New Holland on *Farringford* and spent time inside the fire boxes with fellow fireman 'Ozzie' Osman, cleaning them out and removing all the fire bars ready for inspection. Terry Hopper relieved me in the afternoon and told me that, following a conversation we had had the year before, he was taking some GCE courses.

They were short-handed in the buffet on *Farringford,* so I worked there for a couple of days, then returned to the stokehold on the *Lincoln Castle*. On Friday 2nd July I was booked on a cruise that finished up at New Holland at 1.50am

and slept in the third class saloon below the aft deck, waking at six on the Saturday morning very grubby indeed. There was just time to go home and have a wash before booking on at 1pm for an afternoon shift. On Sunday 4th I worked with Terry Hopper as leading fireman on a cruise for the Railway Correspondence and Travel Society, followed by two regular crossings between New Holland and Hull.

I left the Humber ferries in July as Katharine and I were going on a long camping trip to the USA and Martyn Ashworth, who had already approached the ferry manager about a summer job,

Wingfield Castle seen from the deck of *Lincoln Castle* on a crossing from Hull to New Holland in 1973. New Holland Pier can be seen on the left. *Kirk Martin*

'Stoker John' pitches one of the two 'wing' fires on *Wingfield Castle* in 1973. The notice on the wall instructs stokers to build fires at New Holland and pitch them lightly at Hull. The starboard bunker is behind the fireman. On *Lincoln Castle*, with the fireman facing the stern, this would be the port bunker. *Kirk Martin*

Wingfield Castle on the Humber with Hull Docks in the background. *Geoff Plumb*

The author in the stokehold of *Lincoln Castle*, firing a cruise to Grimsby. *Kirk Martin*

One of the two lower central fireboxes on *Lincoln Castle* with the heavy fire door open and also the two ash pan doors open. *Kirk Martin*

was taken on in my place. Martyn was to stay with *Lincoln Castle* full time from 1976 to 1977, thus working through the winter and gaining experience in the engine room as leading fireman on several occasions. (He tells his story in Chapter Eight.)

We returned to Hull in September 1977 because I was taking a post-graduate university course, and I became once again involved in the campaign to save *Lincoln Castle*. As I shall explain later, the Humber Paddle Steamer Group had been wound up at the end of 1976 and a new group, the Save the PS Lincoln Castle Campaign, had been launched at a meeting at the New Theatre on 16th April 1977. I became responsible for publicity, producing leaflets and posters.

The situation changed suddenly on 13th February 1978: *Lincoln Castle* was withdrawn from service with a serious boiler problem which threatened to end all hope of her continued operation on the ferry service. On 23rd March 1978 I joined Barry and Esther Beadle of the former HPSG, and crew member Chris Braithwaite, in the studio of Radio Humberside for a phone-in show about the efforts to save the vessel. In April the Save the PS Lincoln Castle Campaign organised a petition. That it obtained over 5,000 signatures in a few days attests to the level of support.

Despite all this local activity, *Lincoln Castle* languished in Alexandra Dock and, with no money forthcoming to repair her boiler, she never returned to service. The first paddle steamer had come to the Humber in 1814 and the year 1978 saw the end of 164 years of paddle steamers on the estuary

and the demise of the last coal-burning paddle steamer in regular service in Britain. In fact Russell Plummer, in his 1975 book *Paddle Steamers in the 1970s*, suggested that she may have been the last coal-fired paddle steamer in the world operating an all-year-round ferry service.

When it opened in 1981, the Humber Bridge was the longest suspension bridge in the world. Between 1974 and 1996 it also helped to weld together the very separate communities of North Lincolnshire and East Yorkshire – which had always viewed each other with some ambivalence across the Humber Estuary – by means of the short-lived County of Humberside.

Over the years I have returned to Hull many times and stood on the remains of Corporation Pier to look out across the Humber Estuary. There is something sadly missing without the familiar sight of two paddle steamers passing each other midway in their journeys between Hull and New Holland. I have visited both *Tattershall Castle* on the River Thames, enjoying a pint in the much-altered and refurbished bar, and the superbly restored *Wingfield Castle* in Hartlepool, where she is now preserved as part of the Maritime Experience. In 1978 I had been living in London and unable to follow the move of *Lincoln Castle* to the foreshore at Hessle and then to Alexandra Dock in Grimsby, but in 2010 I visited her there, where she had formerly been a floating restaurant. What happened to her in Grimsby forms an extraordinary conclusion to the story of the last paddle steamers of the Humber.

The author getting some fresh air on deck of *Lincoln Castle* whilst returning to Hull after a cruise to Grimsby, 28th July 1974. *Kirk Martin*

Katharine firing *Lincoln Castle* for one round trip. Was she the only woman to fire a Humber paddle steamer? *Kirk Martin*

The author with Hassan on *Lincoln Castle* in Alexandra Dock, Hull, in 1978. *Kirk Martin*

Chapter Two

EARLY FERRIES OF THE ESTUARY

The Humber Estuary, with its strong tidal currents and shifting sandbanks, forms a natural border between the counties of Lincolnshire and Yorkshire and drains a vast area of the Midlands and the north-east of England, extending to over 9,000 square miles, via the rivers Ouse, Aire and Trent, among others. The estuary has long been a barrier to movement between north and south, unless a long detour is made to the west to a point narrow enough to bridge or shallow enough to ford. It is thirty-seven miles from the point where the Rivers Trent and Ouse come together to create the Humber, to its mouth at Spurn Head. The river is two miles wide at Hull and over seven miles wide where it joins the North Sea.

The Humber forms a natural highway as well as a barrier, and the remains of prehistoric craft dating from the Bronze Age were discovered at North Ferriby in 1938 and 1940. Other craft dating back to before 2000 BC have been found more recently, submerged in the mud. Boats such as those would have been used for trade up and down the Humber as well as for ferrying people, animals and goods across

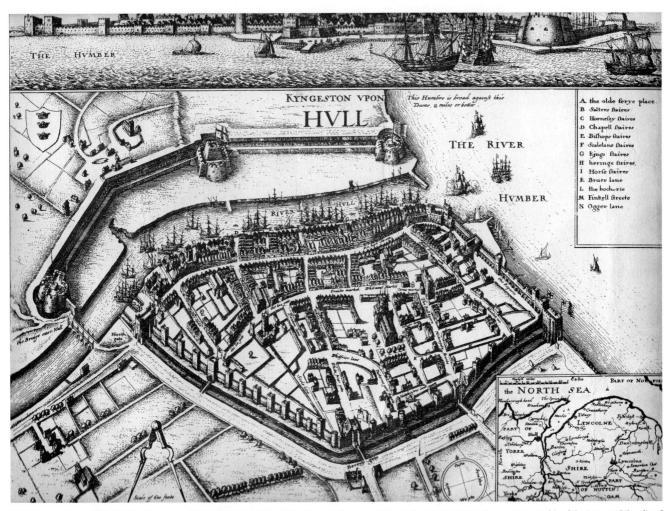

Detail from a plan of Hull c1640 by Wenceslas Hollar. North is to the left. The River Hull runs north to south to enter the Humber on the east side of the town and the site of the ferry pier is on the right. In the foreground the town walls follow the line of the later Town Docks. © *British Library Board, Maps 177.L.2*

A View of Barton Ferry, engraved by John Hassell in 1801 from an original oil painting by T. Bradley. A stagecoach is leaving the Waterside Inn and the ferry is getting ready to set off across the Humber from the jetty in the foreground. *Hull Museums*

it. Rodney Clapson, historian of Barton-on-Humber, has described these craft, measuring some 50ft long, as among the oldest plank-constructed boats in the world.

The Celtic Parisii occupied a large area on the north bank of the Humber and another tribe, the Corieltauvi, or Coritani, settled in an area extending from the south bank. Traces of a village at North Ferriby were found during archaeological excavations in the 1930s. The settlement was on relatively high ground, where the Humber cuts through the Wolds, and there is evidence of a similar settlement on the south bank of the Humber at South Ferriby. It seems likely that a primitive ferry operated at this point.

With the coming of the Romans, the Ninth Legion – under Quintus Petillius Cerialis, governor of Roman Britain from 71AD – advanced north from Lindum (Lincoln) to establish a settlement near Winteringham on the south bank and, crossing the Humber – which the Romans called Abus – established another at Petuaria (Brough) in the area occupied by the Parisii tribe on the north bank. This was part of the campaign to extend Roman rule across the north of Britain and the territory of the Brigantes. They might have forded the river on this occasion, but they certainly had a ferry at this point later on, known as the Transitus Maximus, or 'great ferry'. The Roman Ermine

Street from Lindum (Lincoln) to the newly-founded town of Eboracum (York) crosses the Humber here, bestowing greater importance upon the ferry.

After the Roman legions left Britain early in the fifth century, there were incursions of Picts and Scots from the north and west and the country was overrun by Angles, Saxons and Jutes from across the North Sea. In the Early Middle Ages England was a collection of warring kingdoms and one of these, Northumbria, had the Humber for a large part of its southern boundary with Mercia to the south. The origins of the name 'Humber' are obscure, but in the Anglo-Saxon chronicle of 872 it is referred to as *Humbre*.

Later, Vikings from Denmark and Norway attacked and then settled large areas of Britain, particularly in the east, including the lands north and south of the Humber Estuary, which became part of the Danelaw. A ferry had long been operating between North and South Ferriby, but during the reign of the Danish King Cnut the southern terminus had been moved to Barton-on-Humber. In September 1066 hundreds of ships made their way up the Humber, carrying the troops of Tostig Godwinson and Harold Hardrada, King of Norway, to their defeat by King Harold Godwinson at the battle of Stamford Bridge. A few weeks later Harold was defeated at Hastings.

At the time of the Norman Conquest there were ferries operating between Barton and Hessle, as well as from South to North Ferriby, and in 1069 the operator of the Ferriby ferry was paying £3 a year to de Gaunt (also spelled de Gand or de Gant), the Norman Lord of the Manor of South Ferriby and nephew of William the Conqueror, who also had the rights to the Barton to Hessle ferry. As Alun D'Orley explains, this crossing became the most important: it was on the main road through Lincolnshire to the village of Barton Waterside on one side of the Humber, and from Hessle northward on the Yorkshire side of the estuary. D'Orley states that the ferry was 'much used by Royal Personages travelling along the great high road to visit Cottingham and Beverley, before Hull had even commenced'. According to the Domesday Survey of 1086, land and mills in Barton, as well as the ferry, were in the hands of Gilbert de Gand, and his descendants held the ferry until 1298, when it reverted to the Crown.

Hull, a relatively minor fishing settlement in the marshy ground near the confluence of the Rivers Hull and Humber, was recorded in the Domesday Survey as Myton, or Mitune, part of the Hessle Hundred and one of the estates of Ralph de Mortimer. In the late twelfth century the monks of Meaux Abbey, seven miles to the north, began to acquire land at Myton, until then a small hamlet, from the Camin family. The monks were improving the land around the River Hull and needed to establish a port for the export of wool.

The course of the River Hull was altered in the thirteenth century. Originally it flowed south to a point a quarter-of-a-mile north of Stoneferry, where it turned westwards for some distance before turning again almost due south to enter the Humber near the little fishing village of Wyke. It was decided to make a new watercourse from the point where the Hull turned westwards straight into the Humber. This resulted in a deeper, faster-running stream and also improved the drainage of the land. The old riverbed silted up and ceased to be navigable; the fishermen of Wyke then moved eastwards to the banks of the new river, which provided safe anchorage for their boats.

In 1193 a large amount of wool was gathered from several monasteries as a contribution towards the ransom for Richard I after he was captured on his return from the crusades; this was collected 'at the port of Hull'. The names Wyke and Hull both seem to have been in use at this time. The new port began to be preferred by trading ships over the harbours at Hedon and Ravenser (or Ravenspurn). In 1275–6 accounts show that sixty-seven cargoes left the port, including over 4,000 sacks of wool and 100 hides. For several years only Boston and London contributed more than Hull to royal customs revenue. Imports included wine, much of which was taken on to York, with some being destined for its archbishop.

In 1293 Edward I acquired the port and town of Wyke and part of the grange of Myton from the monks. This gave

View of Barton Creek today with Joe Irving's boatyard, formerly Clapson's boatyard, on the left and the Humber Bridge in the background. *Kirk Martin*

him a useful port at which to supply his troops during their move north towards Scotland. New streets were laid out and, in the fourteenth century, town walls were built, which were only demolished during the construction of the docks many centuries later. Henceforth the town was known as the 'King's town', or Kingston upon Hull. The town was governed by a royal keeper or bailiff, one of whose duties was to maintain the banks of the Humber, which were prone to flooding the town's low-lying land. The town was granted borough status by royal charter in 1299, and the burgesses were made responsible for the running of affairs. A quay was constructed by 1302, later known as the King's Staith.

By the fourteenth century Hull had become an important east coast port, exporting wool, cloth and lead and importing timber, corn and flax from the Baltic ports and wine from France. Owing to concerns about difficulties with the existing ferry between Barton and Hessle, a royal charter issued by Edward II was granted to the wardens and burgesses of Hull to operate a ferry between Hull and Barton. In his *History of Hull*, published in 1798, Tickell states that:

> In the ninth year of this King's reign [1315], Robert de Sandal, being custos, or warden of the town, the King, at the request of the burgesses of Kingston upon Hull, and after inquisition made, was pleased to found a passage, or Ferry, to and from the town of Barton-on-Humber in Lincolnshire, to bring and carry over men, horses, beasts, &c. belonging to the said towns, and for the advantage of the travellers; and gave the profits thereof to the Wardens and Burgesses, their heirs and successors, forever; every single man, to pay one halfpenny; every horseman, one penny; every cart, going over with two horses, two pence; &c. This grant was made at Lincoln, the 28th day of August, in the aforesaid year.

In the face of this, the Barton men jealously guarded their right to continue operating a ferry across to Hessle, on what had become an important link on the road north to Beverley and York and also, in 1316, obtained a grant from the Crown to operate a ferry between Barton and Hull. After disputes between them and the men of Barrow, who also operated a ferry to Hessle, in 1371 it was agreed that the Barton ferry was to be the only one from the coast of Lindsey, with the exception of the original ferry from Barrow, which was for the inhabitants of that village only.

Clapson points out that four ferries were using Barton Haven at this time: the Barton to Hessle and Barton to Hull ferries, both owned by the Crown (as Lord of the Manor of Barton) and farmed out to lessees; the ferry between Hessle and Barton, owned by the Lord of the Manor of Hessle; and the ferry between Hull and Barton, owned by Kingston upon Hull. Clapson also states that competition between the Hessle and Hull boats was a great source of dispute in Barton for many years.

In 1440 Hull gained corporate status with thirteen aldermen, one of whom would be the mayor, replacing the 'best burgesses'. The corporation's Hull to Barton ferry was let to an operator who initially paid a proportion of the tolls to the town chamberlains. The rent of the ferry dropped from an average of £18 in the first half of the fifteenth century to about £8 in the second half, and from about 1482 it was let at a fixed rent. It became known as the South Ferry, to distinguish it from the North Ferry over the River Hull, which had been granted to the burgesses of Hull by a charter of 1299. Over the years the corporation's ferry was operated by various lessees. Whilst the North Ferry may not have survived the building of the North Bridge across the River Hull in 1541, the ferry to Barton remained important. Rents did gradually increase, but tolls were not raised until 1656. Clapson mentions that the first recorded coach service through Barton ran in 1654 and that the journey from London to Hull, via the ferry, took around five days.

A lengthy description of the Barton ferry accompanies the famous print of *A View of Barton in the County of Lincoln* by Hassell (from an original oil painting by Thomas Bradley) currently held in the Ferens Art Gallery in Hull. It mentions that, 'though it has been the practice of different Authors' to represent crossing the Humber 'as extremely dangerous, yet we do not find on Record any misfortune till the year 1640, when Mr Andrew Marvell, lecturer of Hull…[and father of the famous poet and Hull MP] together with other passengers, were lost in a Storm'.

From 1640 the lessee of Hull Corporation's Barton ferry was obliged to provide six men to operate the service, and to maintain the landing staiths. From 1667 the lease demanded that one ferry cross on every tide, and as early as 1673 the corporation proposed that a crane should be erected to load and unload coaches – a feature that was to continue into the twentieth century with the craning of motor cars. The lease of Barton's ferry to Hull also changed hands many times. Lessees included the Godfrey family during the reign of Elizabeth I and, from 1624, William Smithsby, who held it for thirty-one years.

Sir John Hotham's refusal to give King Charles entry into Hull in 1642 was said to be the first act of aggression in the Civil War. During this time Hull was kept for Parliament whereas most of Yorkshire was a Royalist stronghold. Fleeing from Royalist forces in 1642, Sir Thomas Fairfax, the Parliamentary general, crossed the Humber from Barton, and the following year Oliver Cromwell also crossed the Humber from Barton to Hull. According to Clapson, 'In August 1645 a Royalist raiding party was sent from Newark to take prisoners and destroy the Barton ferry boats which were providing a vital means of transport for troops, supplies and news to and from Parliamentary forces in Hull'. The raid appeared to have been a success and the ferry boats were burnt.

The ferry service revived after these tribulations and remained important throughout the remainder of this turbulent century. However, Tickell describes a dispute of a local nature that arose in 1680 between the ferrymen of Barton and those of Hull, in which the following complaint was made by the men of Barton to the Privy Council in the form of a letter to the Mayor and aldermen of Hull:

> We are credibly informed that of late great disturbance and interruption has been given by your officers, and those you employ in the ferry boats belonging to your town, to the loss of his majesty's ferry-boats at Barton-on-Humber; and that your said officers, and others under your authority, injuriously and maliciously hinder the landing of passengers and goods at your staiths, to the great diminution of the profits of his majesty's said ferry, contrary to the ancient usage, and in violation of the undoubted rights of the crown.

A response, signed by the mayor, George Crowle, stated:

> We called the farmers of our town's ferry before us; and have examined how the differences arose between the queen's ferry at Barton and ours at Hull. It fully appears to us from the examination, that the first obstruction and cause of the trouble, was occasioned and given by the ferry-men of Barton, who, it appears, dealt very uncivilly and unkindly with our ferry-men; not only affronting, hectoring and abusing them, but also this whole town. It is therefore very probable, that ours might answer them again with the like incivilities and unkindness. But we have now reconciled all differences between them; and they have promised all love and respect to each other in carrying on this affair.

Even without these disputes, the Humber was always a very treacherous stretch of water to cross, with the sediment brought down from the many rivers feeding into it adding to the extensive mudflats that were a constant hazard to shipping. The skippers of the early ferries needed a thorough knowledge of the sandbars and tides in order to navigate safely across the Humber in all weather conditions.

In her 1697 tour through England, Celia Fiennes visited the area:

> The buildings of Hull are very neate, good streets, its a good tradeing town by means of this great River Humber that ebbs and flows like the sea is 3 or 4 mile over at the least, it runs 20 miles hence into the Sea and takes in all the great Rivers, the Trent Ouise Aire Don the Derwent and the Hull, and carries much water that a man of warre of all sorts can ride...the Humber is very salt always it rowels and tosses just like the Sea, only the soile being clay turnes the water and waves yellow and soe it differs from the sea in coullour, not else; its a hazardous water by reason of many shoares the tides meete, I was on it a pretty way and it seemes more turbulent than the Thames at Gravesend.

Daniel Defoe mentions Grimsby and Hull in his fascinating *A Tour Through the Whole Island of Great Britain*, which gives a picture of the country in pre-industrial times. The book was first published in the 1720s, although it may have been based on travels as early as the 1680s. In Letter 7 Defoe describes Barton as 'a town noted for nothing that I know of, but an ill favoured dangerous passage, or ferry, over the Humber to Hull'. He continues:

> In an open boat, in which we had about fifteen horses, and ten or twelve cows, mingled with about seventeen or eighteen passengers, called Christians; we were about four hours tossed about on the Humber, before we could get into the harbour at Hull; whether I was sea-sick or not, is not worth the notice, but that we were all sick of the passage, any one may suppose, and particularly I was so uneasy at it, that I chose to go round by York, rather than to return to Barton, at least for that time.

In the 1720s – just as in 1371 – the people of Barton were becoming jealous that their monopoly position in north Lincolnshire was being infringed by others, including the ferries at Barrow and Hull. A petition to the Duke of Newcastle in 1722 stated that:

> whereas the…Ferry of Barton hath formerly been, and of right still is, ye only Ferry for carrying passengers on the River Humber…of late the said Ferry hath not only been encroached upon by the Ferrymen belonging to Barrow Ferry in pretending theirs to be a Publik Ferry… but also by the Hull Ferrymen taking and carrying over from Barton Shore such passengers & their merchandize as ought to goe in the Barton boates.

The outcome of the petition is not known.

From 1723 the Royal Mail was carried from London to Barton before crossing the Humber by ferry to Hull. The ferry was becoming widely known and began to be mentioned in the press beyond the local area. In 1776 it was reported in several newspapers, including the *General Evening Post* of 10th February, that 'a gentleman who arrived here from Hull, on Saturday evening' had related the following:

> A number of passengers, who wanted to cross the ferry to Barton, on the Lincolnshire side, about six miles over, ventured last Wednesday forenoon in an open oared boat, to the number of 13, including the boatmen; they had not got more than two miles before they were set fast in the ice, and from the severity of that night is it supposed they all perished, as no assistance could possibly reach them.

Tickell, writing in 1798, outlined the complex nature of the tolls charged for using the ferries eighteen years earlier. It is hardly surprising that there were occasional disputes between the Barton and Hull ferrymen, given that both companies operated ferries on the same route and each had to agree to pay a part of their toll income to the other:

The following statement of the tolls paid to the owners of the ferries from Hull to Barton, belonging to the mayor and burgesses of Kingston upon Hull, and from Barton to Hull, belonging to George Uppleby, esquire, lessee under the Crown, as settled and agreed by the owners of the respective ferries, may perhaps, not be unacceptable to many of our readers.

Strangers, going from Barton to Hull, in Hull boats, pay six-pence; four-pence of which is returned to the Barton ferry-men.
   Strangers, going from Hull to Barton, in the Barton boats, pay six-pence; four-pence of which is returned to the Hull ferry-men.
   Inhabitants of Hull, going from Barton to Hull, pay nothing to the Barton ferry-men.
   Freemen of Hull pay six-pence for a man and horse, in the Hull boat; and inhabitants, who are not freemen, pay eight-pence.
   If a stranger and his horse be carried from Barton to Hull, in the Hull boat, he pays one shilling, the whole of which is paid to the Barton ferry-men.
   If a stranger and his horse be carried from Hull to Barton, in the Barton boat, he pays one shilling, the whole of which is paid to the Hull ferry-men.
   If an inhabitant or freeman goes in the hoy, he pays four-pence; if in the horse boat, without a horse, two-pence.
   If a Barton man pass from Hull to Barton in the horse boat, he pays one penny to the Barton ferry-men; and if from Barton to Hull, he also pays one penny to the Barton ferry-men.
   If a Barton man goes in the hoy from Barton to Hull, he pays four-pence, one penny of which is paid to the Barton ferry-men; but if he goes from Hull to Barton, in the hoy, he pays four-pence; all of which, is kept by the Hull ferry-men.

Signed:
B[enjamin] B[laydes] Thompson, mayor.
G[eorge] Uppleby, lessee of the Barton ferry under the crown.

In 1786 Uppleby sub-let the Barton to Hull ferry to a company operating a coach service between Barton and London, his own lease being renewed by the Crown in 1792. In 1795 the corporation had to withdraw the lease of the Hull to Barton ferry from one of its tenants and, in 1796, it also purchased the lease of the Barton to Hull ferry from Uppleby for £2,900, and leased it to the proprietors of a coach service between Barton and London.

One of the difficulties facing the operators was the tendency of the harbour at Hull to be so overcrowded with boats that the ferry could not reach the landing stage and passengers often had to walk across several vessels or use smaller craft to reach

The Waterside Inn, Barton, built in 1715. Stagecoach services from as far afield as London connected here with Hull and Hessle Ferries. *Kirk Martin*

The Waterside Inn, Barton, viewed from Barton Creek. *Kirk Martin*

the shore. It was believed that this problem would be solved when the corporation completed a small basin for the sole use of the ferries and the market boats. In 1799 the corporation negotiated with the Crown to purchase enough land at South End, the former artillery ground, to carry out improvements to the area around the jetty and, under the provisions of the Ferry Boat Dock Act of 1801, a pier was built parallel to – although not connected to – the shore, which made landing alongside the shore easier in times of rough seas. The streets around the area were improved by the same Act and a dock master was appointed in 1805. From 1809 the area was extended, using the soil excavated by the creation of New Dock (later known as Humber Dock) and several new roads were laid out to the south of Humber Street and named in honour of the naval and military heroes of the time, including Nelson and Wellington.

The *Hull Directory* for 1803 lists the large number of passage and market boats then in operation in addition to the ferries:

From Barrow arrives every Tuesday and Friday and sails again the same day; From Burton Stather arrives and sails the first Market day after every new and full moon; For Ferriby Sluice, Rawcliffe, Winteringham and Whitten sails twice a week; Gainsborough sails twice a week; From Grimsby arrives on Monday and Thursday and sails on Tuesday and Friday; From Howden arrives first Market day after new and full moon; From Weighton Lock arrives and sails first Market day after new and full moon; For West Farney sails every Wednesday; From Whitgift arrives first Market after new and full moon and sails the same day; From Selby arrives and sails generally on Saturdays; From Stallinborough arrives and sails every Tuesday.

In addition, Thomas Dent is reputed to have established his ferry service between New Holland and Hull in 1803. There were so many boats transporting passengers and goods across the Humber that (it was claimed) there was not a single village along the banks of the river without its own market boat. They made regular journeys to Hull, and some sailed twice a week to transport the Tuesday and Friday market traffic. Occasionally legal action was taken against them by the owners of the ancient ferries, but nevertheless they continued to operate, forming an important part of the local economy.

The *Hull Guide* of 1806 stated that the Barton ferry was operated by 'not less than four large boats of 45 ton burthen and several smaller ones which will take between fifteen and twenty five persons each'. Alongside the passenger boats there were horse boats, capable of carrying four gentlemen's four-wheeled carriages, an equal number of gigs and up to fifty horses on each tide. Boats usually made the passage in forty to fifty minutes, and seldom took longer than two hours. A typical entry in the weekly newspaper *Hull Packet* announced that on Tuesdays the ferry sailed to Barton at eight o'clock and back to Hull at eleven o'clock, and 'three quarters of an hour later every succeeding day'. There is a similar entry for the Grimsby packet-boat.

As previously mentioned, Hull Corporation had withdrawn the lease of the Hull to Barton ferry from an unpopular tenant in 1795, and the following year it purchased the lease of the Barton to Hull ferry. Over the course of a century the rent of the corporation's ferry rose from £30 in 1719 to £300 in 1813, although this now included the rent for the lessee's house at South End. In 1813 the *Hull Advertiser* announced that the lease of the Hessle to Barton route was to auctioned at the Paragon Inn:

The Ancient Ferry from Hessle to Barton-upon-Humber…And also a Public House called the Ferry House near to the Landing-place at Hessle aforesaid. This Ferry has for a great number of years been much used by Farmers, Grazers, Beast Drovers, &c. frequenting the Fairs and Markets at Beverley, &c. being the direct Road from Barton into all parts of Lincolnshire and will be Let on Lease for a term of three or five Years…

In October 1814 Hull Corporation applied to increase ferry fares, because the expense of 'keeping up the boats, and of sailors' wages, are now greatly increased; and there can be no doubt that formerly all the horses, carriages, and passengers were conveyed across the river in one and the same boat. Now, there are three or four boats, and one of them provided with suitable accommodation purposely for passengers'. Commenting on this application, Mr James Allan Park, attorney-general of Lancaster, was of the opinion that 'the Corporation have not the power for increasing the rates of passage', and, 'if larger boats, or more of them, or a greater number of hands be wanted, the increased passage will pay the additional boats'.

In 1821 the corporation sub-leased both ferries, at a rent of £800 per year, to Thomas Walkden of Barton and his associates Boyce and Chaplin (some sources say 'Boyes and Chapman'). The lessees purchased the paddle steamer *Waterloo* at auction and constructed a new jetty at Barton, extending 200 yards into the river. It also offered connecting coach services to London and, from 1823, carried the London mail on this vessel.

A reference to the ferries in 1834 states that the corporation paid the Crown £236 yearly and leased the ferries to Boyce, Chaplin & Co, including a clause that a steamboat should be operated at least twice a day at a fare of one shilling per passenger.

An engraving of 1843 said to depict an early New Holland ferry. *Author's collection*

Chapter Three

THE FIRST PADDLE STEAMERS

Legend has it that, in 1788, Robert Fourness (or Furness) and James Ashworth (or Ashton) constructed an early steam-powered paddle boat at their yard at Wincolmlee in Hull. Trials were conducted along the River Hull to Beverley with some success. They then supposedly built another steam-powered craft, took it to London for trials on the River Thames, and sold it to the Prince Regent. The two men were definitely granted patents for steamboats, but the rest of the tale may be apocryphal. According to the Maritime Historical Studies Centre at the University of Hull, 'If such stories could be properly verified then the River Hull could lay claim to being the cradle of steamship technology, but apart from the patents, no real contemporary evidence has ever been found to support such assertions'.

What we know for sure is that in 1803, as Trevithick experimented with steam power on road and rail, William Symington was already operating a paddle steamer called *Charlotte Dundas* on the Forth & Clyde Canal. She successfully towed two seventy-ton sloops against a headwind for over nineteen miles on the summit level of the canal to Glasgow, thus proving the value of steamboats as a commercial proposition. American engineer Robert Fulton was also interested in the development of steam-powered vessels. He initially carried out trials in revolutionary France, where he launched a successful steamboat on the Seine in 1803, his experiments enjoying the support of Napoleon. Fulton went on to build the first commercially successful steam-powered boat – *Clermont* – which operated from 1807 along the Hudson River between New York and Albany, a distance of 150 miles.

Fulton had studied the engines of *Charlotte Dundas*, and he was in touch with Henry Bell, who in 1812 launched *Comet* on the Clyde. This craft was built by John Wood & Sons, with a boiler constructed by Sir John Napier & Sons, and an engine by John Robertson; all three firms being based at Glasgow. *Comet* was the first commercially successful steamboat in Europe, and in 1812 she was operating regular advertised trips on the Clyde. Her engine has survived and is currently held at the Science Museum in London.

Just two years after *Comet*'s successful launch, the *Rockingham and Hull Weekly Advertiser* described how a steamboat, 'most commodiously fitted up with two cabins for passengers', had arrived on the River Severn. In the same year the wooden steam paddle sloop *Caledonia*, built by Stuart of Dundee for the same John Robertson who supplied the engine for *Comet*, was manufactured for the Humber. Her dimensions were: '64 feet keel, 13 feet beam, 7 hold'. (This *Caledonia* is not to be confused with another ship of the same name built by J. & C. Wood of Glasgow in 1816, which operated on the River Thames in London before becoming – according to author Frank Burtt – the first paddle steamer to operate on the Rhine.) In September 1814 the *Hull Advertiser* reported *Caledonia*'s progress down the east coast:

A steamboat from Dundee, intended for the Humber, arrived in the Tyne on Saturday week, passing the bar, on which a heavy sea was running, in a capital style. She is 10 feet longer than the Tyne steam packet, draws only 3½ feet of water when loaded, and made her passage on Sunday from South Shields to the Quay at Newcastle, against the tide in 1 hour and 20 minutes.

The paper noted that *Caledonia* had arrived in the Humber that morning and was intended for use 'betwixt' Gainsborough and Hull. The paper featured her again on 15th October 1814, three days after she went into service:

The steamboat…has during the week been exhibiting her capabilities on the Humber, and it appears that with wind and tide against her, her speed is considerable. On Wednesday she went off to Gainsborough, and the weather being favourable, reached Burton [upon] Stather in the space of an hour and a half, travelling at the rate of 14 miles per hour.

The following May, the *Rockingham* reported that *Caledonia* went

from hence up the River Ouse to Naburn, about 4 miles from York, with intention of proceeding to that city, but the lock was not sufficiently wide to admit of her passing through it. The packet had arrived from Hull on the same day, making the whole distance in that time of 122 miles.

Caledonia and another paddle ship called *Humber*, were offered at a public sale held at the Wellington Hotel in Hull on 11th July 1815.

In September 1816, when *Caledonia* was just two years old, her axle broke in two between Hull and Grimsby. According to the *Morning Post* the passengers were 'taken out, and conveyed to Grimsby by some fishing boats which happened to be near'. *Caledonia* was still making news in April 1820, when the *Bury and Norwich Post* reported that 'on Tuesday se'nnight' she 'ran from Hull to Selby, a distance of 54 miles, in the short space of four hours'.

In the years following *Caledonia*'s arrival, the increase in the number of steam-powered craft in the area was phenomenal. Paddle steamers were soon operating on a variety of cross-Humber services, and also to inland towns, via adjoining rivers such as the Trent and the Ouse. The 1817 edition of *Battle's New Hull Directory* listed seven steamers then working the Humber:

The *Caledonia* sails every day to Grimsby.
The *Waterloo* sails every Tuesday, Thursday and Saturday to Selby.
The *Albion* sails every Monday, Wednesday and Friday to Gainsborough.
The *Humber* sails every Monday, Wednesday and Friday to Selby.
The *British Queen* sails every Tuesday, Thursday and Saturday to Gainsborough.

The *Maria* sails every Tuesday, Thursday and Saturday to Gainsborough.
The *John Bull* sails every Tuesday, Thursday and Saturday to Thorne.

Before the operators had offices, local pubs or shops sold tickets and accepted parcels. (*Caledonia*, *Waterloo*, *Albion* and *Humber* used the London Tavern on Queen Street; *British Queen* used the General Elliot, High Street, *Maria* used Mr J. Cook's on Humber Street and *John Bull* used the Humber Tavern, also on Humber Street.) There were also market boats sailing to Barton and Barrow, as well as packets going to Brigg, Brough, Burton upon Stather, Ferriby Sluice, Garthorpe, Grimsby, Howden, Selby, Skitter, Swinefleet, Weighton Lock, Whitgift, Whitton and Wintringham, many of which sailed only once a fortnight.

About this time paddle steamers began operating on longer routes around the coast and, eventually, to the continent. In 1821 the *Kingston*, built by Pearson's of Thorne, with engines by Overton of Hull, was operating the Hull to London service for the Hull Steam Packet Company, and in 1823 she was joined by the *Yorkshireman*, which later inaugurated a regular packet service to Antwerp.

The *British Queen* of the Gainsborough and Hull Steam Packet Company. The vessel was built in 1815 by J. & H. Smith & Sons of Gainsborough. Passengers are enjoying the trip, drinking and being entertained by musicians, whilst a man stands at the stern, steering with a long tiller. *National Maritime Museum, Greenwich*

The steam packet *Rockingham*, which operated on the Hull and Thorne route in the 1820s. She had the typical flush deck of the early steamers, with no cabins above the deck. From a painting by Thomas Henry Binks. *Hull Museums*

In 1821 Hull Corporation leased the Barton to Hull ferry for £800 to Thomas Walkden of Barton and his associates Thomas Boyce and William Chaplin, both of London, and others involved in operating the coach service between Barton and London. The following year this company became the first to use a steamboat on the Barton to Hull route, when it replaced its hoy with the *Waterloo* in 1822. Built in 1815, the year of the famous battle, it was described by the *York Herald*:

At the head of the vessel is a gilt figure of Britannia, holding the Imperial eagle of France in chains, over which the British Flag is seen flying with triumphant splendour. At the other end is a bust of the Duke of Wellington, in the midst of trophies of victory; over which the union flag is also flying. On each side is a wheel of paddle, to impel the vessel, by means of the engine and steam, but carefully covered so as to prevent water from incommoding the passengers. On the deck, which is 76 feet long by 21½ feet broad there are several seats neatly fitted up, for the convenience of passengers. Below are two cabins, a ladies' dressing room, and other conveniences. The best cabin is well lighted, and above 14 feet long by about 12 feet broad, round which are seats stuffed and covered with crimson cloth; an oil cloth on the floor, the sides panelled and neatly painted; with a brass stove at one end. Between the two cabins is a small room, in which are engine, &c., the weight of which, including the whole of the iron work, is stated to be 25 tons; and from it the chimney ascends 33 feet above the deck.

The Barton to Hull route had been improved considerably by the introduction of the *Waterloo*, as well as by the development of better landing facilities at Hull. According to a comment in the *Hull Advertiser* in December 1821, the change to steam 'appears to have met with the general approval' and was said to have 'materially benefited the town by making communication with London more direct and much more reliable than hitherto'.

Battle's New Directory of 1822 listed eleven steamers operating on the Humber: *Aire, Caledonia, Leeds, Favourite, Humber* and *Waterloo* sailing to Selby; *Albion, British Queen* and *Nottingham* sailing to Gainsborough and *John Bull* and *Rockingham* sailing to Thorne. These boats generally left Hull three days a week, returning from their destinations on the alternate days. The 1823 *History, Directory & Gazetteer of Yorkshire* provides detailed information about nine steamboats, including the names of their masters (or captains) as well as the destinations and sailing times (please see Appendix II). *Waterloo* had switched from the Hull to Selby route to the Barton to Hull crossing, and was replaced in 1826 by *Royal Charter*, built by J. & H. Smith and Sons of Gainsborough. Since 1823 the company had been conveying the Royal Mail to and from Hull, Thomas Walkden having offices in Hull to facilitate this. The Barton to Hessle ferry was still important and Hessle could also boast warehouses and the aptly named Ferry Inn.

As early as 1820, Hull Corporation had tried unsuccessfully to forbid the carriage of passengers and goods in private boats. When such a service started from Barrow, near New Holland, in 1826, the corporation stated that this was not permitted under the charter of 1315; however, this was not the case: as they were providing a service only to Barton, private boats were allowed to operate from other settlements on the Lincolnshire bank.

By the time the 1826 *Directory, Guide and Annals of Kingston upon Hull* was published, the number of vessels had increased to twenty. It listed *Albion, British Queen, Dart, Eagle, Hero, Maria, Mercury,* and *Trent* working to Gainsborough; *Aire, Calder, Caledonia, Duke of Wellington, Favourite* and *Leeds* to Selby; *John Bull* and *Rockingham* to Thorne; *Royal Charter* and *Waterloo* to Barton; *Elizabeth* to Glandford Bridge and *Graham* to Grimsby. The author commented:

> The application of steam to the purpose of navigation has assisted materially to increase the prosperity of Hull. The rapidity with which vessels are impelled by this powerful agent, and the excellent accommodation afforded to passengers, together with the moderate charges for fares, have no doubt induced thousands to visit Hull, who would never have ventured on the uncertain passage by sailing packet or made the journey by coach.

In August 1826 the *Hull Packet* carried an item on the newly built paddle steamer *Dart*:

> On Saturday morning last, was launched from the ship-yard of Henry Smith, Esq., of Gainsboro', a most beautiful and superior strong built steam-packet, called the *Dart*, intended to ply between Hull and the above place, in conjunction with the *Mercury*, at present justly considered the quickest running steam-vessel on the Rivers Humber and Trent.

The *Mercury* left Hull shortly after 5am, with a party of invited guests who were landed at Gainsborough at 8.15am, allowing one-and-a-half hours to witness the launch of the *Dart*. They arrived back at Hull at 2pm, 'having run the distance of 108 miles in little more than seven hours, including stoppages at the different ferries to deliver and take in passengers and parcels'.

The *Eagle* came up for sale in November 1826. According to an advertisement in the *Hull Advertiser*, she was 'Two years old, in a complete state of Repairs, with an Engine of superior make by Overton & Co. And a new Boiler extremely strong'. The steamer had been 'constantly plying betwixt Gainsboro' and Hull, and is now lying in the dock at Hull, where she may be inspected'.

The risk of explosion on these early craft was ever near. *Graham* was involved in a tragic incident on 7th November 1826. She had left Grimsby for Hull, under the command of Captain Valentine Morvison, when her boiler exploded. A report in the *Hull Advertiser* three days later provides a fascinating glimpse into the operation of the steamers.

> The *Graham* left Grimsby at about eight o'clock on Tuesday morning, on her passage to [Hull]. At that time, the *United Kingdom*, [under] Captain Oman, the largest and most magnificent steam vessel, which plies between Leith and London, and which left the latter city on her voyage to Leith on Saturday, was riding in the roads, having been prevented from making her passage northwards, by the violence of the wind from the North, and the roughness of the sea. The *Graham* proceeded directly towards her, in order to take passengers, &c, for the district, and also those who, from the previous detention of the vessel by contrary winds, wished to proceed overland. She arrived alongside about half past eight, and in ten minutes from that time, while the transference of luggage and passengers was actively taking place, the boiler of the *Graham* suddenly burst with a tremendous explosion. The scene of alarm and confusion which followed was of the most appalling description. The deck of the *Graham*, at that moment, was literally swarming with passengers. She left Grimsby with about forty, and had received nearly the same number from the *United Kingdom*. Many of these, by the violence of the shock, were raised from their feet – some of them to a great height, – and precipitated into the Humber, the tide at that time running strongly.

The *Hull Packet* provided an equally vivid description of the explosion:

> Horrible to relate, she had hardly been in this station ten minutes, when her boiler burst with a tremendous explosion, opening in the middle, like the two halves of a book, tearing up the deck in the vicinity, and consequently producing a scene of confusion and distress, of which those persons present can alone form an idea. Several, both men and women, were fairly lifted into the air, and thrown into the water. One man [William Mellins], who had the moment before jumped on board the *United Kingdom*, was killed outright, by a large splinter of iron projected that way, which, we are told, actually passed between Lord Elibank [a Scottish baronet] and Col. Howard [brother-in-law of the Lord Advocate of Scotland], whilst they were in the act of assisting a lady into the *Graham*. One man had his skull

severely fractured, and several others were severely bruised and scalded. Of those who had been forced into the water, Mr. [John] Cundill, a Baptist preacher of Hull, was taken out in a dying state, and expired in a few minutes. Four others were eventually found to have lost their lives, whose names are Richard Jenny, John Blow, John Potter and John Wray, whose bodies we are not aware have yet been found. Much greater indeed would have been the mortality, had not Captain Oman, of the *United Kingdom*, had two boats at the time alongside his vessel, fully manned.

Mr Cundill appears to have drowned after swimming until he was exhausted. Mr Blow, an elderly man, was well known locally as the owner of a luggage boat which sailed between Hull and Grimsby. His death left eleven children fatherless.

The inquest, held on 9th November, not only gives details of this incident but also conveys a very human story of paddle steamers on the Humber in the 1820s. Witnesses included Thomas Dowes, a mate on the *Graham* for about eighteen months, who steered the vessel from Grimsby out to the *United Kingdom*. He told the inquest that the boiler had been examined and repaired at Selby about a fortnight before. Samuel Waltham, foremast man on the *Graham*, stated that,

> The paddles had stopped, and steam was escaping at the time. He saw the boy take the weight off the safety valve as soon as the *Graham* was alongside the *United Kingdom*. The steam then escaped in the usual manner… [Waltham] heard the engineer order the weight to be taken off, when the vessel was making fast. The valve was open, and the steam was letting off, in the way usual when coming into port at Hull or Selby.

George Stephenson had been an assistant engineer (fireman) on the *Graham* for five years. He had never known a boiler to burst in port. There was no gauge on board (though it was usual to have one and the vessel formerly had one), and so they guessed the degree of pressure in the boiler by the weight on the safety valve. Stephenson stated that he 'had took the weight from the safety valve by order of the engineer, and the steam was escaping in the usual way'. Jacob Urwin, engineer of the *Graham*, 'took command of the engine, and stopped it, on coming alongside the *United Kingdom*'. The weight was removed from the safety valve by the boy before the engine was stopped. He had gone onboard the *United Kingdom* a minute previously, curious to see her engine, and was upon her paddle box, about to return to the *Graham* when the boiler exploded. Urwin stated that the *Graham*'s boiler had 'given way more than once' and, from the first, he had 'never considered' the boiler a good one. In fact, he had even 'represented to the owners that it was defective'. When Urwin took charge eighteen months previously the weight on the safety valve had been 56lbs; he had taken off 20lbs 'not thinking the boiler strong enough', and it had remained at 36lbs ever since. He 'considered the boiler then safer, but

always had a dread upon him'. Contradicting his fireman, Urwin stated that there was indeed a gauge, but did not use it because 'the safety valve was a better gauge'.

Valentine John Morvison had been master of the *Graham* for only three weeks and had not had the boiler examined, for he had 'often gone down to Grimsby, in a heavy gale, in two hours'. He admitted that he knew 'nothing of the cause of the accident, or of the management of steam engines, but had particularly cautioned the engineer to be careful'.

Passengers on the *Graham* deposed that no steam was escaping by the safety valve, but they could not see if there was a weight upon it. None of the crew was near the engine at the time of the explosion.

James Overton, who had built the engine, described the exploded boiler as 'entirely rent asunder in the middle of the top, and both the sides of the top turned open like a pair of folding doors. The boiler, as to thickness, appeared to be much decayed at the top, particularly where the rent took place'. He judged the boiler as sufficiently strong to bear the customary working pressure. 'If the weight on the safety valve was 36lbs. the pressure on the boiler would be 3lbs. per square inch, against the atmosphere, supposing the steam in its ordinary state'. Had the valve been 'open and free', he believed that 'no explosion could possibly have taken place'. He thought the cause of the accident was 'the safety valve not doing its duty'. He suggested that, 'Some weight placed upon it – a passenger's foot or luggage' may have been the cause. A problem with the safety valve may have caused 'a trifling rent', but not an explosion. He 'admitted that the engineer should have been with the engine if there were likely to be any difficulties'.

The verdict of the jury was manslaughter against the engineer and the owners. The deaths were deemed to have been caused by Jacob Urwin 'grossly and criminally neglecting his duty as engineer' and by Richard Clay, the acting agent and manager of the *Graham*, 'grossly and criminally failing to remove the boiler from the said vessel' and permitting it 'to be used after frequent representations made to him of its dangerous and imperfect state'. A subscription list was launched to aid the families of the victims.

In 1828 the original *Caledonia* was up for sale again, having changed hands at least once before. An advertisement described her as 'in excellent repair, and well found in other respects'. Also on offer were 'several shares in those well known Steam Packets, *Aire* and *Favourite*, regularly plying between Hull and Selby'. *Caledonia* was to be auctioned at the Humber Tavern, and interested parties were asked to 'enquire of Messrs. G. Malcolm and Son, High Street, or of the auctioneer, 16 New Dock Walls'.

On the longer route between Hull and Grimsby, a ferry had been established in the thirteenth century by a royal charter of Henry III to the mayor and burgesses of Grimsby, and they let the ferry to 'suitable persons'. G. Bernard Wood, in his *Ferries and Ferrymen*, points out that in 1828 a steam packet named *Pelham* commenced operation between the two towns. In April the *Hull Packet* described *Pelham*'s inaugural run. Although fourteen years had passed since the arrival of *Caledonia*, there was clearly still a great deal of excitement surrounding the introduction of a new steamer.

She left the pier, at eleven o'clock, in the presence of a large concourse of spectators, who appeared highly gratified at the gallant style in which she started. To add to the gaiety of the scene, the bugle band of the 83rd regiment, now lying at our citadel, were stationed on the deck, and, on the vessel being loosed from her moorings, struck up the cheering and martial strain of *Rule Britannia*. The morning was delightful. She got under weigh with a favourable breeze with colours flying, and after exhibiting herself down the river, she returned and took in an additional number of passengers, who were all anxious to partake of the hilarity of the day. As she passed the *Bee* and *Lapwing* cutters she fired a salute, which was returned in the most handsome manner by both.

On arrival at Grimsby at about 3pm, the ship was greeted by 'a great assemblage of company'.

The *Pelham*, with about 100 gentlemen on board from Hull, made her appearance, with colours flying from stem to stern, and was welcomed on her arrival by the cheers of the assembled multitude; at the Lock, she fired a salute, and received a great addition to the number of visitors. She then, with nearly 700 passengers on board, proceeded up the Dock as far as the Custom-house

quay, fired another salute, and returned to the Lock, in fine style, amidst immense cheering, and fortunately, without the slightest accident. The bugle band from the Garrison at Hull played most delightfully all the time.

A rival concern must have won the ear of a councillor, for another steamboat, *Sovereign*, began operating in competition with *Pelham*. G. Bernard Wood comments, with irony, that instead of working the service alternately from the two Humber terminals (the most sensible way to operate) the boats would race each other across. From this ungainly contest *Pelham* emerged victorious.

In 1831 a radical character called James Acland moved to Hull. Sheahan, writing in 1864, states that he 'distinguished himself as the self-elected champion of popular liberty', and continued:

His trade was agitation, and for about three years he managed to keep the townspeople in a state of turmoil. He attacked every institution and every individual member of each institution; but to make war against the corporation of the town seemed to be his chief aim. He published a weekly periodical, called the 'Hull Portfolio, or Memoirs and Correspondence of James Acland, its Editor and Proprietor'; and in it he attacked almost everybody of position in the most scurrilous manner.

The Barton to Hull route had been operated since 1821 by Thomas Walkden's company, which enjoyed sole rights. The vessel used was the steamboat *Royal Charter*, and the fare was

Hull from the Humber c.1837, by John Ward. Note the paddle steamer *Pelham* tied up by Minerva Pier. *Pelham* worked mainly on the Hull and Grimsby route. *Hull Museums*

one shilling for a return crossing. But Acland claimed that the fare of just one halfpenny, granted by King Edward five hundred years earlier, should still stand. According to some sources he encouraged people to turn up at the ferry and demand the halfpenny fare, but the crews refused to let them board. In the autumn of 1831 Acland started a rival service to that offered by *Royal Charter*. At first he used the *Victory*, but after she was found to have a defective boiler he hired the *Aire* from Furley & Co. of Gainsborough. Renaming the vessel *Public Opinion*, Acland operated it with the arms of Hull Corporation displayed upside down on the flag and paddle boxes. Sadly, his planned fare of a halfpenny had to be raised eight-fold, to fourpence, and would later be increased to sixpence. On 13th September the *Hull Packet* reported:

In an attempt to destroy the monopoly of the Barton Ferry the newly christened steam packet 'The Public Opinion' plied between Hull and Barton on this day, carrying about 500 passengers at 4d a head each way, with the regular packet charging a shilling. Some opposition was made on the Barton side at first in the handling of the passengers.

This 'opposition' consisted of barricades being erected to prevent *Public Opinion* from landing, but, with help from the public, Acland removed them. As the rival ships raced to the landing-places, collisions occurred. At noon on 31st October *Public Opinion* 'ran into the *Royal Charter* carrying away her paddle box, breaking her wheel paddle and the iron axle in which they moved'. Those words, from the *Hull Packet* of 1st November, were elaborated upon in a lengthy letter from an outraged eyewitness, who had never before seen 'a more wanton, wilful, malicious and mischievous attack on, and destruction of, private property'. The captain of *Public Opinion* had, he said, 'put on all the steam and force he possibly could, to put his helm hard over, and in a most dastardly and illegal manner, ran his vessel most foully into the *Charter*…endangering the lives of all on board'. A slower steam packet, the *Coronation*, took the place of the *Charter* whilst she was repaired, which delayed the London mails.

Acland's account of the collision in his own newspaper (the *Hull Portfolio*) differed from that described above:

In only one of the many collisions which have taken place, has the packet of the monopolists received injury. This was on Sunday 6th November, on the passage from Barton to Hull. We left Barton at 11.30am against the flood. Both vessels crossed to Hessle to avail themselves of the slack water along the Yorkshire coast. They were side by side the entire distance, the *Public Opinion* being without [i.e. on the outside of] the *Royal Charter*. Each had her sail up. At the pottery, a full half mile from the dock basin, we lowered our sail, getting half a length ahead. The *Public Opinion* was making for the north east extremity of the jetty, its usual place of destination. It was required of the *Royal Charter* for her to get round

the east jetty to her berth in the harbour, that she should get out into the river. But she kept between the shore and my packet half a length astern. She should have lowered her sail, stopped her engine for a quarter of a minute, and gone round our stern. The captain of the *Royal Charter*, however, ported his helm, and his bow came into contact with my paddle box, and he was forcing us out of the way to our station, and the *Royal Charter*, being between us and the west jetty – there was not room for her there – she was out of her usual course, and she got her desserts, a squeeze against the jetty and an injury to her larboard beam, paddle wheel and shaft. A tremendous shout of applause from the hundreds of people on the pier rent the air as we reached our berth at the end of the east pier and the *Royal Charter* sheared off and was taken in tow by her co-adjutor. This is the only instance of damage sustained by the *Charter* and it can most satisfactorily be shewn that this injury was consequent on the attempt of her captain to shove *Public Opinion* out of her course.

As the corporation was bound to support its lessees, a warrant was issued and *Public Opinion* was seized. Alun D'Orley describes the seizure by 'bum-bailiffs', the passengers being transferred to the *Royal Charter*, which had come alongside. Although *Public Opinion* escaped the bailiffs' grasp on that occasion, the vessel was later seized again and taken to Barton before Acland was able to regain command. According to Sheahan:

Legal proceedings were taken against him in the King's Bench [at York], by the Corporation for libel; the case came on in February, 1832, and was adjourned till the next term. Acland returned to Hull in triumph, and was met by a body of 20,000 men, with music and banners, who went in procession through the town. At the close of these proceedings he harangued the multitude from a balcony in the Market place. On the last day of the following month a trial took place at York respecting the Barton ferry.

In early April 1832 the *Hull Packet* carried a lengthy report of this trial, which makes fascinating reading, not least because of its descriptions of the operation of steam ferries on the Humber. The jury found in favour of the plaintiffs (the corporation) but awarded it damages of just one farthing, the equivalent of awarding a penny today. When Acland requested that he be spared the costs, the judge replied, 'No, it is a question of rights, and such a course is not usual'. Unable to pay his costs, which amounted to £270, Acland avoided arrest by barricading himself in his house in Queen Street.

According to the *Victoria History*, 'the trial over, Acland's popularity waned as he was forced first to raise his fare to 6d and then to withdraw the *Public Opinion* in disrepair'.

The *Royal Charter* regained its monopoly of the Barton to Hull crossing but, according to the *Hull Advertiser* a meeting of the Guardian Society took place in August 1832 to discuss lowering the fares. Mr T.B. Smith stated that the town was indebted to Acland, and so 'it was unjust that he should be incarcerated for the costs' of the trial. An amendment to a proposal on the fares was sought for donations, but it was pointed out that there was already a subscription list raising the money, although many of the members were happy to contribute, pointing out that much had already been raised by the poorer people, who rarely used the ferry to Barton. Sheahan – writing thirty years or so after the event – takes up the story:

> On 1st October, 1834, we find him writing from the Hull gaol, asking his followers, if any were left, 'for assistance in his hour of need', but his day had passed; his best friends had become his enemies; the mask had fallen; the charm was broken; and Acland's occupation was gone.

Acland had been active in Hull at a time of reform throughout the country. The Great Reform Act of 1832 swept away the rotten boroughs and established a middle class franchise in urban areas, whilst the Municipal Corporations Act of 1835 modernised local government. In Hull the old corporation was swept away, to be replaced by a newly elected body more accountable to the people.

The concern over the fares did not go away and a petition of 970 signatures was presented by members of the Guardian Society to the mayor and aldermen, asking that the fares on the Barton ferry be reduced.

> Mr Alderman Bolton remarked on the respectability of the deputation, and the number and respectability of the signatures attached to the memorial. He said it was the wish of the corporation, in their capacity as trustees, to attend on all occasions to any complaints or suggestions that might emanate from the inhabitants of the town… In regard to the ferries, it was not to be kept out of view that they had very considerable expenses to defray; they had to make good, and keep in repair the landing places both here and at Barton, and, unless funds were at their disposal, it was impossible those objects could be attained in that effectual way required for the public accommodation.

Sadly, the financial situation of Walkden's company in Barton was not healthy and, by 1831, it was unable to pay its rent to the corporation, although the corporation was still obliged to pay its rent to the Crown. It was calculated at a public meeting that the receipts of the ferries together would not clear £2,400 that year, against expenses estimated at about £2,700.

These financial difficulties were exacerbated by developments at New Holland. The first ferry service to Hull was commenced in 1803 by Thomas Dent, who occupied land close to the main drain outlet into the Humber (the creek later took his name). He built a house and large shed and, using a small craft, operated a ferry with one assistant. A correspondent to the *Lincoln, Rutland and Stamford Mercury* in December 1848 mentioned Dent's undertaking:

> This primitive state of things lasted for some time, when the convenience of the landing afforded by the creek, the isolated position of the spot, the paucity of the inhabitants, with other collateral advantages pointed it out as an eligible place for the debarkation of smuggled goods, more especially of Holland's gin, and it was notoriously used as such, and hence it obtained the name New Holland.

In 1825 Joseph Brown of Barton and some influential friends bought land near Oxmarsh Creek in Barrow, just west of New Holland, formed a company called the New Holland Proprietors, purchased a small boat, and began operating a ferry to Hull. Under the terms of the 1315 charter, Hull Corporation was powerless to prevent them. The following year they built the Yarborough Arms, which was for many years the only public building in New Holland, and from 1828 there was a daily service. This scheme had Acland's support and would doubtless have benefited from his campaign against the fares charged on the Barton to Hull route. The New Holland proprietors increased their capital by involving more shareholders, and also by instigating plans to purchase a steamer and improve road access to New Holland. In August 1832 the *Hull Advertiser* reported that the steamer *Magna Charta* was running three return trips daily, with an extra one on market days. Not long afterwards a daily 'hoss' (horse) boat was introduced for the carriage of livestock. The Yarborough Arms was extended and joined by a house built for the ferry superintendent.

By then the approach road to New Holland had also been upgraded, allowing regular coaches to serve the ferry, and a jetty had been constructed, although a proper pier had to await the coming of the railways. Coaches that ran from New Holland reflected the names of the paddle steamers: *Pelham* ran to Boston and *Magna Charta* to Nottingham via Lincoln; *Age* initially ran to Boston but was later diverted to Lincoln. However, a major problem at New Holland was the lack of a suitable landing facility, as at low water great areas of mudflats were exposed.

By 1833 Robert Hall, landlord of the 'Yarborough Arms Inn & Hotel, coaching and posting house', was inviting the public to use the frequent sailings of *Magna Charta* to spend 'the Day, or any part of the Day' in New Holland. 'An exhilarating Trip across the Water', he wrote, 'at the trifling charge of fourpence or sixpence…enables every description of person to enjoy, in a few minutes, the beauties of the country'. He offered tea gardens, a spacious bowling green, quoits and skittle-grounds, cricket and 'pigeon matches', and promised that 'a band will occasionally attend'. Customers would also find 'grateful relaxation', 'a good larder' and 'well-aired beds', as well as an 'open carriage landau…expressly purchased for the purpose', to convey parties to local attractions.

engrossing and it is not an infrequent occurrence for the beautiful and noble scenery on either side [to be] but little noticed by the steam boat passenger between Gainsborough and Hull. This is in many instances caused by the difficulty of gaining information in the midst of animated discussions on politics, farming, trading, scandal and religion.

NEW HOLLAND FERRY,
The *NEAREST ROUTE* to and from the *METROPOLIS* to *HULL*,
BY THE NEW ROAD TO BRIGG.

THE YARBOROUGH ARMS INN & HOTEL
COACHING AND POSTING-HOUSE.

ROBERT HALL, having Taken and Entered upon the above Premises, which have lately been much Enlarged, and newly Furnished them, in the best style of Comfort and Accommodation. R. H. having formed a connection along the whole line to Lincoln, so as to ensure the greatest dispatch, has provided
A BAROUCHE, POST CHARIOT, POST CHAISES, with able HORSES and careful DRIVERS.
☞ *A GOOD LARDER, WELL-AIRED BEDS, AND EXTENSIVE STABLING.*
CHOICE WINES, SPIRITS, ALES, PORTER, &c.
PUBLIC DINNERS
At the shortest Notice,—a large handsome Room being lately added to the House.
PRIVATE PARTIES immediately Accommodated.
•₊• A BOWLING-GREEN and CRICKET-GROUND, which are admirably adapted for Pigeon Matches, &c.
R. HALL hopes, by strenuous exertions, to render this delightful spot a constant source of Recreation and Amusement, during the Summer Months, to the Inhabitants of Hull and Neighbourhood.
Carriages to Thornton College; Mausoleum, and Picture Gallery, Brocklesby.

NEW HOLLAND FERRY.

NEAREST ROUTE TO BRIGG, BY THE NEW ROAD.

LONDON ROYAL MAIL.
IN consequence of the LONDON BAGS being to be forwarded by this Ferry, the

MAGNA CHARTA STEAM PACKET,
On and after MONDAY, the 26th May,

LEAVES HULL, EVERY DAY.	LEAVES NEW HOLLAND, EVERY DAY.
1st Trip Seven o'Clock	1st Trip—Half-past Eight o'Clock
2nd— Quarter before Ten o'Clock	2nd — Eleven o'Clock
3rd— One o'Clock	3rd — Half-past Two o'Clock
4th— Four o'Clock	4th — Seven o'Clock

N.B. No Trip at Seven o'Clock on SUNDAYS, the first Passage commencing at a Quarter before Ten on that day.

MAGNA CHARTA COACH,
To Brigg, Lincoln, Nottingham, Derby, Lichfield, and Birmingham, every Day, except Sundays, at Seven o'Clock in the Morning.

PELHAM COACH,
To Limber, Market-Rasen, Wragby, Horncastle, Boston, Lynn, and Norwich, every day, Sundays excepted, at One o'Clock, P.M.

HULL CHORAL SOCIETY.

THE FOURTH PUBLIC CONCERT of this SOCIETY will be given at the Public Rooms, on WEDNESDAY EVENING, the 28th instant, at Seven o'Clock.

PRINCIPAL VOCAL PERFORMERS:
Mrs. CUMMINS
Mr. KNOWLES
And Mr. BROOK (from the Lincoln Concerts.)
PRINCIPAL FLUTE, WITH SOLOS,
Mr. RICHARDSON.

Tickets, 3s. each, to be had at the usual places.
•₊• Subscribers to the Society have Free Admission, and Two Free Tickets.
ROBERT BOWSER, Secretary.
Hull, May 14, 1834.

PUBLIC NOTICE.

SPECULATORS are daily foisting on the Public CHEAP and SPURIOUS Macassar Oil as the Genuine.
To PREVENT such vile Imposition ATTENTION to the following is solicited.
THE LOWEST PRICE of the ORIGINAL MACASSAR, or ROWLAND's OIL, is 3s. 6d. per bottle The Label has the words "Rowland's Macassar Oil," and between those words are the same words minutely and curiously engraved 24 times, also the Name and Address in Red on Lace-work,
A. ROWLAND & SON, 20, HATTON GARDEN, Counter-signed ALEX. ROWLAND.

An advertisement for the Yarborough Arms in New Holland, *Hull Packet.* **May 1834.**

The *Hull Packet* reported in August 1835 that a member of the crew of *Magna Charta* had rescued a woman who had thrown herself into the Humber from the East Pier just after his vessel had arrived. John Ellerthorpe 'immediately jumped into the water, and succeeded in bringing her to the pier steps. She was evidently very much in liquor, but the rash act appeared to be one of determined self destruction, which, but for the praiseworthy exertions of Ellerthorpe, there is reason to fear would have proved successful'. This was one of about forty lives Ellerthorpe saved in his long seafaring career, and his story is included in Chapter Eight.

A small booklet entitled *The Trent and Humber Picturesque Steam-Packet Companion*, issued by John Greenwood in 1833, provides some interesting descriptions of travel on the steamers, complete with a map and delightful illustrations. The author points out that, when travelling by steamboat,

Where a number of fellow travellers are congregated together; the social picnic not unusually becomes

John Ellerthorpe

In October 1833 the leases of the Barton to Hull and Barton to Hessle ferries expired. Neither the corporation nor the coach proprietors were interested in continuing the service. Thomas Walkden acquired the leases of both, plus the corporation's Hull to Barton ferry and the two steamboats then in use on the service.

There was serious concern in Hull about leasing the ferries. In June 1834 the *Hull Packet* reported that the Barton Ferry Committee (BFC) held a meeting at the White Hart tavern in Hull, where it decided to send a deputation to London to meet several MPs, the secretary of the General Post Office (GPO) and the commissioners of His Majesty's Woods and Forests and Land Revenues (who represented the Crown). The GPO intended to test sending mail via the Barton–Hessle crossing and also via the rival route from New Holland to Hull, before opting for 'whichever way should ultimately prove the best for the interest of the Town of Hull'.

The deputation's report was presented at a crowded meeting at the Cross Keys in Hull on 22nd September 1834. Attendees were opposed to the ferry being leased for another three-year period, and wanted to end the ferry monopolies. The *Hull Packet* reported that John Gresham had 'great hopes' that the ferry could be 'thrown open to public competition', but this 'had been unfortunately prevented' and 'to their astonishment they found published in the papers the willingness of the corporation to lease the monopoly for three years longer'. The BFC was adamant that the lessees could not adequately cope with the large number of people who wished to travel over to Hull, particularly on market days. The corporation was concerned that increasing competition would see a return to sailing boats. The BFC disagreed; not only would steamers be used 'but they would be much more commodious and comfortable'. The article continued:

> The report of that deputation [concluded] that 'unless the ferry monopolies on the Humber are quickly destroyed, and the most vigorous measures instantly adopted for the improvement of the landing-places at Hull and New Holland, and more especially at Hull, the chief point of transit from Lincolnshire to Yorkshire, will be removed from Hull to Hessle'.

The local MP, Matthew Davenport Hill, moved the first resolution: 'That the report now be adopted; and the committee be thanked for their continued exertions to throw open the Barton Ferry'. He also claimed that 'the water ought to be as free as the land' and 'a person ought to have as much right to have a steam packet on the water, as to run a stage coach on the high road'. George Pryme, MP for Cambridge and professor of Political Economy at its university, stated that 'it was incumbent on anyone who possessed a monopoly of any kind, to show most distinctly and clearly that the public benefited by it'. The meeting passed a resolution to send a deputation to the corporation to ask if it intended to surrender its monopoly, to consider the level of compensation, and to construct a new ferry boat dock in Hull.

Hull Corporation was well aware of the need to improve landing facilities in Hull, as the *Hull Advertiser* reported in December 1834:

> An order was passed, we understand, at a full bench of the Mayor and Aldermen of this borough, held on Tuesday, the 2nd inst., for making a landing place, for the convenience of the steam packets and other craft engaged in the trade of this port, on the foreshore opposite the cattle market (the vacant ground lying to the west of the Patent Slip and Aydon's foundry) agreeably to a plan submitted to the bench. This plan,

we have reason to believe, comprises a jetty, by which vessels will be enabled to land their passengers at any state of the tide. It was also determined at the same bench to construct at the present ferry boat landing (which most of our readers are aware has been recently cleaned out and deepened), two additional flights of steps, between the Minerva and Vittoria Hotels, in such places as may be considered most convenient for the landing of passengers.

The Humber was also busy with steamers arriving at Hull from inland towns on the Humber and connecting waterways. Edward Parsons, in *The Tourist's Companion; or the History of the Scenes and Places on the route by the Railroad and Steam Packet from Leeds and Selby to Hull* of 1835 (the Leeds and Selby Railway having opened the previous year) mentions several steam packets:

> The *Eagle* and the *Lion* steam packets pass daily between Goole and Hull, and vice-versa, with goods and passengers, leaving the former place at ten am and the latter to suit the tide. The *Eclipse*, a steam packet upon a new construction and light draught of water, plies from and to Hull daily, with passengers only, leaving the former place at ten o'clock am as the tide may permit, and the latter place on the arrival of the passengers from the interior. The *Calder* and *Echo* steam packets are employed in the daily conveyance of goods to and from Goole and Hull.

GENERAL COACH AND MAIL PACKET ESTABLISHMENT,
NEW HOLLAND FERRY, NEARLY OPPOSITE TO HULL.

THE London Royal Mail Route, being the shortest and quickest Road to the Metropolis, as decided by his Majesty's Post Master General,

AT REDUCED FARES.

THE MAGNA CHARTA COACH TO LONDON every day, at Seven o'Clock in the Morning, from the Cross Keys, through BRIGG, LINCOLN, NEWARK, GRANTHAM, and STAMFORD, arriving at the Saracen's Head, Snow Hill, at Seven the following Morning.

☞ This is the only Coach that leaves Hull for London on a Sunday, the Mail excepted.

THE AGE DAY COACH TO LONDON, leaves the Cross Keys, Hull, every day (Sundays excepted) at Four o'Clock in the Afternoon, after the arrival of the Wellington from Scarborough, arriving at the City Arms, Lincoln, at Ten o'Clock the same Evening ; leaves Lincoln the next Morning at Six o'Clock, through GRANTHAM, STAMFORD, HUNTINGDON, BIGGLESWADE, and reaching the Belle Sauvage, Ludgate Hill, at Ten o'Clock that Night, combining safety, comfort, and despatch.

THE MAGNA CHARTA COACH TO NOTTINGHAM, DERBY, BIRMINGHAM, and BRISTOL, every day from the Cross Keys, Hull, at Seven o'Clock in the Morning.

☞ This Coach arrives at the May-Pole, Nottingham, at Half-past Six o'Clock, whence passengers are forwarded the same Evening to Derby, as well as Manchester, arriving at the latter place in time to proceed by the first train of Carriages to Liverpool the following Morning.

THE PELHAM COACH, from the Cross Keys, Hull, every day (Sundays excepted) at a Quarter-past Eleven o'Clock, through CAISTOR, MARKET-RASEN, WRAGBY, and HORNCASTLE, to the Peacock Inn, Boston, from whence Passengers are forwarded to Lynn, Norwich, and all parts of Norfolk, Suffolk, and Cambridge.

New Holland, July, 1835.

MAGNA CHARTA STEAM PACKET

LEAVES HULL	LEAVES NEW HOLLAND
At Seven o'Clock Morning, with Magna Charta Coach Passengers.	At Nine o'Clock Morning. Two o'Clock Afternoon with London Royal Mail, Magna
Quarter-past Eleven, with London Royal Mail and Pelham Coach Passengers.	Charta, and Pelham Coach Passengers.
Four o'Clock Afternoon, with Age Coach Passengers.	Seven o'clock Evening with Age Coach Passengers.

Tuesdays and Fridays (Hull Market Days) an Extra Trip from New Holland at Twelve and Hull at One o'Clock.

 HORSE BOAT

FOR CARRIAGES AND CATTLE,
Leaves Hull Two Hours before High Water, and New Holland at High Water.

N.B. At New and Full Moon it is High Water at Six o'Clock, both Morning and Evening, and One Hour later every following Day.

YARBOROUGH ARMS, NEW HOLLAND.

This delightful spot possesses every accommodation for Recreation and Pleasure, having a spacious Bowling Green, Grounds for Cricket and Pigeon Matches, &c.

☞ Parties taken to Thornton College, Brocklesby, and the Mausoleum at Limber.

⁎⁎⁎ Post-Chaises, able Horses and careful Drivers, a Barouche, Gigs and Saddle Horses, at a Moment's Notice.

Vans and Carriers to all parts of the Country.

Performed by　NICHOLSON & CO., New Holland.

A newspaper of 1835 advertising coach and steamer services from Hull and New Holland.

BARTON FERRY.

THE BARTON FERRY COMPANY being desirous to afford every facility to the Public in crossing the Humber to and from HULL, BARTON, and HESSLE, beg to state that on MONDAY, the 2nd of MAY next, they will commence making FIVE PASSAGES per DAY from HULL and BARTON, to continue during the Summer Months.

FROM HULL TO BARTON.		FROM BARTON TO HULL.	
Laurel, Steam Packet,	7 0 A.M.	Laurel, Steam Packet,	9 0 A.M.
Ditto ditto	10 30	Ann Scarborough, do.	11 0
Ann Scarborough, do.	1 0 P.M.	Laurel	1 30 P.M.
Laurel	4 0	Ann Scarborough	4 30
Ann Scarborough	6 0	Laurel	6 30

FROM BARTON TO HESSLE.		FROM HESSLE TO BARTON.	
Ann Scarborough	6 0 A.M.	Ann Scarborough	6 30 A.M.
Laurel	12 0	Laurel	12 30 P.M.
Ann Scarborough	3 0 P.M.	Ann Scarborough	3 30

In addition to this a Packet will leave BARTON for HULL every TUESDAY and FRIDAY, at SEVEN o'Clock in the Morning, for the Accommodation of the Fruiterers. A TOW BOAT built expressly for the Conveyance of CARRIAGES, HORSES, and CATTLE, to and from BARTON and HESSLE, is now in use ; on which they are Towed over with despatch and safety at any hour of the Day, except at low water of Spring Tides, and the difficulty attending Landing at that time will be obviated when the Pier about to be erected is completed.

The Company take the opportunity, in announcing the above arrangements, to state they are determined that every accommodation shall be provided, to ensure to them the patronage and support of their Friends and the Public in general.

An advertisement from the *Hull Packet*, April 1836 for the Barton Ferry Company.

The Barton route remained a major concern in Hull. The *Hull Packet* of 1st April 1836 reported a meeting of the town council in which a Mr Gresham said that the lessees of the Barton ferry had endeavoured to obtain a twenty-one-year lease directly from the Crown, bypassing the corporation. Had they succeeded, 'it would have caused considerable embarrassment to the council and the public'. The council would not take any steps without consulting the Barton Ferry Committee. By 15th June the council resolved that 'the report of the Hull and Barton Ferry Committee be received; that the thanks of the meeting be given to the committee for their attention to the interests of the public; and that the report be referred to the property committee for their immediate consideration'.

There was clearly a difference of opinion between the people of Hull and those of Barton regarding the monopoly status of the ferries. In September and October 1834 the *Hull Packet* reported that two meetings in Barton had resulted in the formation of a company to take over the lease of the ferries from Barton to both Hessle and Hull. The members claimed that, if improvements were made to the landing places at Barton and Hessle, the ferry would be able to accommodate all those wishing to cross. They opposed an open competition for the ferries and declared their conviction that, 'a Lease of these Ferries to either a Company or to an Individual, by securing an obligatory attention to the Ferry duties, will be of greater advantage to the Public than by throwing them open'.

The corporation agreed to let Thomas Walkden operate the ferry 'at a nominal rent of 20s. per annum [but] in deference to the opinion of the town, and of account of matters then passing…they declined letting the ferry at present for any given time'. (Walkden had long had an interest in the Barton ferry, coaching services and the Waterside Inn at Barton. He and a group of other men, some as far afield as London, had formed the Barton Ferry Company in 1835 to improve the landing facilities and operate the ferries to Hessle and Hull.)

An advertisement in the *Hull Packet* in April 1836 announced that, from Monday 2nd May and 'to continue during the Summer Months', a service would commence operation between Hull, Barton and Hessle, using the steam packets *Laurel* and *Ann Scarborough*. There were five services between Hull and Barton and three between Barton and Hessle, with the two vessels visiting all three places during the day. In addition to this, a packet would leave Barton for Hull every Tuesday and Friday at 7 am to accommodate fruiterers. A tow boat, which had been built for the conveyance of carriages, horses and cattle, could be taken at any time of the day, apart from during the low spring tides. The advert promised that 'the difficulty attending Landing at that time will be obviated when the Pier about to be erected is completed'.

However, by July the Barton Ferry Company was complaining about losses resulting from the activities of certain people in Hull, an oblique reference to the Barton Ferry Committee. The improved service it offered seems not to have lasted beyond the summer. On 26th August the company announced that it was reducing the service and not improving the landing places at Barton, because Hull Corporation was 'unable to make up their minds' on the proposition of the Barton Ferry Committee that the corporation should either 'take the Ferries into their own hands, build the jetty at Barton, and do as much for the accommodation of the Public as the present Tenants are doing; or that they should withdraw their opposition, and allow the Barton Ferry Company to make the necessary improvements, and continue the management of the Ferries'.

The disputes about leasing the Barton ferries were sidelined somewhat by developments to the east. In 1836 New Holland became the chosen route for the conveyance of the London mail and the Barton Ferry Company was dissolved the following year. Thomas Walkden, who had taken over the steamers and the ferry in his own name, died in December 1839, leaving his Barton ferry interests to his daughter, Ann. According to Clapson, 'the ferries were taken over by James Clapson the younger, who was occupying the Waterside Inn'. He adds, 'A consortium of businessmen including Smith Wormold of Barton, Esquire, and James Clapson the elder, of Barton, farmer, had bought another ferry, the *Duncannon*, built at North Shields in 1841. The steam packet *Royal Charter* was taken out of service in 1845 and replaced by the *Duncannon*'.

Steam tugs Lightning and Hecla by Hull Victoria Pier, 1860. Tugs were occasionally used as ferries. The painting gives a clear view of the Victoria (or Corporation) Pier at this time when a roof had been added to the old pier but before the new pier was built, with an upper deck promenade, in 1882. *Hull Museums*

With all these difficulties, Ann Walkden was declared bankrupt in 1851. Generous locals raised a subscription of £814, which was invested to give her £60 a year for life. Walkden's assignees worked the ferry until his affairs were wound up. Later, the North Eastern Railway (NER) became the owner of the Barton to Hessel ferry until it was succeeded in 1856 by Messrs. Hill, Stamp and Drust.

Paddle steamers, although now a regular sight on the Humber, were still relatively new technology and, as with the *Graham*, disaster struck again. On 10th June 1837 the *Manchester Times & Gazette* described an explosion at Hull on board the Hull & Gainsborough Steam Packet Company's steamer, *Union*:

THE PELHAM STEAM PACKET COMPANY return thanks to their numerous Friends and the Public in general, for their kind support during the last nine years to the PELHAM Steam Packet in the HULL and GRIMSBY Ferry, they now beg to inform them they have purchased the superior Steam Packet
UNION,
of Sixty-Horse power, which they are fitting up in splendid style, with Two AFTER CABINS and ONE FORE CABIN, for PASSENGERS, which they intend to put into the Trade with the PELHAM, to ply between HULL and GRIMSBY: they will thus have two powerful Packets, which will enable them to accommodate the Public; and they respectfully assure their Friends that no attention shall be wanting, and no expense spared to merit a continuance of that distinguished support which they have hitherto experienced.   THOS. WINTRINGHAM,
Grimsby, March 20, 1837.   Managing Owner.

The *Pelham* and the *Union* are mentioned in a March 1837 advertisement in the *Hull Packet*.

Sales by Auction, &c.

FOR SALE BY PRIVATE CONTRACT,

THE well-known and uncommon fast Steam Packet SOVEREIGN, about 130 Tons Builders' Measurement, and an Engine of 40 Horse Power, built in Hull in 1831, of the very best materials, by the present Proprietors, under particular inspection; and is considered by competent judges to be one of the strongest and best built Vessels on the Humber. Her Hull and Machinery having had a thorough overhaul, and a new Boiler put into her, and being employed in a very easy trade, with every possible care taken of her, she is equal to a new Vessel in all respects; she has superior Accommodation for Passengers, having three Best Cabins and one Fore Cabin, with very large Deck room, and is of very light draught of water. Is now plying between Grimsby and Hull, and may be seen at the latter place every day, and further information known on application to
Hull, June 16, 1837.   ROBT. KEDDEY.

The paddle steamer *Sovereign* was up for sale in June 1837 as described in the *Hull Packet* of that date.

It is our painful duty to record this week one of those awful and appalling visitations of Providence which are from time to time occurring – a catastrophe more fatal in its character, and more deplorable in its nature than, perhaps any which has been known in this town…It had been announced that the *Union* would leave Hull for Gainsborough at a quarter-past six, by which time a great many passengers were assembled on board the vessel – the number being larger than usual, on account, probably, of Retford fair, which is much famed, being held this week. The steamer at this time was lying in the Humber dock basin, close alongside the East Pier. The morning was beautiful; the passengers in all the buoyancy of expectation were anticipating their voyage; preparations were being made for the quitting of the shore, when with one loud crash the deck of the quivering vessel was rent to shivers, while devastation and death were spread thickly around. One moment put an end for ever to the bright hopes of numbers, and rendered many a father childless, many a child an orphan, and many a wife a widow. For some moments after the explosion a dense white vapour prevented the eye from beholding the full extent of the awful calamity, but when the partial mist had cleared away, a most distressing sight was presented. Numbers of human beings were struggling in the water, endeavouring to escape a threatened death, – others were stretched, mangled and bleeding corpses, on the quay and vessels in the neighbourhood, – while some were shrieking in agony, having received wounds and scalds of the most dreadful nature. The water rushed into the opened seams of the ill-fated vessel, and, in a few minutes after the explosion, she went down. Boats were, fortunately, near at hand, and they put off and afforded assistance to the unfortunate sufferers, while they preserved peace and order among the crowds who immediately assembled.

Nine men (including a stoker) and four women were killed in the explosion, and a great number were left seriously injured. Six more casualties were to die later, including the ship's stewardess and her maidservant. Some were thrown a great distance by the force of the explosion:

It was observed that the body of a man was lying on top of the house of Mr Westerdale, mast and block maker, a distance of sixty yards from the *Union*. Ladders were immediately procured, and with some difficulty the body was lowered into the street. It was then recognised to be the shattered and disfigured corpse of Joseph Matthews, the foreman of a crane on the quay, a few feet from the 'berth' in which the *Union* was lying.

Goods and pieces of machinery were also hurled from the vessel:

A large bale of goods, weighing about 2 cwt. was carried, by the violence of the explosion, over the roof of Mr.

Westerdale's house, and fell in the timber yard. The top of the boiler, in an almost entire state, was deposited in the open space in front of the Minerva-terrace 15 or 20 yards from the vessel. The safety-valve was carried as far as Wellington-Street, a distance of about 80 yards, where it stuck, and severely damaged the booking-office of the York Steam Packet Company. The weight, which had been attached to the safety-valve, was found in Humber Street, where it had alighted on the steps of Mr. Veltmann's house, several of which were broken.

An eye witness account appeared in *The Times* on 9th June:

When I arrived upon the spot, hundreds of people had collected, and I observed the paddle-boxes of one of the Gainsborough packets just above the water, the whole of the packet being immersed…I observed some men bearing away a corpse upon a board, and another was just bringing up from the wreck…I found several medical gentlemen upon the spot, and in the water floating about were articles of furniture and clothing, hats and bonnets…I heard it stated upon the pier, that the accident arose from the boiler having scarcely any water. If such be the case, I presume that some part of the iron had become red hot, when, by contact of the boiling water, steam of the very highest intensity would be instantly formed, and the explosion then would be inevitable…I think it is quite evident that the men who are employed as engineers on board steam-packets ought to be intellectual men, of virtuous habits, well acquainted with the laws of heat, and deeply impressed with the responsibility of their office.

Another correspondent to *The Times* had spoken with a group of people who had escaped injury because they were on the fore end of the vessel:

The boarding plank had not been taken away, and, notwithstanding the consternation they were in, they had presence of mind to rush on shore by the plank before the vessel sank, which was the case immediately…[One passenger] informed us that for several years he has had to attend and manage steam-engines; and, although an illiterate person, he appeared to me to understand the nature of steam power. He informed us, and his wife vouched for the truth of the statement, that on going on board a few minutes before the vessel was blown up he observed to her that the engine had too much steam and too little water, the safety-valves emits a peculiar sound, quite different to what it does when there is sufficient water in the boiler.

The most common cause of boilers exploding was excessive pressure caused by the over-weighting of the safety valves, a practice that would not be permitted today. However, the five-day inquest into the first thirteen deaths concluded that

Hull from the Humber, 1874 by Henry Redmore, showing a Humber sloop and a square-rigged keel either side of a large, square-rigged ship, whilst a paddle steamer sets off from Corporation Pier. *Hull Museums*

the explosion on the *Union* was caused by 'gas generated by the small quantity of water left in the boiler; some part of which getting red hot, the combustible atmosphere ignited with a tremendous explosion'. The coroner's jury found Joseph Gamble, engineer of the *Union*, guilty of several counts of manslaughter. Gamble subsequently stood trial at Yorkshire Summer Assizes, where he was acquitted.

The Humber Union Steam Packet Company's agents, Hudson & Cobby, inserted a notice in the local papers stating that they had no connection with the vessel (as had been reported) and, at the same time, took the opportunity to point out that their own steamships were provided with 'two practical and experienced engineers and, therefore, their machinery could not even temporarily be in charge of an ignorant fireman, as is too frequently the case'.

In the following decade the ferry service between New Holland and Hull would be in the ownership of a railway company, ushering in a new era on the Humber.

Chapter Four

THE RAILWAYS AND THE FERRIES

Hull was first linked to the growing railway network in 1840 with the opening of the Hull and Selby Railway, later to become part of the York and North Midland Railway and subsequently the North Eastern Railway. The Hull and Selby Railway had a station at Hessle, which was mentioned in *White's Directory* as being suitable 'for the convenience of passengers &c. coming or going by the ferry boats, one of which is a steam packet sailing to and from Barton twice a day'. (Later the railway was to have a direct interest in the Hessle to Barton ferry.) It offered a circuitous route to London via the Leeds and Selby and other railways, and in 1844 the journey to London took over twelve hours. It was later shortened to around seven hours, after railway developments on the south bank of the Humber via the ferries to New Holland.

The area around New Holland, originally served by connecting coach services, was to be completely transformed by the development of railways. On 27th July 1846 four companies came together by an Act of Amalgamation to form the Manchester, Sheffield & Lincolnshire Railway (which, in 1897, would become the Great Central Railway). The four companies were the Sheffield, Ashton-under-Lyne & Manchester Railway; the Great Grimsby & Sheffield Junction Railway; the Sheffield & Lincolnshire Junction Railway and the Grimsby Docks Company, the oldest of the four and the company largely responsible for the development of the commercial docks in Grimsby.

However, the connection with the Humber ferries started two years earlier. The Grimsby Docks Company and the Great Grimsby & Sheffield Junction Railway shared several directors – namely, Lord Worsley, Richard Thorold, Michael Ellison, George Heneage and James Wall. In 1844 the provisional committee of the Great Grimsby company had discovered that a line under the control of the infamous George Hudson – the 'Railway King' – had made a bid for the New Holland ferry service. Talks with the New Holland proprietors established the asking price of £11,000 for the ferries, which included at New Holland the Yarborough Arms and gardens, stabling, coach houses, a granary, a fold yard, piggeries, a seven-acre field, foreshore, a jetty, a wharf, a warehouse and coal yard and, at Barrow, a public house, warehouse, granary and a two-acre field. George Dow, in his detailed, three-volume history of the Great Central Railway, describes how the provisional committee made an offer of £10,000 for the ferries, which was declined. The threat from

George Hudson added some urgency to the proceedings, however, and the committee asked Robert Smith of Ancaster to carry out a survey of the ferry properties. In his report of 1st January 1845, included in the GG&SJR's minute-book (held in the National Archives) Smith stated that, even if the projected Grimsby railway 'or any other line south of the Humber' did not go ahead, it was 'a most valuable property… and likely to increase'.

> The net annual revenue at present, after deducting all expense and maintenance, he had calculated at £420… and the purchase money, he had calculated, would be £11,820 – he would have no objection to take an interest in it himself at that valuation. The meeting having carefully considered the whole matter…the purchase should be concluded without delay and instructed the solicitor to complete it accordingly at the offer of £11,000.

However, at a meeting with the ferry owners on 10th January, the provisional committee repeated the offer of £10,000. This time, the sellers agreed the reduced price. The Goxhill ferry was also purchased, for the sum of £300.

In an advertisement published in the *Sheffield & Rotherham Independent* in January 1845, the directors of the GG&SJR announced that they had, 'on their own responsibility' purchased the whole of the 'valuable property and privileges in the ferries from New Holland and Barrow to Hull, with land and buildings at both landing places, deeming it most important to the success of the undertaking that the property be at once secured by them, and essential to the future working of the railway that the arrangements for the ferry service should be taken under their control'. This seems to imply that the provisional committee had made the purchase on behalf of the GG&SJR, to be held in trust until the Act of Parliament was secured. However, the secretary, Lt. Col. John Hambly Humfrey, was instructed to make no reference to the purchase of the Humber ferries in the company records. The committee's solicitor, Mr Hinde, who had himself put £500 towards the purchase, was advised that, 'after 1st January 1845 you must be taken as acting for the parties in their private capacity and not as the provisional committee of the Great Grimsby & Sheffield Junction Railway'. The scheme had become a private speculation involving fourteen members of the provisional committee. Humfrey, who had originally agreed to become a shareholder before changing his mind, was invited to take up shares but he, along with William Smith, of the solicitors, and Dr Bartolomé, refused to become involved.

The Great Grimsby & Sheffield Junction Railway Act received Royal Assent on 30th June 1845. Soon afterwards a resolution was passed by the new railway's directors, to purchase the Barrow, New Holland and Goxhill ferries, and the associated landing places, land and buildings. At the first shareholders' meeting, held on 27th August, it was agreed that the New Holland ferry should be purchased, but because some of the directors were also owners of the ferries, the negotiation of the purchase price was to be entrusted to John Rodgers, William Smith, Mark Favell and Thomas Newmarsh. The ferry owners nominated Messrs Ellison, Woodcroft and Howe to meet the company representatives and offer the undertaking for sale for £21,000, the railway company paying all the expenses, legal and otherwise. As George Dow points out, with eight out of the eleven members of the railway's board being also the owners of the ferries, it was a case of the vendors also being the purchasers, despite hiding behind the facade of Rodgers, Smith, Favell and Newmarsh. The three board members who were not ferry owners instructed Lord Worsley to write to the solicitors (who were acting for both parties) to let them know that they were happy with the sale and the price, mentioning that 'the gentlemen had possessed themselves of the Ferries at considerable risk'. On 8th October the board of the GG&SJR approved the price. The purchase was ratified at a meeting of the directors, eight of whom were amongst the fourteen owners of the ferries. In less than nine months the trustees of the company had made a clear profit of £11,000, with little risk to themselves. This was at a time when railway mania was raging through the country, with numerous railway schemes being promoted, many of which were never built.

The railway ownership of the New Holland route had an impact on Barton. This was graphically illustrated by an item in the *Morning Post* in November 1845, which noted the competition between the GG&SJR and the promoters of the Hull and Lincoln Direct Railway, which had taken control of the Barton and Hessle ferry. The latter held the contract for the Lincoln and Hull mail, 'but, under direction of the Post-office, have to run the coach down to New Holland, thus avoiding their own ferry'.

This arrangement has been in force since the making of the New Holland road, some years ago, by which the nearest route to Hull was obtained; but the owners of the Barton ferry now meet the mail at the junction of the New Holland and Brigg roads, and bring the passengers down to the Barton Ferry, by omnibus, cross the Humber to Hessle, and thence come by special train to Hull. It appears that by the shorter ferry and four miles of railway, with the special engine, the passengers reach Hull twenty minutes to half an hour before the mail bags. The Grimsby and Sheffield people, on the other hand, are prosecuting the construction of their railway, and as an earnest of what they will do for the convenience of Hull,

are running steamers ten times a day, each way, or twenty passages daily, between New Holland and Hull.

Despite the dubious methods by which the GG&SJR had acquired the Humber ferries, it is undeniable that railway ownership was beneficial. Plans by John Fowler, dated 1845 and currently held at the East Riding Archives and Local Studies Service, show the proposed pier and railways at New Holland, and also the proposed pier to the west of the Humber Dock Basin at Hull. However, the plan for a longer pier in Hull was objected to by navigation interests, and was never built as planned, although the new full length pier at New Holland was constructed.

At a meeting of shareholders of the GG&SJR, reported in the *Sheffield & Rotherham Independent* in May 1845, it was pointed out by the chairman that,

when passengers got to the Humber, if there was no ready communication across it, he was afraid they would regard the Humber as such an impediment, that they would prefer some of the old routes. This bill had been strongly opposed by some parties at Hull, but particularly by the Barton people, from the idea that it would interfere with the ferry there. The bill had been altered in committee, but he thought had passed in such a form, that it would be extremely useful, and give the Company not only a profitable ferry, but an immense advantage in the communication between their railway and Hull, where passengers would have the advantage of railway communication with other places.

Progress was continued by the company's successor, the Manchester Sheffield & Lincolnshire Railway, on its formation in 1846. The first section of line, between Grimsby and New Holland, was opened on 1st March 1848, whilst at the same time the East Lincolnshire Railway line between Grimsby and Louth was opened and was leased to the Great Northern Railway. The MS&LR and the GNR shared the operation of trains between Louth and New Holland.

Under the GG&SJR's Humber Ferries Act of 1846, the MS&LR was able to carry out works at New Holland and Hull to improve the ferries across the Humber and the proposal was to construct not only extensive piers but floating pontoons at both terminals. However, on 17th March 1848 the *Hull Packet* reported the findings of the Admiralty on the proposed development at New Holland and the restrictions that would be placed on any pier to be built at Hull:

The works proposed and the provisions of the bill which affect the jurisdiction of the Admiralty are: 1st – The erection of a pier at Kingston-upon-Hull. 2nd – The enlargement of the whole works at New Holland. 3rd – The regulation of pilotage of the port of Great Grimsby...

At New Holland...an open pier upon timber piles projecting 1,380 feet into the river from high water,

Sketch of the original extended New Holland Pier, showing a paddle steamer and sailing vessel using the old jetty at New Holland, in contrast with the new extended pier, which allowed trains and steamers to connect in deep water. *Illustrated London News, 15th April 1848, Alf Ludlam collection*

or about 600 feet below low water...is now nearly complete, and its outer end will reach into a depth of eight feet at low water or 38 feet at high water at ordinary spring tides. No extension of this pier is proposed by the present bill, but powers are taken in section 4 to make additional piers, wharfs, and also a basin, in and adjoining to, New Holland creek. As the latter works will not offer any obstruction to navigation they have their lordship's assent.

At Kingston-upon-Hull, it is proposed to construct an open pier on timber piles, projecting 1,010 feet into the river Humber, from the line of high water, and about 730 feet beyond the line of low water spring tides, exclusive of floating stages or caissons, which will extend about 40 feet beyond making a total length of 1,050 feet. The pier is to leave the shore at a point 342 yards west of the principal entrance to the Humber Dock Basin...

Across its outer end, three floating stages or caissons, 450 feet in length, by 40 feet wide, are to be secured by piles within which the stages are to rise and fall with the tide, which latter, on an equinoctial spring, ranges from 27 to 30 feet. Communication with the caissons, at low water, will be effected by inclined roadways, on a slope of about 1 in 7, lying on the east and west sides of the main pier.

Notwithstanding the River Humber is more subject to silting than any other river in the United Kingdom, and that silt is the great evil from which the harbour now suffers, their lordships regret to observe that it is in evidence that the Hull Dock Company take out of their docks and basins, and deposit annually in the channel of the river, 80,000 to 100,000 tons of mud, some of which occasionally dropt within a cable's length of the entrance to the Dock Basin, or nearer the shore than the site of the proposed jetty.

Their lordships are fully alive to the necessity and importance of a low water pier at Hull, in order to keep up steam communication, but we are of the opinion that this desirable object may be obtained by a shorter pier, and by dredging a channel up to it, without sacrificing the more important interests of navigation. It appears in evidence given before the surveying officer, that no less that 17,874 vessels cleared inwards and outwards at the port of Hull during the past year, a great part of which entered and sailed from the Dock Basin, distant only 340 yards east of the proposed jetty. Also, it is to be remarked that it is highly desirable for the interest of all parties in Hull, as well as to secure the proper scour of the river, that a straight line of foreshore should be laid down, up to which all works should be advanced, and beyond which none should be permitted to project. Their lordships, therefore, cannot permit that either the proposed pier or any other work should project into the stream beyond a line starting from the south west pier of the Dock Basin at Hull, and drawn westward to the bend in the shore at high-water mark of spring tides on the south edge of the Hull and Selby railway embankment at Dairy Coates Brickfield. With this condition their lordships assent to the bill.

The developments at New Holland, including a picture of the new pier, were presented in the *Illustrated London News* in April 1848. Although the issue's main feature concerned the large demonstration for electoral reform by the Chartists which had taken place in London, the improvements on the Humber were given ample space, emphasising the benefits of the new works:

It was and is common, at present, first to attain a steamer by a boat, then cross the river, and then retake a boat to land on the other side…Men, women, cattle, and merchandise are subject to this inconvenience and delay…But the Bill we have already alluded to proposes, by the erection of piers of enormous length, to supersede this. Already, the railway has reached the ferry on the south side of the Humber: and, instead of all the personal discomfort which our illustration graphically makes clear, a pier upwards of 1500 feet long is extended into the river and is already in use; and an application is before Parliament to enable a corresponding accommodation

Detail from *A Bird's Eye View of the Town of Kingston Upon Hull* (1880) by Frank N. Pettingell, showing the Minerva and Victoria Piers and the Humber, Railway and Prince's Docks. There is a paddle steamer at Corporation Pier. The proposed new pier, extending 1050ft into the Humber, would be 340 yards to the west of the Humber Dock Basin to the left of the picture. *Hull Museums*

Victoria Pier, Hull (1882) by Thomas Dudley, depicting paddle tugs busy in the Humber while two paddle steamers are tied up at the pier with its upper deck promenade. *Hull Museums*

to be erected on the northern side of the Ferry…When all the arrangements are completed, the passage of three miles across the Humber may be made in the shortest time and with the least trouble to the passenger. The most timid lady, instead of stumbling over wet stones – slipping over landing planks – getting in and out of boats, subject to damp shoes and their baneful consequences, will have merely to descend under cover into the saloon of a rapid steamer, and, after a journey of fifteen minutes, ascend again under covered steps on the opposite side of the river.

Before the construction of a pier at New Holland, boarding the ferry by plank was always perilous and sometimes even fatal. In February 1836 the *Hull Packet* described an incident in which a woman who had become inebriated in the Yarborough Arms – 'where her loose conversation was notorious' – had slipped from the plank and fallen into the mud, pulling her elderly companion Mr Anthony (a 'dealer in gingerbread and nuts') in with her. Mr Anthony was saved, but she drowned and her body was not found for some time. The crewman who was supposed to supervise the boarding passengers was subsequently sacked.

The railway-owned ferry service had been provided since 1845 by the two original steamers, *Magna Charta*, built in 1832, and *Falcon*, dating from 1836, and was expanded in 1848 by the purchase of two second-hand paddle steamers,

the *Queen* and the *Prince of Wales*, from operators based on the River Thames. Built in 1842 and 1843 by Ditchburn & Mare of Blackwall, they had iron hulls and were almost 100ft in length. The latter craft were not in service in time to be mentioned in the 1848 *Stephenson's Directory*, which lists the following craft on the Humber: the *Railway* for Boston; the *Albion* for Brigg; the *Columbine, Lindsey* and *Atlas* for Gainsborough; the *Calder, Duke of Wellington, Eagle, Leeds* and *Echo* for Goole; the *Pelham* for Grimsby; the *Falcon* and *Magna Charta* for New Holland; the *Don* and *John Bull* for Thorne and the *City of York, Ebor* and *Arrow* for York.

The new pier at New Holland was designed by John Fowler, chief engineer of the Manchester, Sheffield & Lincolnshire Railway. (His future works included the Metropolitan Railway, opened in 1863, and the Forth Bridge, completed in 1890. He was also involved in a scheme for a railway tunnel under the Humber, although this was abandoned.) At the landward end, New Holland Town station had four through-tracks. A fine, red-brick building with a shallow slate roof and a decorative stone entrance stood on the east side, just north of New Holland Town signal box. An apex-roofed canopy protected the platform and, on the other side, a flat-roofed shelter was provided. A footbridge stood at the southern end of the platform.

Constructed of timber, the pier was thirty-two feet wide and 1,375 feet long, with two lines of rails as well as a carriageway and a footpath along its entire length. The tracks along the pier were bounded on either side by extensions to the Town station platforms, which eventually became the Pier station platforms. On the east side of the pier was a pedestrian walkway; on the west side was a wider access road. At the pier end there were three tracks, the middle one being a siding. A crane was provided for transferring goods to trolleys for loading on and off the ferries. At New Holland Pier station the buildings were of timber construction. The more substantial of the two, which stood on the east side, had refreshment rooms, and a canopy similar to the one at the Town station.

As reported by the *Railway Chronicle*, in February 1848 several directors of the Manchester, Sheffield & Lincolnshire Railway travelled from Hull to New Holland in one of the company's newly purchased boats. After admiring the pier and adjacent dock, they and their friends proceeded to the Yarborough Arms for breakfast, then:

At 10am the party took their places in a train of five carriages, for Grimsby, a distance of 16 miles…About six miles from New Holland we reached a spot where the junction will be formed with the line from Gainsborough and Sheffield. Passing into the Brocklesby domains, which the line intersects for nearly eight miles, we came to Ulceby, where the New Holland branch joins the main line by forming one side of a triangle…We arrived at Grimsby at about 10.45am and were met on the platform by the Mayor and corporation of that ancient borough and a party of Directors of the East Lincolnshire Railway'. The directors then travelled to Louth before returning to Grimsby for dinner. They mentioned that when the Great Northern Railway opened from Louth to Peterborough, passengers will be able to travel direct to Hull from the Metropolis, saving nearly 40 miles in distance and about 10 shillings in money.

In December 1849 a pontoon was installed at the end of New Holland Pier. This rose and fell with the tide, making the transfer between rail and river much easier at all stages of the tide. Constructed entirely of wrought iron, except for the platform, the pontoon had watertight bulkheads, and at the time was the largest of its kind in the country. Manufactured by locomotive engineers E.B. Wilson & Co. at a cost of £17,500, it was 400 feet long, 52½ feet wide and eight feet deep, weighed almost 700 tons and had a deck area of 20,000 square feet. The pontoon was conveyed in sections from Wilson's works in Leeds along the Aire & Calder Navigation to Goole. There it was reassembled and launched sideways into the River Ouse. The launch caused a great deal of excitement, as reported in the *Hull Packet*.

She went sideways down the slip most beautifully into the water, and after floating about twenty minutes in mid-stream, was brought to the shore and entered by a band of music and several hundred visitors. The national

anthem was played. The company then retired, and immediately afterwards six steamers…were attached to her cables, and brought her down to New Holland in the short space of three hours and a quarter.

Once secured there were two tubular iron bridges that connected the pier to the pontoon, each 140 feet long, ten feet wide and ten feet deep.

Despite the triumph of these developments at New Holland, the method used to purchase the ferries was still bothering some people and, in June 1850, the Manchester, Sheffield & Lincolnshire Railway's shareholders met at the Corn Exchange, Manchester, and drew up a resolution condemning those members of the board of the GG&SJR who had been involved in the purchase of the ferries. According to Dow, the directors of the MS&LR were ordered to 'make immediate application to the parties who participated' for the repayment of the £11,330 exacted, with interest, and, 'failing the success of such application legal steps be taken by the Directors against all or any such parties to compel a refund of such overcharge'. As far as Dow was aware, this was promptly done and the whole of the money was eventually paid back.

MANCHESTER, SHEFFIELD, AND LIN-COLNSHIRE RAILWAY.
CHEAP PLEASURE TRIP BY RAILWAY AND SEA!
TO SPURN POINT AND BACK THE SAME DAY,
FROM SHEFFIELD, WORKSOP, RETFORD AND
GAINSBRO'.
A SPECIAL TRAIN will leave the Bridgehouses Station, Sheffield, on M O N D A Y, June 24th, at 6 a.m., calling at Worksop at 6.40, Retford at 7.10, and Gainsbro' Station at 7.30 a.m.
On arrival at New Holland the Passengers will embark from the New Iron Floating Pontoon, on Board one of the Company's Steamers, which will at once proceed to Hull. The Company's Splendid New Iron Steamer the "Sheffield," of 150 Horses power, will leave the Corporation Pier, Hull, for the Sea Trip, at 2 p.m. precisely, and will proceed along the Yorkshire Coast to Spurn Head and Lighthouse, returning by way of the Lincolnshire Coast, and after calling at the Corporation Pier, Hull, about 5.30 p.m. to take up the Passengers who have remained there, she will proceed at once to New Holland, from whence the Return Train will immediately Start, Arriving at Sheffield about 9 p.m.
The "Sheffield" is fitted up in the most luxurious style, with Deck Saloon, and is the most magnificent and fastest sailing Steamer upon the Humber. Refreshments will be Provided on Board, and a Band of Music will accompany the Steamer.
FARES THERE AND BACK, INCLUDING THE
STEAM-BOAT TRIP:
First Class.   Covered Carriages.
From Sheffield........   7s.   ..   4s.
„ Worksop ....   6s.   ..   3s.
„ Retford ....   5s. 6d.   ..   2s. 6d.
„ Gainsbro'........   4s.   ..   2s.
Persons wishing to visit Grimsby instead of Hull, may do so with the same Tickets, by alighting at Ulceby, and proceeding from thence by any of the Regular Trains, and Returning by the Regular Train at 5.30 p.m. to meet the Special Return Train. The same Tickets will also be available to Return from Hull and Grimsby by any of the ordinary Trains up to WEDNESDAY Night.
Omnibuses meet the Trains at Grimsby for that beautiful Sea-bathing place Cleethorpes, distant only Two Miles.
The Tickets for Grimsby will entitle the holders to view the Works of the New Dock, now being constructed there.
The Committee of the Zoological Gardens, Hull, will Admit Persons shewing their Trip Tickets, for 6d. each.
Early application for Tickets is necessary, as to ensure punctuality, a limited number will be issued.
JAMES ALLPORT, General Manager.
Manchester, June 12th, 1850.

The Manchester, Sheffield and Lincolnshire Railway were organising pleasure cruises as early as 1850 as shown by this advertisement from the *Sheffield and Rotherham Independent*, of 15th June that year.

As mentioned earlier, plans for a pier to the west of the Humber Dock entrance in Hull were opposed by the dock and shipping interests, who feared that the longer pier would interfere with access to the docks. The GG&SJR, and later its successor, the MS&LR, had powers to establish proper landing facilities at Hull but, because these were not acted upon, it was found that at low tide there was insufficient water for steamers to approach the quays and passengers were obliged to embark and disembark using small boats. In February 1848 the *Hull Packet* reported on the official inquiry into the MS&LR's proposal for landing places in Hull. Since April Captain Charles Bailey, master of the New Holland ferry, had followed the instructions of Stephen Court, the resident engineer at New Holland, to 'keep a log showing the difficulties he had to encounter in landing at the piers in Hull, specifying clearly every time he was not able to land, giving the depth of water &c'. Court himself had several times travelled on ferries which had run aground at the Ferryboat Dock pier in Hull, and 'had also seen a great number of other steamboats aground, in fact no less than seven at one time'. As an engineer, 'he was of the opinion that a pier built on the same principle as that at New Holland would be no obstruction at all'. Captain Bailey believed that 'the New Corporation Pier was not high enough, and at high water steam-packets were in danger of having their paddle wheels broken'. The side wheels of the paddle steamers were always vulnerable in this situation.

Opposing the railway company's proposal to construct the new pier, Mr Reynolds of the dock company had pointed out that the existing Corporation Pier was quite sufficient, that the proposed longer pier to the west of the Humber Dock Basin would deposit people away from the centre of the town (the area now referred to as the Old Town) and oblige them to cross the dock bridges. It would also, for the sake of pleasing a few ferry passengers, impede access to the docks and destroy shipping in Hull. The town clerk asserted that the town's main concern was to protect shipping. He recalled the history of the Corporation Pier:

Until November 1845, there was only a breakwater, which formed the Ferryboat dock, wholly unconnected with Nelson Street, and the only landing was at the Quay. This was found to be very inconvenient. On November 20th that year, the Town Council passed a resolution for the construction of the new pier, and to communicate with any railway company for co-operation. A plan for a low water jetty was proposed by the Manchester Sheffield & Lincolnshire Railway Company, similar to that now submitted by them, and which at that time the Corporation deemed impracticable. In December, a deputation of the Council met with several of the railway directors and several thousand pounds were promised in aid of the work, which promise, however, was never fulfilled.

He complained that, despite this, the railway company had tried to compulsorily purchase land in Wellington Street. This

Engraving of the *Old Manchester*, built in 1849 by Robinson & Russell of Millwall, published in the *Illustrated London News*. She was known as *Old Manchester* from 1855 when a new vessel of the same name was built for her owners the Manchester, Sheffield & Lincolnshire Railway. *Alf Ludlam collection*

was opposed as it was felt it would be for the construction of a jetty, to the detriment of shipping. There was a genuine concern that any pier would cause masses of mud to build up and obstruct the dock entrance, as it was well known that the estuary was laden with sediment. In fact whole islands – such as Whitton Sand and Sunk Island – had formed, disappeared and reappeared in the Humber.

In July 1848 the *Hull Packet* stated that any pier built 'was not allowed to project beyond the line agreed by the Admiralty, and also that no tubular bridge or caissons would be allowed'. The existing pier, or breakwater, known as the Ferryboat Dock, which stood out in the water to the east of the Humber Dock entrance, had been linked to the shore by a platform in 1847, thus forming a proper pier against which ferries could moor. According to Dow, the unsatisfactory situation for the ferry boats was eased after April 1856 when the Manchester, Sheffield & Lincolnshire's general manager, Edward Watkin, offered the Mayor of Hull an annual payment of up to £40 towards the cost of proper landing facilities at Corporation Pier.

The MS&LR had its own offices in Hull, situated at Walkington's Lodgings, which were acquired for £850 in January 1849. In August, 7 Nelson Street, close to the pier, became the company's booking office for passengers and parcels, the clerk living in the upper floor. The company acquired the neighbouring property in May 1854 and constructed a new building in 1880, which continued to serve the ferries for a century (it has since been converted into flats). Goods traffic to and from New Holland was dealt with at Limekiln Creek, where the MS&LR's depot in Hull was connected to the NER's depot by a horse-operated line crossing Wellington Street. Between 1856 and 1858 the MS&LR's premises were operated by the NER under an agreement between the two companies.

The railway line from Barton-on-Humber to New Holland opened in 1849 and, in the same year, the MS&LR inaugurated a ferry service between Hull and Grimsby, using the newly constructed iron paddle-steamers *Manchester*, built in London, and *Sheffield,* built in Gainsborough. They were also used on the New Holland service. According to an article in the *Sheffield & Rotherham Independent* that September:

Mr Fowler visited all the principal ferries in England and Scotland, to acquire a knowledge of the various descriptions of boat already in use; and having thus made himself acquainted with all the improvements hitherto introduced into modern steam ferries, he made a design for two powerful steamers, the entire construction of one of which was entrusted by the company to Messrs. Robinson and Russell, engineers and iron ship builders, Millwall; and the hull of the other to Messrs. H.E. Smith and Son, of Gainsborough, with engines to be furnished by Messrs.[J.G.] Rennie, of London.

Russell was well known for his knowledge of hull design, whilst Smith had experience of building paddle steamers for the Humber. Later the two vessels were given a competing run on the Thames by 'a cruise round the Nore Lights and back again. It was arranged that when the boats arrived off Erith, they should be laid alongside each other, and a regular trial of speed should take place'. *Manchester* was the fastest, although *Sheffield* arrived earlier (she had turned at the same time as *Manchester*, which was further downriver).

Manchester was 150 feet long and double-ended with large paddle boxes and two rudders. These rudders were described at the time as 'peculiarly strong and accurate pieces of workmanship; the rudder posts forming what are called snuff-box joints, and the rudders themselves forming part of the line of the vessel, so as not to be distinguishable from its natural form when used as a bow'. She also had a large passenger saloon on the deck, fitted with plate-glass windows. *Sheffield* was also built with two-cylinder, oscillating engines. She was lengthened to 160 feet during construction and was not delivered until 1850. Neither vessel was very successful, *Manchester* being particularly difficult to manoeuvre. They were both superseded in 1855 by boats given the same names, theirs being changed to *Old Manchester* and *Old Sheffield*.

The year 1850 saw some animosity between the MS&LR and the Great Northern Railway when the former joined the 'Euston Square Confederacy' against the latter. Some GNR trains were obstructed from using the New Holland branch, over which they had been granted running powers in 1848. During this time the older Barton ferries struggled on against the ever-increasing competition from the New Holland route. The Barton to Hessle ferry was first closed in 1851. The MS&LR considered purchasing it but decided against doing so. The ferry was briefly re-opened in July 1852 by the York & North Midland Railway, which had taken over the Hull & Selby Railway, and it carried out some improvements to the Barton jetty in the hope of being able to compete with the MS&LR route via New Holland. Despite this, the ferry was again closed, although a meeting was held in Barton on 4th March 1856 in an attempt to revive it and the MS&LR ran some trips between Hull and Barton, although they were not maintained. In 1858 the Crown Estates leased land and the ferry rights to William Wilkinson for £500 and he also purchased the Waterside Inn and land from James Clapson. By this time the Barton ferry was no longer carrying passengers, although livestock and general goods were still taken over the Humber to Hessle and Hull. By the 1890s a sailing sloop was being used on this route.

Perhaps the greatest moment in the history of Hull's Corporation Pier was the visit of Queen Victoria and Prince Albert on 13th October 1854. Arriving by train at Paragon station, the royal couple were welcomed by civic dignitaries and, after a night at the station hotel, drove through town to the pier, passing the crowds amassed en route. Sheahan, writing just ten years later, describes the scene:

At the entrance of Corporation Pier…Her Majesty was received by the Mayor, Recorder, and Town Clerk (the Mayor bearing the Mace), and ushered up the roofed

Postcard view of a paddle steamer alongside Minerva Pier, Hull, in the early twentieth century. The pier is crowded and a second boat appears to be ready to come alongside as soon as there is room. *Author's collection*

way of the pier, the floor of which was covered with a rich velvet pile carpet…Here the cheering of the multitude was so great that the national anthem, which was played by the military bands, could scarcely be heard.

Queen Victoria knighted the Mayor of Hull in a short ceremony held close to the great lamp on the pier. Afterwards the local dignitaries accompanied the royals on a trip through the docks on board the royal steam yacht *Fairy*. Although renamed Victoria Pier in honour of the visit, the new name never really caught on and it continued to be referred to as Corporation Pier, a tradition followed by this book.

By the 1850s the steamers *Queen* and *Prince of Wales* had been sold and the Humber ferry was being operated by a hired-in paddle steamer called *Petrel*, as well as the original *Manchester* and *Sheffield*. These craft were replaced by the new *Manchester* and *Sheffield*, built by Martin Samuelson of Hull, in 1854. The renamed *Old Manchester* was sent to the

Mersey in 1858 to operate between Garston and Liverpool, returning to the Humber the following year. The *Old Sheffield* was sold to a new owner on the Thames in 1863.

By 1860 the New Holland to Hull ferry had become established as the principal river crossing. There was a need for repair facilities and, in 1867, the MS&LR built small workshops at Grimsby; these were placed under a marine superintendent, the first of whom was George Copley. New Holland itself was an increasingly important railway town. As well as facilities for the ferries, an engine shed had been built in 1847 alongside the triangle, formed by the lines to New Holland Town, Barton and Grimsby and by 1872 forty-five passenger and twenty goods trains were being handled each day. Only in 1887 did Grimsby – rather than New Holland – become the terminus of the main line from Manchester. In 1912 Immingham's new shed took over the maintenance tasks formerly carried out at new Holland, which became a sub-shed of Immingham, finally closing in 1938.

Chapter Five

THE BUSY HUMBER

The Mercantile Navy List for 1857 includes the following paddle steamers, over thirty tons, working on the Humber: at Gainsborough the *Atalanta*, *Columbine* and *Harlequin*; at Hull the *Manchester*, *Chesapeake*, *Magna Charta*, *Royal Albion*, *Old Sheffield* and *Sheffield*; at Thorne the *Don*; and at Grimsby the *Pelham*. The *Atalanta*, built in 1851, was a remarkably long-lived steamer, featuring in the Mercantile Navy Lists and Lloyd's Register from the 1850s right through until 1927, amassing seventy-six years of service. Many of these paddle steamers were built locally. The building of sailing ships had long been a major industry on the Humber and Sheahan, writing in 1864, mentions the prominence of shipbuilding in Hull:

Iron ship building has for several years been one of the most important branches of trade in Hull, and at present it is in a very flourishing state…The great iron shipbuilding and engineering firm of Martin Samuelson and Co. commenced business in Hull in 1849 as marine and general engineers, millwrights and iron and brass founders. In 1854 they extended their premises, and added to their already large establishment, the iron ship building business.

After the *New Manchester* and *Sheffield* of 1854, Samuelson built two further paddle steamers for the Humber ferry service: the *Liverpool* in 1855 and the *Doncaster* in 1856. Sheahan continues:

There is another great iron shipbuilding and marine engineering establishment here, belonging to Messrs. Charles and William Earle. Twenty years ago these gentlemen established their Junction Foundry, situated on the Prince's (formerly called the Junction) Dock side. Here the firm make the marine engines, &c. for their ships. In 1852 Messrs. Earle commenced the building of iron ships, and their fine ship yard, on the bank of the Humber, covers an area of eight acres, exclusive of the new patent slip, which the firm recently built for the Dock Company, from which they lease it…

Both yards constructed large screw, or propeller-driven, vessels for ocean trade as well as paddle steamers. Samuelson's premises were situated at the western end of Victoria Dock, close to the mouth of the River Hull on the site of the old Hull Citadel; Earle's yard was to the east of Victoria Dock, where they originally launched into the dock itself but, in 1863, the yard was extended to include a slipway directly into the Humber, which was more convenient and allowed for the construction of larger craft.

In the 1850s steamers were serving many other towns on the Humber and associated rivers, particularly in connection with the developing railways. A Goole newspaper advertisement of 2nd June 1856 announced that:

The public are respectfully informed that the New Steamer 'Empress' which has been built in London expressly for the conveyance of passengers between Goole and Hull is now on the station, and will leave Goole every weekday morning on the arrival of the first train, and return from Hull in time for the 6.30 train for Leeds, Wakefield, etc. At no time will she leave Hull before 3 p.m., but according to the tides the time in Hull will vary from 3 to 6 hours. Fares, Best Cabin 1s.6d; Fore Cabin 1s. To Hull and back on the same day 2s and 1s.6d. The Empress has been built under special superintendence on the model of the noted fast Thames boats with the engines by the celebrated Messrs Miller and Ravenhill, and as she had been fully tested for speed and draught of water, and will be confined exclusively to the conveyance of Passengers, the Public may depend on the regularity of this conveyance.

In 1860 *Royal Albion*, built by Martin Samuelson in 1855, was operating the Hull to New Holland service, along with *Liverpool* and *Doncaster*. In 1874 the latter two were fitted with new engines by Lairds. In 1873 *Magna Charta II*, built by T. Charlton of Grimsby, who also provided the engines, was added to the ferry service. *Manchester II* (or *New Manchester*, the prefix and suffix not being shown on these vessels) was the standby vessel, although she was expensive to run, having two boilers and oscillating engines which consumed six tons of coal a day.

Disaster struck when the pontoon at New Holland was destroyed and sunk in a violent storm which hit the Humber during the night of 18th October 1869, also causing severe damage to local shipping. Four days later the *Hull Packet* reported:

On Tuesday morning the nine o'clock steamer from New Holland brought intelligence of the sinking of the Manchester, Sheffield and Lincolnshire Railway

Doncaster in the horse-wash, alongside the eastern end of Hull Corporation Pier. *Brian Peeps collection*

Doncaster pulling away from Hull Corporation Pier and passing some steam boats, November 1911. *Hull Daily Mail*

Company's pontoon at that place. An announcement was at once made that the traffic be stopped at low water, it being impossible to land passengers from Hull. It appears that the pontoon sunk whilst the steamboat was leaving New Holland, the passengers having been shipped in the harbour in consequence of the storm. It was almost entirely submerged, and part at least of the 'tube' through which passengers have to pass to it from the railway. It was first thought that the failure in the strength of the structure was entirely owing to the violence of the storm and various sensational rumours were afloat…but inquiries which were held proved that there were defects in the pontoon itself which might in part account for the disaster, though the consequences might not have been so serious had it not been for the violent state of the weather.

The first dramatic attempt to raise the pontoon was reported in the *Sheffield and Rotherham Independent* on 10th November 1869. Following the advice of one of the company's masters, Captain Hollingsworth, nineteen lighters were brought over the sunken pontoon and chained to it.

By half-past four most of the lighters were pretty well down in the water, and in a few minutes more it was seen that the whole mass moved upward with the rising tide. Half-an-hour more passed away, and still the lighters continued to float…Meantime the tide increased in strength, and it began to bubble and foam amongst the lighters in a manner which showed what a fearful strain was put upon the vessels. Exactly at five o'clock the action of the tide forced the pontoon out from the dolphins which for the last twenty years have kept it in position. The eastern end was the first to move, and as the vessels were seen to swing out into the open river the large number of spectators gave three hearty cheers. Soon the whole was floating well out, but the tide, which was flowing with unusual force, caught the east end of the pontoon, and swung it athwart the stream with such violence that the lighter at that end was almost submerged. The two men stationed on board were afraid that the vessel was about to sink, and they cut the lashings which held the chains together. The effect was to throw a sudden strain on the next lighter, which was also liberated, and the next, and the next. Cutting adrift then became general, and such a scene ensued as is rarely witnessed. The men on board the lighters appeared to become nervous. The man at the head would cut his chain adrift before the man at the stern could do so, and the result was that the end of the vessel first liberated flew high into the air, the lighter for an instant standing almost perpendicular…Before the last lighter had been cut adrift, the pontoon was once more at the bottom, but it is now out of the way of the passenger traffic, which has been most seriously interfered with since the accident.

The pontoon was finally raised at the third attempt using twenty-two lighters and a number of tugs. Once afloat the whole mass moved onto the beach at high tide where, according to the *York Herald* of 11th December 1869, 'It is intended to repair the pontoon and replace it in its old position, and for this purpose a huge gridiron will be constructed by the company's permanent-way men on which it will be placed. It is believed that in two months the pontoon will be floating in its old place'.

During this time there was talk of replacing the pontoon with an old paddle steamer called *Stockport*, after removing and selling its engines and using its saloons as waiting rooms, but the idea was dropped. (*Stockport*, like *Sheffield III*, was a former American Civil War blockade runner, purchased by the MS&LR in 1866 for continental services. Both ships were sold in the 1870s.) However, eventually it was decided not to repair the pontoon, despite the enormous efforts that had been made to raise it. In January 1870 the *Leeds Mercury* reported that:

it was found to be greatly strained and damaged. Having regard to its originally defective construction, and liability to similar accidents hereafter if the old structure were repaired, the directors have decided to provide improved permanent landing place, which they consider every way preferable to the adoption of a pontoon.

From this time, until the improvements of the 1930s, New Holland Pier had sloping ramps against which the ferries moored at different states of the tide. These are clearly visible in pre-1930s photographs.

In March 1875 the *York Herald* reported that *Manchester II* had run into and sunk the steamer *British Hero*, which was subsequently successfully raised and repaired. Later in the same year *Manchester* ran aground and broke her back. She was replaced by *Manchester III*, built by Goole Engineering & Shipbuilding Co. Ltd in 1876.

The pier and landing arrangements at Hull were still causing concern at this time. In October 1875 the *Hull Packet* reported that a committee was considering filling in the ferry-boat dock and constructing a promenade in its place, adjacent to the Minerva pub, a plan that had been repeatedly raised over a number years. There were questions about this from several committee members.

Mr Williamson asked where they would put the ferry-boats, &c, if they did away with the dock. The Chairman said it was no use making an objection. They had got an Act of Parliament to fill up the dock, and it must be done. Mr Williamson: Where do you suggest putting the market-boats and sloops? The Chairman said he suggested that the old harbour should be cleaned out, and those vessels put there.

Further debate took place about extending the pier:

The steamers *Grimsby* (1888) and *Cleethorpes* (1903) moored alongside New Holland Pier. Note the slope used to reach the ferries before the new pontoon of 1935.
Photograph reproduced courtesy of North East Lincolnshire Council Library Service

The *Grimsby* tied up at New Holland Pier with a train in the station. There is a further paddle steamer close behind her and two more funnels on the other side of the pier.
Photograph reproduced courtesy of North East Lincolnshire Council Library Service

Mr Williamson next inquired whether the pier was going to be carried out further than at present. If not they would always have a complaint such as Alderman Seaton had been making as to the awkwardness of landing sometimes at low water. The pier ought to be taken twenty feet further out. The Chairman said it was not intended to take the pier any further out than at present, as, for one reason, they had no power to do so without an act of parliament, or permission from the Conservancy Board.

In late February 1879 the *Hull Packet* reported the corporation's continuing deliberations over the issue of filling in the Ferry Boat Dock and installing a pontoon, with one councillor claiming that:

Unless the mouth of the river Hull was altered so as to allow the tide to come by the entrance it would be utterly impossible to get a better flow in front of the pier… Vessels going down the river at the present time had a very great difficulty in keeping clear of the pier, and if, as it was proposed, a pontoon for landing purposes was placed further out into the river the difficulty would be very much increased. Another great objection to the pontoon was that it would be almost an impossibility to keep it clear, as mud would gradually collect, and so prevent it rising and falling with the water, as it should do.

The problem of mud fouling the pontoon was still being faced by one ferry manager in the 1970s as is revealed in Chapter Eight.

There was also concern over the total cost of the project to the ratepayers as the dock company would not fund the proposed improvements. It was moved:

> That it is inexpedient to spend the sum of £70,000 in filling in and reclaiming the site of the Ferryboat Dock on the plans prepared by the Borough Engineer; under the instructions of the Ferryboat Dock Committee of the Hull Town Council, and that the Corporation be requested to obtain the services of Mr James Abernethy, C.E. of London, to report upon the best method of dealing with the Ferryboat Dock… his fee for the above not to exceed 150 guineas; or if it be found that there is no absolute compulsion on the part of the Corporation to fill in the dock, that the present piers and landing-stages be efficiently repaired, and the dock cleaned out, if necessary, at a

minimum cost, and that the drain [outlet] be carried into the Humber.

Mr Elam, chairman of the Ferryboat Dock Committee, urged them to carry out improvements as the Act of Parliament to fill in the dock had been handed down in 1872 and they would have to 'get rid of that before they could get rid of their obligation to fill in the dock'. Alderman Willows pointed out that one plan for filling in the dock

reclaimed 3,800 square yards of land, which would be utilised for widening Nelson Street, and provide 30 feet quay outside of the promenade. The design included a wrought-iron pier, with inside and outside landing stages, in place of the heavy structure existing, and upon this would be erected a covered gangway, with two rows of shops or offices for the Manchester, Sheffield and Lincolnshire Railway Company, either of which would bring in a considerable revenue.

He also suggested that this plan would retain the water space for smaller craft.

A battle raged between those who wanted improvements and those who were concerned about committing ratepayers to an ongoing charge of interest payments on the money raised to pay for the work. Not until 4th December 1882 was the *York Herald* able to announce that:

View of Hull Corporation Pier in the late nineteenth century, from a postcard showing the upper promenade of the new pier opened in 1882. The upper deck of the promenade, demolished in 1965, was popular with spectators. *Author's collection*

The new Victoria Pier, Hull…has been undergoing reconstruction, the original structure having fallen into a very dilapidated condition. The tender of Messrs. Storry and Jagger, of Hull, amounting to several thousands of pounds, was accepted by the Corporation, and it is only due to the contractors to say that they have carried out their arduous undertaking in a manner which reflects the greatest credit upon them, and a special word of praise is due to the Borough Engineer for designing such an elegant structure as that which has been reared on the site of the landing stage which for so many years past was anything but a credit to the third port in the kingdom. On Saturday the pier was formally declared open by the Mayor (Alderman Leak), in the presence of a large concourse of spectators. The Ferryboat Dock Committee, who have had the work under their immediate control, assembled at the Town-hall shortly before noon, and from thence proceeded to South End, and there forming in procession, and proceeded by the Chief Constable (Mr. J. Campbell), and the sword and mace of the Corporation, the Mayor and a large number of the members of the Council ascended to the upper portion, the band of the police force, under Mr Dodgson, in the meantime dispensing 'sweet music'. The procession being halted at the southern end of the pier, Mr Councillor Myles Raven called upon the Mayor to declare the pier open to the public.

This new pier included a covered promenade on two levels (the upper level was demolished in 1965).

There were always challenges in operating the ferries across a busy estuary. On the night of 24th November 1881, the steamer *Liverpool* was involved in a collision with the keel *Jane and Mary*, causing the latter to sink. The Board of Trade inquiry was reported in the *Hull Packet and East Riding Times* in December. The *Jane and Mary* was carrying a cargo of about sixty-six tons to Sheffield, and was crewed by a man and a boy.

About a quarter to seven, the weather being dark and clear, and the wind blowing strongly from the SSW, the keel was running from New Holland before the wind, with the intention of getting into Hull for shelter. She was not carrying any lights at all. The Liverpool was crossing from Hull to New Holland, with a crew of seven hands, and about 50 passengers, when she saw the Jane and Mary right ahead, about 60 yards distant, running before the wind. The order was at once given to reverse and stop the engines, and [it was] believed the order was given to put the helm hard-a-port. Before, however, the steamer could be stopped, she struck the keel, and the latter sank almost directly.

Captain Hollingsworth of the *Liverpool* (the man also responsible for the successful method of raising the New Holland pontoon) stated that every endeavour had been made to avoid the collision. His vessel had a lookout and good lights. The keel also had a lookout, but was under no legal obligation to carry lights. However, its captain had made no effort to warn the *Liverpool* by showing a light. The inquiry exonerated Captain Hollingsworth of any blame.

In 1888 Earle's of Hull built the *Grimsby II*. She was the first to have a steel hull, and was said to be so powerful that she could complete the crossing in just seven minutes. (The first *Grimsby* owned by the railway company was a screw steamer and not one of the paddle steamers used on the ferry service.)

A devastating fire occurred at New Holland on Sunday 13th January 1895. The *Hull Daily Mail* reported that:

> Considerable damage was done, a portion of the Pier and the Pier station of the Manchester Sheffield and Lincolnshire Railway Company being destroyed…The fire broke out at an early hour in the morning. It was 6 o'clock when the alarm was given. Many persons were then aroused from their slumbers… Now and then, as the piles beneath the platform were burnt away, they let fall a large mass of lighted timber, which fell into the waters…The Company's paddle steamer Manchester went across from Hull with her hose and very valuable aid did her crew, with a good staff of assistants, render. There were many willing helpers from Grimsby, the Company's fire brigade being amongst the number…There was a great anxiety for some time as to the safety of the Company's steamers. The Grimsby was moored at the west end of the pier… and the Liverpool and Magna Charta were on the other side. It may certainly be said that the Grimsby had a narrow escape, for the ropes by which she was fastened to the pier were burnt.

Due to the difficulty in landing passengers after the fire, a special train was run via Doncaster. The damage was extensive and it required considerable work to restore a normal service. By 31st January 1896 an emergency timetable was still in operation, and the MS&LR made special arrangements for the conveyance of cattle, sheep, carriages and carts. It was only on 27th March that the *Hull Daily Mail* was able to report that 'Plans for the erection of refreshment-rooms, waiting-rooms and necessary offices were laid before the Barton magistrates on Monday and passed'. Rebuilding was not completed until 1898, three years after the disaster.

Photographs taken around the turn of the century show a pontoon moored against the pier at Hull, to which steamers could attach lines, whatever the state of the tide. According to the *Victoria County History*, a pontoon had been moored at Corporation Pier in 1877. It appears that, despite its convenience for ferry operators, a pontoon could cause problems: in July 1899 Hull Corporation brought an action against the MS&LR for mooring a pontoon against the pier in contravention of its rights. An item in the *Yorkshire Herald*

The paddle steamer *Liverpool* moored to the pontoon at Hull Corporation Pier. *Author's collection*

on 4th July explained that the railway company 'had rights only on the Lincolnshire side of the river. Those which they possessed on the north, or left, side of the Humber were by leave and licence' of the corporation. The following year the railway applied for the right to continue using the pontoon.

The Manchester Sheffield & Lincolnshire Railway was renamed the Great Central Railway (GCR) in 1897 with the building of the new London extension, which opened through to Marylebone station in 1899. Its fleet of paddle steamers all lasted into the next century, the first to go being the *Liverpool*, which was broken up in 1905. *Doncaster* and *Manchester III* remained in service until 1913 and 1914, whilst *Grimsby II* and *Magna Charta II* lasted until 1924. According to Dow, *Doncaster* was sold for £600 in 1914 to Hans Trouve of Boulogne. She was by then the longest-serving ferry on the Hull to New Holland crossing, having sailed on that route for fifty-seven years.

Inevitably, the old Barton ferry service deteriorated over the years and, as late as 1891, Thomas Stamp was carrying

Hull Corporation Pier, with ferries and packets. Note the pontoon moored alongside the pier. The training ship *Southampton*, on the right, was built in 1805, and was used to train orphan boys for service in the Royal Navy and Merchant Navy. She was towed away and scrapped in 1912. *Photograph reproduced courtesy of North East Lincolnshire Council Library Service*

Hull Pier with two paddle steamers, possibly the *Magna Charta* on the left and the *Grimsby* on the right, alongside the pontoon which appears to have been made from an old steamer hull or barge. People need to cross several small bridges to reach the furthermost ferry. Note the Humber sloops in background. *Brian Peeps collection*

The *Killingholme* alongside the pier at Hull. Note the crane on Minerva Pier and also that the floating pontoon has been removed. People seem to be very interested in an event which is taking place out of site of the photographer. *Brian Peeps collection*

The Pier, Kingston upon Hull by Thomas Jacques Somerscales, 1922. Note the Humber sloop and a tug on the left, and a paddle steamer, possibly the *Grimsby*, leaving the pier. *Hull Museums*

goods between Barton and Hull, not in a steamer but in the sailing sloop *Bee*. By this time all trade had ceased between Barton and Hessle, although the crossing between Barton and Hull continued to be used into the twentieth century, finally ceasing in the face of increasing road competition.

Although the railway-owned ferry between Hull and New Holland was important, two independent companies were still operating paddle steamers on the Humber at the beginning of the twentieth century. These were the Gainsborough United Steam Packet Company and the Goole and Hull Steam Packet Company. The former owned *Columbine*, *Atalanta* and *Isle of Axholme*, built in 1848, 1851 and 1860 respectively. *Atalanta* spent time each summer at Bridlington and Scarborough and was used for cruises. The Goole and Hull company owned *Lady Elizabeth* and *Empress*, both built in 1856, and *Her Majesty*, built in 1860. A new *Empress* was built in 1893. The Gainsborough company ceased trading in 1905 and its steamers were bought by the East Coast Passenger Service, which sold *Isle of Axholme* to the Goole and Hull company in 1912.

In 1903 the GCR commissioned the construction of a new ship, *Cleethorpes*, from Gourlay Brothers of Dundee; this was the first new vessel to operate the Humber ferry service in the new century. She was originally going to be a twin-screw steamer but, owing to the shallow water and shifting sandbanks, was built as a paddle steamer, as was customary on the Humber. Richard H. Coton described her as 'possibly the most attractive of all the Humber paddlers', having 'an open

foredeck, a single, well-raked funnel forward of the paddles, and a full width passenger saloon aft with a promenade deck above it'. Brian Peeps, archivist of the Humber Keel and Sloop Preservation Society, has a copy of a diary kept by Arthur Rushforth, a joiner on the ferry service based at New Holland around the turn of the twentieth century. One entry mentions the new arrival.

October 6th 1903. Launch of PS Cleethorpes from Gourlay Bros. Trial trip November 5th. Arrived New Holland Sat November 21st about 12.15 midday, and whilst swinging round the East pier end she pulled her forward port gangway door overboard; a diver came round from the Grimsby November 27th and got it up same day. She went for a spin on Weds Dec 9th. Started on the ferry on Sat Dec 12th. First trip with passengers was 2.20pm.

Despite this investment, not everyone was impressed with the railway and ferry service operated by the GCR. A letter in the *Hull Times* in September 1910 gives a very poor impression of crossing the Humber:

I think it is high time the Board of Trade step in and do something for the poor unfortunate passengers that are compelled to travel with a company like the Great Central Railway, who advertise rapid luxury travel. As for the first thing, their carriages are lost in dirt, and not fit for a passenger with a decent dress to enter; and secondly, the miserable state of things you have to put up with when you arrive at the beautiful place of change called New Holland Pier, which, in my opinion, is far more miserable to look at than Hedon Road Gaol, with waiting rooms like convict cells, offering just a glimmering of light; and thirdly, when you board the so-called passenger steamer it is more like a farmyard than a passenger boat, dirty by being used for the conveyance of worn out horses consigned for Germany or Holland, let alone beast and sheep, and worst of all the carriers' luggage, comprising for the most part of poultry which are generally well covered with a little insect which is most troublesome to passengers.

At the beginning of 1911 Hull Corporation was preparing to build a new pontoon for Corporation Pier. The GCR had offered to pay £1,500 per annum for the use of the facilities. There was a feeling on all sides that improvement was needed to the service, including the steamers then in use. According to the minutes of a meeting held by the GCR Steamship Committee at Marylebone on 26th January 1911:

It was reported that the Company's ferry steamers Cleethorpes, Grimsby, Manchester and Magna Charta

are old vessels and out of date for dealing with the Hull New Holland traffic, and a drawing was submitted by the Port Master of what is considered the most desirable type of vessel for the service, the design showing the double ended steamer with steering at either end, by which a good deal of manoeuvring would be avoided, and the arrival and departure to and from piers greatly facilitated.

Records in the National Archives show that tenders for two new ferries were sought by the GCR from a number of builders, including Caledonian Shipbuilding & Engineering Co.; William Denny & Brothers, Dumbarton; G. Rennie & Co., Greenwich; Ailsa Shipbuilding Co. Troon; John I. Thorneycroft & Co., Southampton; and Earle's Shipbuilding and Engineering Co., Hull. The latter three were the only firms able to provide a tender for the cost of building one or two ships, and Earle's was selected. A letter dated 21st July 1911 stated that Earle's would build two new ferries at a cost of £17,050 each, which was lower than the quotes from the other two yards.

The new paddle steamers, launched from Earle's in 1912, were *Brocklesby* and *Killingholme*. They were double-ended, enabling them to steam equally well in either direction, having rudders at each end. A spacious promenade deck

A model of *Killingholme*, clearly showing the rudder in the bow which allowed her, like Brocklesby, to work in either direction. *Killingholme* was built by Earle's Shipbuilding and Engineering Company, in Hull in 1912 and survived both world wars. *Hull Museums*

Killingholme, newly painted for the opening of Immingham Docks in 1912. *Photograph reproduced courtesy of North East Lincolnshire Council Library Service*

Brocklesby, built by Earle's of Hull in 1912. *Hull Daily Mail*

with seating was provided for both first and third class passengers. A first class saloon, with rectangular windows and a large dome skylight, was situated on the main deck, with an open-well double staircase leading to a lower saloon. A refreshment bar was also provided. A large cabin for third class passengers below the main deck had rectangular port lights similar to those in the first class accommodation. The captain had his own chart room with access to the bridge. Provision was made for carrying cattle, with portable fittings being provided, and also cars, although these had to be craned on board the vessels as was usual.

Many writers have described these two new steamers as the ugly ducklings of the Humber ferry service. Duckworth and Langmuir call them 'the ugliest monstrosities imaginable, each being double ended, very broad, and with a ridiculous chimney like funnel abaft the paddle boxes. An unusual feature was the slinging of the life boats over the paddle boxes'.

Killingholme was painted white when George V and Queen Mary visited the area for the opening of Immingham Docks. She had a new name – *Queen Mary* – painted on either side of her bows, but this was later removed, as the statutory period had not been allowed for a change of name. Alun D'Orley describes this event:

On Monday 22nd July 1912, the Immingham Dock was formally opened by King George V. The Killingholme, dressed like a Royal Yacht, was boarded by the King and Queen at the lock gates, which were opened by an electric signal, operated by His Majesty. With the King and Queen standing alone on the upper foredeck, the Killingholme steamed round the new dock, to tremendous cheers and applause from the thousands of spectators. It must certainly have been a day to remember, with the sun shining, the dock ablaze with coloured flags and bunting, and the brilliant scarlet dress uniforms of the Territorial Army, who proudly lined up on the dock side.

The king later surprised everyone by bestowing a knighthood upon Sam Fay, general manager of the GCR, just as Queen Victoria had honoured the Mayor of Hull in 1854. The proud captain for the occasion was Tom Rusling, who later received a letter from the marine superintendent's office at Grimsby, thanking him for 'the excellent manner' in which he navigated the *Killingholme* with the royal party on board, and asking him to 'convey my best thanks to the crew for the helpful manner in which they discharged their duties'.

Captain Thomas Rusling with his crew, including his son Fred, who was a steward, and Walter Ward. *Hull Museums*

PS *Cleethorpes* — renamed HMS *Cleethorpes* — armed and equipped to work as a sea plane carrier during the First World War. © *Imperial War Museums*

Sir Sam Fay wrote a similar letter, and both – along with photographs of Captain Rusling – are held in the archives of the Hull Maritime Museum.

At one time the GCR considered running steamers from Hull to Immingham. This idea proved impractical, however, and so instead it proposed to build six new boats – of lighter draught and faster than the existing ones – as well as constructing a railway line direct from New Holland to Immingham; this opened for goods and passenger services in May 1911. Hull was also expanding its port facilities at this time and George V opened the King George Dock, to the east of Alexandra Dock, in 1914.

During the First World War *Killingholme*, *Brocklesby* and *Cleethorpes* were converted for use as seaplane carriers. They were armed with small guns and equipped with derricks for lowering planes into the water for take-off and for retrieving them when they returned from their sorties. *Cleethorpes* was noted as far away as the Mediterranean, and it is claimed she was also used as a ferry in Mesopotamia. *Killingholme* was torpedoed by a German U-boat just off the mouth of the Humber, with the loss of nine lives. She was lucky to have been hit only in the paddle wheel and, after being towed back to Earle's yard, was repaired. The incident was recalled twenty-three years later, in a reminiscence of *Killingholme's* mate, published in the *Hull Times* in April 1939:

[H]e was serving aboard the Humber tug Central No. 2, (at the time) which was called to the stricken ferry's aid. 'It was blowing half a gale when we found

her,' he said. 'She was rolling badly, and her starboard side, around the paddle-box had been shattered by the explosion. It looked…like a matchstick that had been trodden on. There was bloodstained wreckage everywhere, and on her deck were nine bodies covered by Union Jacks. It was a horrible sight…I hope I'll never see another like it'. The Killingholme was towed into Immingham, her war service over, but was later repaired and put back into the ferry trade. She had been saved from complete disaster by her paddle-box, which took the full force of the explosion. The mate joined her after the war and has now served 20 years in the ship he helped to save.

To cover for the absence of three ferries during the war, the old *Grimsby II*, built in 1888, was returned to service, with

Killingholme, showing damage sustained when acting as a sea plane carrier during the First World War. © *Imperial War Museums*

Brocklesby with a vehicle on the stern deck. *Photograph reproduced courtesy of North East Lincolnshire Council Library Service*

the 1873-built *Magna Charta II* being used to move cattle and work the fish trade across the river. Another paddle steamer, *Mermaid*, also arrived on the Humber. Built in 1891 for the Thames, she was brought north by the Goole and Hull Steam Packet Company. She was powered by simple, two-cylinder oscillating machinery, said to be the last of this type on the Humber, with a single chimney behind the paddles. Used at first on the Hull to Goole service, by late 1916 she was chartered for use on the New Holland route. In the same year the Goole and Hull company acquired the *Essex*, built in 1896 for the Great Eastern Railway's Ipswich to Harwich service and sold for Thames excursions in 1913. She had funnels fore and aft of the paddles and a passenger saloon with a promenade deck above that was almost the entire length of her hull. Like the *Old Manchester*, she was said to be hard to manoeuvre. She was sold to a new owner in Greece in 1918, after which she does not feature in Lloyd's Register.

In his *Decline of the Paddle Steamer*, Richard H. Coton mentions that the Goole and Hull company's final purchase, in April 1919, was the former Clyde steamer *Lady Rowena*, built in1891. Along with *Mermaid*, it operated excursions from Hull as well as running the ferry service between Goole and Hull. Coton points out that, with the changing patterns of traffic and the disruption caused by the war, the company was wound up after the 1919 season. *Lady Rowena* was moved to Swansea and *Mermaid* went to the Shannon.

Cleethorpes heading out across the Humber from Hull in the 1920s. *Hull Daily Mail*

The Inglis-built *Frodingham* (1895). Originally called *Dandie Dinmont*, she was renamed in 1928 when moved to the Humber from Scotland. *Photograph reproduced courtesy of North East Lincolnshire Council Library Service*

In 1916 the pontoon, which had been moored by the GCR alongside Corporation Pier in 1901, was sunk in a severe gale whilst being towed to New Holland for repairs. Before the war New Holland Pier had given cause for concern and, from 1915, a weight restriction was imposed for locomotives working over the pier railway. It was estimated that twenty-one of the bays needed replacing and, in 1922, temporary repairs were carried out by Logan & Hemingway at a cost of £39,240. In 1923 work was begun in earnest by the newly formed London & North Eastern Railway which, in the railway grouping that year, had incorporated several railway companies including the GCR and the NER, thus uniting the railways on each side of the Humber under one ownership for the first time. Concrete stanchions replaced the wooden piers, but the new Pier Station buildings were constructed from recycled materials. The work took five years to complete and cost £176,463.

In 1924 *Magna Charta II* was finally withdrawn, after fifty-one years' service on the Humber. *Grimsby II* also went that year; she had been the first of the paddle steamers to be built of steel and had worked on the river for thirty-six years. The crews could also have long careers. Dow mentions the record of forty-four years as a captain set by Joseph Chapman, who retired in 1899 at the age of seventy-six. The board of directors awarded him an allowance of 24 shillings a week. Herbert Lee also completed forty-four years' service, but as a

fireman and an engineman. Recruited by the GCR in 1894 at the age of twenty, he served for many years on *Killingholme* before retiring in 1938. In the 'John Humber' feature in the *Hull Daily Mail* in October 1950, Mr Lee recalled that, when the Admiralty requisitioned *Killingholme* during the First World War, he had to explain how to handle her to a naval crew in Albert Dock. He was on board when she made her last voyage to the village of Paull in 1945 to be broken up. Mr Lee died in 1968, at the age of ninety-four.

The *Hull Times* of 1st May 1926 reported that a General Strike had been declared by the Trades Union Congress for the following Tuesday, 4th May, if there was no settlement of a dispute involving mineworkers, who were on strike over the lowering of their rates of pay. The strike went ahead, the railways were seriously affected and, of course, the railway-owned ferry service was implicated. However, after some initial disruption, the *Hull Daily Mail* was able to report on 6th May that a ferry from Hull to New Holland had sailed the previous night. On 8th May the *Hull Times* provided more detail:

Ferryboat communication between Hull and Lincolnshire was re-established on Wednesday night, and there was a further sailing of the ferryboat on Thursday. Prior to this a motor-boat had been plying between New Holland and Hull; the single fare being

5s for each passenger…The New Holland to Hull ferry brought nearly 200 passengers across the Humber at noon, and returned with a further batch. The railway company hope to maintain a skeleton service.

The *Hull Times* pointed out that, once across the Humber, passengers found few trains running. There was a demonstration against volunteer engine drivers, but 'police intervened and order was restored'. A local enterprise was advertising refurbished vans and trucks for immediate sale as 'Emergency Transport for Trades People and Others'. After nine days the General Strike was called off, although the miners stayed out for a great deal longer before giving in to the mine owners' demands. The *Hull Daily Mail* reported on 12th May that the railwaymen of New Holland would be returning to work at 9am the next day.

By 1929 four vessels were working the Hull to New Holland service: *Brocklesby*, *Killingholme*, *Cleethorpes* and *Frodingham*. The *Frodingham*, built by A. & J. Inglis in Glasgow, had started out on the Clyde in 1895 as a North British Railway steamer, the *Dandie Dinmont*, and she became a part of the LNER fleet on its formation in 1923. In 1928 she was renamed and moved to the Humber for the New Holland ferry service. Alterations were made, including the removal of the fore-saloon in order to provide an open deck for carrying cars. At this time eighteen crossings were being made each way on weekdays and seven on Sundays.

Motor cars were by then a regular feature on the ferries and there were difficulties in handling them. In order to load and unload them at Hull, cars had to be driven onto a platform which had ropes attached. The entire platform, with the vehicle secured in place, was then lifted from pier to ferry and vice versa. With the increase in car ownership in the 1920s, this system was in need of improvement, although this had to wait until the following decade.

From 1931 cruises to destinations such as Read's Island and Burton Stather, which had operated before the war, were resumed, although the day-to-day operation of the ferries remained the 'bread and butter' of the company. The LNER letters book for 1930 to 1932, held in the North East Lincolnshire Archives and Records Office, provides a glimpse of the difficulties which could be encountered with steamers. There is some correspondence between Mr C.R. Wharton, at New Holland, and his manager Mr Cookson, the marine superintendent engineer at Grimsby. On 18th July 1932, referring to *Frodingham*, Mr Wharton wrote:

Sir, I have to report that a boiler tube on the above steamer, gave out at noon on Saturday last, when preparing to enter service to relieve the *Killingholme*, for the trip to Burton Stather. The *Frodingham* was re-moored, fires drawn and boiler blown down. *Killingholme* was kept in regular service until 2.30pm and then the service was maintained by the *Cleethorpes*. A new boiler tube was fitted early this morning, boiler filled and the fires set and is now available if required.

Magna Charta II lying derelict after withdrawal in 1924. Note that the number II is not carried but is used in most sources to differentiate the craft. This may also have been the case with Old and New Manchester. *Photograph reproduced courtesy of North East Lincolnshire Council Library Service*

The ferries were back in the news in November 1933, when the *Hull Daily Mail* reported, under the heading: '£125,000 improvements to Humber Ferry. No cost to Hull ratepayers', that an agreement had been reached with the LNER:

New ferry steamers and alterations to New Holland facilities at a cost of £90,000 by the L.N.E.R. and the expenditure of upwards of £35,000 by the Hull Corporation on a floating pontoon at the Victoria Pier, and alterations to the present pier, are the chief points proposed in negotiations explained at a meeting of the Property and Bridges Committee at the Guildhall yesterday…If the negotiations are successful work will start on the scheme almost immediately, as it is being undertaken under unemployment relief considerations but there will be no cost to the ratepayers… A system of low tolls will be sufficient to cover the whole of the interest and sinking fund upon the Corporation's expenditure and the cost of the maintenance and provision of the necessary contingency fund.

The scheme was to involve major landing improvements and the introduction of three new vessels to the ferry service, which would be named after castles in Yorkshire and Lincolnshire.

The *Grimsby* lying derelict after withdrawal in 1924, just before being scrapped. *Photograph reproduced courtesy of North East Lincolnshire Council Library Service*

Cattle bound for Hull Market wait their turn to disembark from the ferry in the 1920s. *Brian Peeps collection*

New Holland Pier in 1925, during rebuilding by the London & North Eastern Railway. Note the steam crane with its bunker of coal. *Brian Peeps collection*

Looking towards the end of New Holland Pier in 1925, during its rebuilding. *Brian Peeps collection*

New Holland Pier in 1925 during rebuilding. Note the rail-mounted crane and the set of narrow-gauge points, which would have been used to carry materials to the worksite. *Brian Peeps collection*

The crane at Minerva Pier, loading cars onto *Killingholme*, 19th August 1933. *Hull Daily Mail*

Chapter Six

THE THREE CASTLES

In 1934 the London & North Eastern Railway placed an order for two new ferries with William Gray & Co., Ltd of Hartlepool. This company had been by founded by John Pushton Denton in 1839, to build wooden ships under the name J.P. Denton. In 1860 Denton constructed *Juanita*, the first of several ships that he was to build for William Gray, a prominent local businessman, and in 1863 the two men formed a partnership to build iron ships. The new company was called Denton, Gray & Co., and the yard was expanded in size.

From 1869, as a result of Denton's increasing ill-health, Gray assumed more direct control. Unfortunately the partnership was something of a gentleman's agreement, which caused some legal wrangling when Denton died in 1871. By 1874 the matter was still unresolved, and the firm was reconstituted as William Gray & Company. In 1883 Gray decided that he should manufacture his own engines and a ten-acre site was leased from the NER. It was there that he established the Central Marine Engine Works.

It was during the ownership of Gray's grandson, also named William, that the company received the order from the LNER for two new paddle steamers for the Hull to New Holland ferry. These were hard times in shipbuilding, and the order from the LNER must have been very welcome. Gray's was an unusual choice for the LNER. Local historian Bert Spaldin has compiled a list of 1,309 vessels built by the company between 1839 and 1961, and *Wingfield Castle* and *Tattershall Castle* are the only paddle steamers noted. The yard continued to construct ships until 1961, when *Blanchland* became the last ship to be launched, and it closed down in 1963.

Mr F.R.C. Cookson, marine superintendent engineer for the New Holland ferries, kept detailed notebooks, currently held in the North East Lincolnshire Archives and Records Office. They record his many visits to Messrs. William Gray's shipyard and the Central Marine Engine Works during the construction of the ferries. They include sketches of valves and paddle design, which he discussed with the shipbuilding staff. He describes one visit in June 1934:

Discussed with Mr Simpson and Mr Cole the results of the Teddington Test Tank trials. Mr Simpson informed me that by modifying the model at the fore end on similar lines for a 215ft vessel and the aft end on similar lines for a 200ft vessel they had been able to obtain a speed of 13½ knots. To obtain this it may be necessary to move the spacing of the accommodation, including the machinery (below decks). Mr Simpson would try to keep the machinery as far forward as possible by moving the boiler feed water tanks to the end of the bunkers.

Tattershall Castle as delivered, with an open bridge and a grey hull, paddle boxes and saloons, in her 1934–1936 livery. *Photograph reproduced courtesy of North East Lincolnshire Council Library Service*

Tattershall Castle at Grimsby. *Photograph reproduced courtesy of North East Lincolnshire Council Library Service*

The first class saloon on *Tattershall Castle*. In common with *Wingfield Castle*, she had a small enclosed bar, seen between the doors at the far end, with a staircase in front descending to the lower forward saloon. *Photograph reproduced courtesy of North East Lincolnshire Council Library Service*

The test tank was one of several at the National Physical Laboratory in Teddington, used to test the effectiveness of different hull designs. On another visit to Hartlepool Cookson noted,

> I asked for the position of the bunker shovelling openings and slides and also deck aft scuttles to be reconsidered. Move scuttle further aft and bunker openings further forward. I asked Mr Cole to pay particular attention to paddle box side openings to make sure paddle crank could be passed through.

In the opening pages of one book, Cookson noted that in July 1934 he visited the PS *Jennie Deans,* along with his manager, Mr Rodger. He sketched the lighting arrangements, including those in the saloon, and mentioned that there were two port lights to the paddle boxes in the alleyways, providing additional light. He also sketched the electric roof lights fitted to the *Waverley* (the predecessor of the preserved paddle steamer of the same name). At a meeting in Hartlepool on 27th July, Cookson asked why the main discharge valve had been placed below the water line. A Board of Trade rule was cited but, upon checking this, it was found to apply only to larger steamers with high discharges which may have flooded the lifeboats when launched.

The new paddle steamers' hulls had a beam of 33ft and 57ft over the sponsons. The length was 209ft 7in overall and 199ft 11½in between the perpendiculars. The vessels were powered by triple-expansion diagonal steam engines developing 1,200 indicated horsepower, incorporating a three-furnace cylindrical boiler, giving them a maximum speed of 13½ knots. They were designed to carry 884 passengers, could accommodate animals and vehicles on the rear deck, and could be operated by a crew of ten men. The pair cost £53,000.

The December 1934 issue of the *London & North Eastern Railway Magazine* carried a comprehensive, illustrated article by E.M. Rutter, port master at Grimsby. Spread over three pages, it traced the origins and history of the Humber ferries before describing the improvements being carried out.

> To those familiar with the Humber Ferry the name no doubt suggests the queer looking paddle boats with tall funnels out of all proportion to their length, ploughing their way across the river, and the wooden landing piers at Hull and New Holland with their awkward and sometimes slippery approaches. They may even have recollections of tedious hours spent in mid-Humber waiting for the rising tide to release the steamer from the muddy embrace of the shifting sands.
>
> We may now briefly describe the steps which are being taken to improve and modernize the Ferry Service between New Holland and Hull. By co-operation with the Hull City Corporation, arrangements have been concluded for improving the pier terminals at Hull and New Holland by the provision of floating pontoons and modern approaches at both landings.

> To anyone familiar with the present steep and narrow slope which has to be negotiated between the steamers and the pier head, it will be realised what a great improvement will be afforded by these new works. At the same time two new paddle steamers of greatly improved design have just been completed, and will be taken into service this month. These boats… are named the *Tattershall Castle*, as representing the Lincolnshire side of the service, and *Wingfield Castle*, the home of the old family of De La Pole, which was so closely connected with the early history of Hull. These vessels have been specially built with a view to the increased comfort of passengers and also to provide more room for merchandise and motor cars. We must not omit to mention the fact that a buffet has been provided in each ship where the weary traveller may refresh himself.
>
> Throughout the preparation of these schemes of improvement, the Railway Company has had the cordial co-operation of the Municipal Authorities at Hull, which is all the more interesting in view of the connection of the people of Hull and the Humber Ferry in former times.

The launch of the new ships in September 1934 was covered extensively by the *Northern Daily Mail*:

> The ceremony of christening the two Humber ferry steamers – the *Tattershall Castle* and the *Wingfield Castle*…was performed at the Dockyard this afternoon in the presence of a distinguished assembly…
>
> Careful consideration has been given to ensure every comfort for intending passengers. A spacious saloon is arranged on the main deck and a smaller one on the lower deck forward for the use of first-class passengers, and a large saloon on the lower deck aft for third-class passengers. The interior furnishings and decorations of the saloons are to be of the most up-to-date type, and a special feature will be the lighting, which is most pleasing and effective. A buffet adjoining the upper saloon where all tastes will be adequately catered for is an innovation which has not hitherto been available on the Humber service.
>
> A large promenade deck is provided for the use of passengers, and provision is made on the main deck aft for the carriage of motor cars, cargo barrows and livestock. The captain will be accommodated on the promenade deck below the navigating bridge, while the crew will be accommodated on the lower deck. Special rooms are provided for the engineer, steward and stewardess…

The triple-expansion steam engines, constructed at Gray's Central Marine Engine Works, are then described and their power and efficiency praised, especially in the context of operating over the fast-flowing and busy estuary of the Humber…

Steam will be supplied by a large three-furnace cylindrical boiler of the return-tube type, working at a pressure of 204lbs. per square inch. The boiler is fitted with hand rocking fire bars, which will be fired with coal under the closed stokehold system of forced draught, air being supplied by a high efficiency fan driven by an enclosed steam engine placed in the engine room...

In order to ensure rapid manipulation of the machinery all the controls are brought to the central platform and conveniently arranged to be handled by one man who will easily control the 1,200 horse-power which the engines can exert on the paddle wheels. The quick manipulation of the engines, the large diameter of the paddle wheels, and the broad convex floats will enable the vessel to be quickly manoeuvred and so speed up the ferry service for which they are intended. The vessels have been built to Board of Trade requirements with special passenger certificates...

The construction of these two vessels, to accelerate the existing service between

Cars being loaded onto *Tattershall Castle* using the crane on Minerva Pier in April 1949, at a time the pontoon was not available for use. *Hull Daily Mail*

An early view of *Tattershall Castle*, in the BTC livery carried from 1948 to 1959 with white paddle boxes, saloon and hull painted white down to sponson level, with black below and a buff funnel with black top. *Author's collection*

Tattershall Castle at Hull Corporation Pier. Note the Victorian upper deck of the pier, which was demolished in 1965. *Author's collection*

Hull and New Holland, is yet another indication of the London and North Eastern Railway Company's enterprise to meeting present day requirements and foresight in anticipating a further development of the traffic between South Yorkshire and North Lincolnshire. Not only will the service be accelerated, but improved accommodation is provided for both passengers and cargo, in addition to which the facilities for transporting motor-cars with special gangway arrangements will enable them to be run aboard and run ashore with ease and rapidity.

In his speech at the launch, Sir William Gray welcomed the Lord Mayor and Lady Mayoress of Hull and expressed pleasure at seeing so many distinguished people present who were connected with the LNER. He remarked: 'It is 29 years since we built for the LNER Co. I am very glad we have revived our connexion with that company, and hope that when more steamers are required we may get our share'. The Lord Mayor thanked the LNER for having instigated the improvements:

We have suffered in silence for a long number of years from the primitive and out of date methods which have obtained at our old pier, and the launching of the two vessels today is an indication that great improvements are now to be made in the service between New Holland and the Hull side of the river.

After mentioning that he had been warned that negotiations with the railway company could be difficult, the mayor stated that he had found it very co-operative. He also knew

that there were 'many reasons for the earlier attitude of the railway company. One of these was the proposal to build a bridge across the Humber'. He continued:

If you saw the vessels now plying between Hull and New Holland you would realise that the appeal to the imagination of the Hull people that these two boats will make will be very great indeed. They are the last word in comfort and efficiency.

Sir Charles Coupar Barrie MP, a director of the LNER, commented that the new vessels 'would save Hull an enormous amount of money which would otherwise have been spent on a bridge across the river, and with the improved service…he hoped little more would be heard about the bridge'. Interestingly, in view of what actually happened, he continued:

It was a great pleasure for me to send the order for these vessels to West Hartlepool and we hope that many more orders will come. If our hopes are fulfilled, it may not be long before we require another vessel in which case I should be only too glad if the order came to Messrs. Gray and Co. (applause).

Hartlepool Central Library holds the original yard books of ships' particulars for William Gray's yard. In these *Tattershall Castle* is shown as order number 1059 and full details are laid out over two pages. The lengths are given as 209ft 7in overall and 199ft 11½in between the perpendiculars with depth, moulded, to main deck of 9ft. 0in. Coal capacity was 18 tons in one bunker and 18½ tons in the other, accommodating 36½ tons in total. The triple-expansion diagonal direct acting steam engine had three cylinders of 18in, 28½ in and 46in, with a 51in stroke. There was one multi-tubed boiler of 15ft 3¾in diameter and 11ft 4⅛in long, with a working pressure of 204lbs per square inch and a water capacity of 26½ tons. The paddles had eight floats, built on the feathering principle, each float being 9ft 4½in long and 3ft 3in wide. The float centres were 11ft 4in in diameter. The keel was laid down on 25th June 1934, the ship was launched on 24th September and her first sailing took place on 2nd November. The pages which referred to *Wingfield Castle*, order number 1060, are the same as far as dimensions are concerned, but the keel was laid down on 27th June. She too was launched on 24th September, but first sailed on 27th November.

Major redevelopment of the terminal facilities at both New Holland and Hull was also commenced. New pontoons would be provided at both piers. Each was to be 150 feet long and fifty feet wide, with connecting bridges twenty-three feet wide and provided with a central, ten-foot wide roadway for the use of motor vehicles, flanked by two five-foot wide walkways. Both the pontoons and the bridges were to be covered, to offer passengers some protection against the elements. At high tide the hinged bridges would be virtually level, and they would have a maximum gradient of 1 in 9 at low tide.

These improvements were well justified when one considers the steady increase in the number of motor vehicle owners willing to pay the ferry fare in order to avoid the round trip of over seventy miles via Boothferry Bridge, a swing bridge near Goole, opened in 1929 on the site of a former ferry. (Prior to

The ship's bell aboard *Wingfield Castle*, denoting that she was built for the LNER in 1934. *Geoff Plumb*

that date motorists were obliged to go via Selby, which was even further.) In 1923, 2,425 vehicles were carried on the ferries; this rose to 12,881 in 1938 and 58,920 by 1955.

The new pier at Hull was under construction from 1935 and opened officially in June 1937. A new scale of charges was introduced, with motorists paying 1s toll instead of the former cranage charge. The public were to pay a penny each to use the pontoon. Ferry tickets bore the words 'toll paid' or 'including toll'. The LNER also began to reconstruct the pier head at New Holland, which would also be provided with a pontoon. The opening ceremony consisted of dignitaries of the corporation and the railway company taking a trip on *Tattershall Castle*, stopping at the new pontoon in order to declare it officially open, and then taking a short cruise.

As the *Hull Times* explained on 5th June 1937, car drivers would be the main beneficiaries:

> For motorists the alterations will provide greatly improved facilities, as the floating pontoons will enable motor cars to be driven straight on and off the ferry boats at both terminals. In addition, the necessity for lifting motor cars on to the ferry boats at Hull by means of cranes will disappear...

However, the pontoon could make life difficult for the staff, as war worker Joyce Watson, who took over a male porter's job on Corporation Pier, told the *LNER Magazine* in 1945:

> I stand on the edge of a floating pontoon, catch and haul ashore a heavy mooring rope. This is quite simple when the weather is calm, but the Humber can be very rough indeed. At these times the pontoon heaves up and down like a boat, and of course the ferry is doing likewise. Catching ropes under these conditions is no easy job, especially if you are feeling very seasick.

As a result of the delivery of two new ferries, *Cleethorpes* and *Brocklesby* were withdrawn (*Cleethorpes* after thirty-one years' service on the Humber). Renamed *Cruising Queen* and *Highland Queen*, they spent a year in Scotland operating trips from Leith for Redcliffe's Shipping Company. Both were scrapped in 1936, as was *Frodingham*, in Belgium. Of the old ferries, only *Killingholme* remained on the Humber for use as a spare ferry and also for the increasingly popular cruises, many of which sailed from Grimsby downriver to Spurn Head or upriver to Hull. *Wingfield Castle* and *Tattershall Castle* also operated cruises on Sundays, when there was less demand for the ferry service.

The Humber ferries could always be called upon to provide assistance in the event of an accident. In December 1938 *The Times* reported that,

> The Hull trawler *Reef-flower* came into collision with the steamer *Hodder* lying at anchor in the River Humber at Hull last night. Efforts were made to beach the *Reef-flower* but she touched a sandbank and sank. The crew,

Wingfield Castle departing from Hull on the afternoon of Tuesday 31st August 1971. *Geoff Plumb.*

Wingfield Castle in the early 1970s, showing the tripod mast on the funnel and the radar fitted to the bridge after the war. *Kirk Martin*

15 in number, were picked up by the ferry steamer *Wingfield Castle* and landed at the Victoria Pier. The *Reef-flower* was owned by the Yorkshire Steam Fishing Company, Hull, and had completed a journey to the Icelandic fishing grounds. She was one of several fishing vessels in the river waiting to berth at St Andrew's dock at high water. It was understood that the *Hodder* was not seriously damaged.

The Second World War was to have grave consequences for the people living along the Humber Estuary. Hull itself was one of the most heavily bombed cities in the United Kingdom. Cruises were suspended for the duration and the ferries concentrated on maintaining the essential link across the Humber.

In 1940 another new ferry, to be named *Lincoln Castle*, was under construction. Three firms were invited to tender: A. & J. Inglis, of Pointhouse, Glasgow, Fairfields of Govan and William Gray of Hartlepool. Inglis won the order. They had already built many paddle steamers for the LNER and would also build *Waverley* in 1946, the world's last sea-going paddle steamer, as well as *Maid of the Loch*, the last passenger-carrying paddle steamer to be built on the Clyde. This was launched on Loch Lomond in 1953 and is currently being restored at Balloch Pier.

A. & J. Inglis had been established in 1847 when brothers Anthony and John Inglis set up a partnership at the Whitehall Foundry at Anderson, Glasgow. In 1862 they moved to a new shipyard at Pointhouse, in Glasgow, where the River Kelvin flows into the Clyde. It became a limited company in 1905 and, in 1919, was taken over by Harland & Wolff, although it retained its own name. It was under the ownership of Harland & Wolff that *Lincoln Castle* was built and launched.

Gauges, clock, engine room telegraph and builder's plate of Central Marine Engine Works, in the engine room of *Wingfield Castle* in 1973. *Kirk Martin*

The starboard paddle of *Wingfield Castle*, showing the mechanism which controls the feathering of the float, enabling it to enter and leave the water at a perpendicular angle for greater efficiency. *Kirk Martin*

Sadly, the yard suffered, as did much of British shipbuilding, in the post-war years, and the Pointhouse shipyard closed in 1962, exactly one hundred years after opening. The area is now the site of the Riverside Museum, Glasgow's museum of transport.

A. & J. Inglis turned to the Ailsa Shipbuilding Company of Troon to build the triple-expansion diagonal steam engine for *Lincoln Castle*. The agreement between the two companies was signed on 5th September 1939. It stated that Ailsa was contracted to construct one complete set of paddle machinery and boiler, complete with paddle shafts, wheels and spare gear, and to deliver and install the foregoing machinery, contractor's engine number 164, on board the vessel known by the purchasers as contract No. 1024P, when afloat adjacent to the purchasers' works at Pointhouse, Glasgow. This agreement is held at the University of Glasgow Archives, and shows that the purchase price for the engine, boilers and paddles was £16,400, to be paid in six instalments, as various stages of construction and delivery were completed. As with the two earlier paddle steamers, the plans of the new ferry owed much to the staff of the marine superintendent's office at Grimsby. By 1940 this was the responsibility of Mr J. Wood, whose signature is to be seen on the surviving plans, numbers TD36/20/7 1–8, held in the archives of the Mitchell Library in Glasgow.

Tom Baxter worked for Telford, Grier & McKay, who carried out the electrical work on *Lincoln Castle*. Although when I met him in 2011 he was ninety years old, he recalled his involvement very clearly.

I was a fourth-year apprentice at the time. I did the main lighting and a lot of work in the engine room. The main electrical board was just behind the engineer's platform. I worked on the ship perhaps up to three weeks or more. Then I was off and away to another job as we used to do

a lot of work on ships in the early days of the war. We worked long hours and at least two 'all nights' a week, getting a bit of a break – sleeping where you could in the engine room. Where the *Lincoln Castle* was built there was an office block in front of her and, on the landward side, there was a plater's shop and by the stern there was another workshop. She was built between these buildings and they must have pushed her across onto the slipway in order to launch her. I wondered if they would launch her sideways but they must have moved her onto the slipway and launched her stern first. When I was on the *Lincoln Castle* I just went to the ship and worked whatever hours were necessary and then went home. We did nothing but work, work, work, and really

Ninety-year-old Tom Baxter at his home in 2011. Tom carried out electrical work on *Lincoln Castle* during its construction in 1940. *Kirk Martin*

The River Kelvin in Glasgow and the Riverside Museum of Transport, which stands on the site of Inglis's yard, where *Lincoln Castle* was built, as seen in 2011. *Kirk Martin*

grafted in that year, 1940. I was doing around 110 hours a week. When I left the *Lincoln Castle* she still wasn't ready. There was a lot of wiring and the light fixtures still to do.

Tom joined the Royal Navy in 1941 and after the war ended he moved to Hull working for a ship repair company and later undertaking electrical contract work on buildings.

Lincoln Castle was launched on 29th April 1940. Being wartime there was far less fanfare than was the case with the Gray-built vessels. She had to undertake a hazardous trip around the north of Scotland, through the Pentland Firth, and down the east coast to reach the Humber Estuary. In fact she encountered storm damage and some compass trouble on her first attempt, and had to return to the Clyde before making a second attempt in a convoy the following year, arriving at Grimsby on 4th July 1941. She entered service between Hull and New Holland on 4th August.

Ariel view of *Lincoln Castle* on Humber ferry service, showing the double wake created by her two paddles as they dig into the water. *Grimsby Telegraph*

Her dimensions were similar to the earlier vessels, her length being 199.7ft with a beam of 33.1ft or 56ft over the sponsons, but she had a completely different layout from *Tattershall Castle* and *Wingfield Castle*. On the earlier 'Castles'

The triple expansion diagonal steam engine of 1940 on *Lincoln Castle*, still hard at work in 1971. *Geoff Plumb*

An unusual view of *Lincoln Castle*, near New Holland Pier, with steam to spare issuing from the safety valve. *Angie Stephenson*

Lincoln Castle viewed over the car deck of Tattershall Castle, March 1972. *D.E.G. Anderson*

the stokehold was aft, close to the car deck, with the fireman facing forwards. The engines were ahead of the boiler with the engineer facing towards the stern, so that the engines effectively went 'astern' when the vessel was travelling forward. On *Lincoln Castle* the engines were situated aft, just ahead of the car deck, with the engineer facing forward and looking over his engines towards the boiler, beyond which was the stokehold where the fireman faced back towards the boiler and the stern of the ship. As a result *Lincoln Castle* had her funnel ahead of her paddles whereas *Wingfield Castle* and *Tattershall Castle* had their funnels to the aft of their paddles. The engine of *Lincoln Castle* was rated at 850 indicated horse power, lower than the other two vessels. She also had a slightly shallower draught than them and was notorious for being difficult to control in high winds.

Just as in the First World War, in May 1941 *Killingholme* was requisitioned for war service. This time she was painted battleship grey and worked with the RAF Barrage Balloon Command at Grimsby, as a support vessel for balloon barges tethered on the Humber (the balloons were flown at vulnerable points to protect the port against low flying aircraft and dive bombers). In the *Lincolnshire & Humberside Transport Review* for November/December 1988, Mr N.J. Drewery recalled:

Lincoln Castle seen from the Marine Café on Corporation Pier in 1976. *Kirk Martin*

The *Killingholme* would spend most of her days moored in the Royal Dock Basin, venturing out into the Humber to take supplies and relief crews out to the RAF barges. I often used to see her at her moorings, as one of my duties was to deliver telegrams to the Fleet Mail Office – a rather grand name for a wooden hut on the dockside of the Royal Dock Basin. On my first visit to Hull at the close of the war I found the New Holland Pier had suffered fire bomb damage. The bomb damage at Hull made a lasting impression on me. An unexploded bomb was being recovered from a site near the market.

Tattershall Castle and *Wingfield Castle* were requisitioned by the Ministry of Transport with the intention of converting them into minesweepers, as were many paddle steamers at this time including *Medway Queen* (currently being restored on her namesake river) but the strategic importance of the Humber ferries was soon realised and they continued their essential work transporting the large number of people engaged in war work on both sides of the Humber and, in

particular, those on the many airfields of Lincolnshire. They also played a significant role in the evacuation of children and young people to rural Lincolnshire from Hull. In the absence of *Killingholme*, the arrival of *Lincoln Castle* as a third vessel must have eased the situation.

Hull was subject to severe bombing, owing to the importance of the docks to the British war effort. Between 19th June 1940 and 17th March 1945 the city suffered eighty-six air raids, which destroyed vast areas. In reports, however, Hull was rarely referred to by name, in an effort to protect the inhabitants and dock complexes. Instead, it was stated that a bombing raid had taken place 'in a north east town'.

Throughout the crisis the ferries continued with their mundane but essential task. As mentioned by Chris Braithwaite, who worked on them in wartime, a black flag would be flown at Corporation Pier when mines had been dropped in the estuary by enemy aircraft and the ferries were under instructions not to operate. Chris tells his story in Chapter Eight.

Lincoln Castle uses the whistle to sound her departure. *Kirk Martin*

This LNER notice was still in place on New Holland Pier in the 1970s. *Lincoln Castle* in the background. *Geoff Plumb*

With the arrival of *Lincoln Castle*, Killingholme became surplus to normal requirements and, after the war, she was sold for scrap. In October 1946 the *Hull Daily Mail* published a photograph of her in the scrap-yard, together with the following caption:

A river friend. Once the delight of Humber holiday trippers, and veteran of both world wars, the aged LNER ferry steamer the Killingholme, has just finished her days in a Yorkshire ship breaker's yard. Sold last year for scrap she is now almost completely broken up. Built for the Hull New Holland ferry service, the Killingholme became a Royal Navy seaplane carrier in World War One, when, despite her shallow draught, she was hit by a torpedo, which destroyed one of her paddles. She remained afloat and returned at the end of the war to her old ferry run.

The three 'Castles' – *Wingfield*, *Tattershall*, and *Lincoln* – were the last paddle steamers to enter service on the Humber.

The Humber ferries underwent several changes of livery during their years of railway ownership. Under the GCR, before 1923, the steamers had black hulls with white paddle boxes and white funnels with black tops; however, whilst in LNER ownership from 1923 the hulls, paddle boxes and saloons were painted grey. *Wingfield Castle* and *Tattershall Castle* had grey hulls, paddle boxes and saloons from 1934 to 1936 and these were repainted black from 1936 to 1948, whilst the funnels were white with a black top, as was the case with *Lincoln Castle* from 1940. In 1948, when the New Holland ferries were taken over by the British Transport Commission, the hulls, paddle boxes and saloons were painted white down to sponson level, with a black hull below, and they carried a buff funnel with a black top. A red band was added from 1959 under the management of the Associated Humber Lines. In 1965 British Rail applied a new livery featuring a blue hull below the sponsons, with a white superstructure and a red funnel with a black top displaying the BR 'double arrow' insignia in white. This remained the livery under Sealink ownership and is how they ended their days on the Humber.

Lincoln Castle ready to depart from Hull Corporation Pier pontoon with light smoke from the funnel. Pilot boat *John Good* is tied up alongside Minerva Pier. *Kirk Martin*

Chapter Seven

THE FINAL DECADES

After the Second World War it was back to business as usual for the ferries. The management of most of the seagoing vessels the LNER owned on the Humber, along with those operated by several other companies working out of local ports, had been transferred to Associated Humber Lines (AHL), formed in May 1935 to rationalise shipping services in the area. These included those of the Goole Steam Shipping Co. (London Midland & Scottish Railway); the Hull & Netherlands Steam Ship Co.; Wilsons and North Eastern Railway Shipping Co. (owned by the LNER); and the LNER GCR section. However, the Humber ferries were not included at this time.

Upon the nationalisation of the railways in 1948, the shipping services of the former railway companies were taken over by the British Transport Commission and operated by the new regions of British Railways; in the case of the Humber ferries this was the Eastern Region. Each region had a marine superintendent, who came under the chief officer (marine) of the Railway Executive.

Ferries on the Humber were always at risk of collision in conditions of poor visibility. Journalist Derek Tyson described the river as 'a treacherous stretch of water, with mists and fogs that blot out everything and make the trip three miles of anxious hooting and peering from the bridge'. Indeed, the ferries had been in the news in November 1933, when the *Hull Times* reported an accident.

Passengers travelling from Hull to New Holland and from New Holland to Hull, on Tuesday, had a thrill when the two LNER ferry boats, the *Frodingham* and the *Killingholme*, collided in mid-stream. The slight fog that hung over the river was no doubt responsible for the accident, for it was not until the boats were three lengths apart that the look outs became aware of each other's proximity. The fog signals and alarm bells were rung, while passengers rushed from the saloons to the decks. The boats put hard astern, though not sufficiently

One of the new pontoons being towed to Alexandra Dock for repair on 8th June 1949. *Hull Daily Mail*

New Holland Pier station, 9th June 1945. LNER locomotive 2909 heads a train for Cleethorpes, whilst a tank locomotive stands in the opposite platform and vans occupy the central siding. *W.A. Camwell, Alf Ludlam collection*

to avoid a stiff jar. A hole about three feet long was torn in the side deck plates of the *Killingholme*, while a large length of the side rail was buckled. The damage to the *Frodingham* was at first thought to be more serious, but the boat continued on its way to New Holland.

After the war, plans were made to install radar. *Tattershall Castle* was selected by the LNER as the first to be fitted, although this was carried out by British Railways in 1948. A full-size wheelhouse was added to the two earlier ferries, which originally had open bridges, although a small wheelhouse had been added during the war (*Lincoln Castle* had been built with an enclosed bridge). *Tattershall Castle* thus became the first paddle steamer to carry radar.

The equipment was installed in January 1948 and the *Hull Daily Mail* reported on the immediate benefits of the new navigational aid:

Today, for the first time in its 100 years of history, the Humber ferry was not delayed by the notorious Humber fog, although visibility was down to 40 yards at periods during the morning. While trawlers, which had left St Andrew's dock, dropped anchor until it cleared, the *Tattershall Castle* steamed steadily and confidently between Hull and New Holland. This morning, for the first time, conditions on the river were bad enough to warrant its use. 'It told me everything I wanted to know', said Captain Norman Waldie, after he had made two round trips. Not until he left New Holland,

at 8.25am, did conditions get really bad and visibility down to 40 yards. But by watching the green ray sweeping over the fluorescent screen installed on the bridge, he was able to bring the ferry boat successfully through the shoals and currents of the Humber, until Victoria Pier loomed out of the mist. The Railway authorities expressed themselves highly satisfied and declared that the *Tattershall Castle* had maintained a normal service.

Distinctive tripod masts were fitted to both *Wingfield Castle* and *Tattershall Castle* in 1954. As Graham R. Hand points out, this was carried out as a result of changed maritime lighting regulations, because neither vessel had been built with a main mast. *Lincoln Castle*, however, had been built with a main mast, which was replaced in 1954.

H.M. Queen Elizabeth speaks to the mayor, whilst Prince Philip talks to the crew of *Wingfield Castle* before embarking by launch to join the Royal Yacht Britannia, moored in the Humber on the 18th May 1957. *Rodney Clapson collection*

Despite the foregoing improvements, the river remained a difficult one for the ferry service, as Charles Dixon pointed out in the *Dalesman* in March 1961:

> The tidal conditions of the Humber probably make this ferry service the most difficult to operate in the whole country. As the fastest running tidal river it has a rise and fall of about 26ft throughout the year, and the low water during certain tides can bring the service to a stop for two or three hours.

Associated Humber Lines had become a limited company in 1957, with a majority shareholding held by the British Transport Commission and, in 1959, AHL took over the management and operation of the Hull to New Holland ferry on BTC's behalf (although its main business was operating cargo and passenger ships between the Humber and the continent). The BTC was abolished by the Transport Act 1962, to be replaced by the British Railways Board (and other boards with responsibility for non-railway transport).

Tattershall Castle alongside Hull Corporation Pier in thick ice in January 1963. These were dangerous and unpleasant conditions for the crew. *Hull Daily Mail*

The Humber ferries continued to be managed by AHL until 1971.

On Saturday 24th March 1962 the Hull trawler *Kingston Diamond* was swept against Corporation Pier. The collision caused damage to the stanchions protecting the pontoon and for a while the ferries were obliged to use the adjacent Minerva Pier, and cars were loaded on and off the ferry by means of the old crane and car-carrying cradle.

In the severe winter of early 1963 thick ice formed in the Humber, reaching 150 yards out from the shore and causing problems for the ferries as they came alongside the pontoons at Hull and New Holland. Decks became slippery and ropes were heavy and stiff with ice. On Saturday 19th January, Corporation Pier was put out of action by fierce winds and fifteen-foot waves. The next day ferries were landing passengers on the west slope, which was undamaged. On that same wild, freezing and stormy Saturday night, *Tattershall Castle* broke free from her mooring alongside Corporation Pier. Fortunately, two crew members, Leading Fireman H.R. Walker and Deck Hand Alan Harrod were on board, and acted quickly to save her. Later, Mrs Harrod told the *Hull Daily Mail,* in one of their 'Flashback' series, that her husband 'ran up to the bridge to avoid the ferry crashing into the pier, at the same time blowing for a tug for assistance but the gale was so strong. However, with the help of the stoker he managed to get the ferry back to her moorings, then the crew was called out'. Mr R.R.M. Barr, general manager of AHL, wrote to each crew member to thank them for their prompt action in saving the vessel. The letters, dated 24th January, have been kept by their families:

> I have read with much interest the Marine Superintendent's report on the incident of the *Tattershall Castle* breaking adrift from her moorings during the weekend gales, and the actions you took which Captain Collier reports was in the highest traditions of the sea and shewed considerable skill and seamanship. I would like you to know that I am extremely pleased and proud of the ability and initiative you displayed. Please accept my sincerest appreciation.

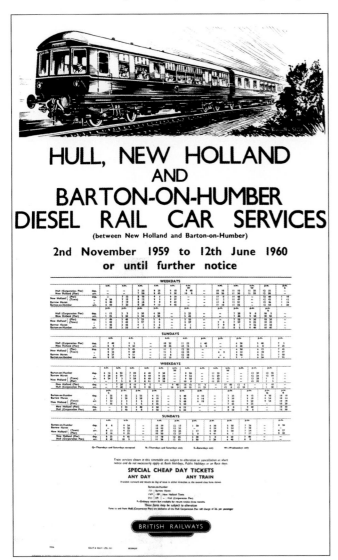

A 1959 British Railways poster advertising Humber ferry and rail services between Hull, New Holland and Barton. *National Railway Museum*

The end of that severe winter did not mean the end of all problems for the ferries because, in June 1963, during the absence of the Corporation Pier pontoon for maintenance, the connecting bridge collapsed into the Humber. The *Hull Daily Mail* broke the news:

> The approach gangway at Hull Corporation Pier which leads to the ferry boat floating pontoon collapsed and sank into the Humber this afternoon. The gangway dipped at a crazy angle into the water, and the end facing the Lincolnshire coast was completely submerged at high tide…It happened as British Transport Docks dredger Telford was about to manoeuvre into position to begin dredging work. At the moment dredging and renovation is being carried out at the pier while the floating pontoon is undergoing repairs in Alexandra Dry Dock. It was expected to return tomorrow.

The incident meant that, once again, ferries were diverted to Minerva Pier. The *Hull Daily Mail* reported that, just before the collapse, a painter called Gordon Robinson had been working between the Marine Café and the connecting bridge.

The letter from Associated Humber Lines to Alan Harrod, thanking him for his actions in getting *Tattershall Castle* back to the pier after she broke adrift in January 1963. *Alan Harrod*

Hull Corporation Pier in June 1963. The connecting bridge had collapsed after the pontoon was removed for repair. *Hull Daily Mail*

Loading cars by crane at Minerva Pier in June 1963. *Hull Daily Mail*

The demolition of the upper deck and promenade of Hull Corporation Pier in February 1965. *Hull Daily Mail*

Tattershall Castle in BR post-1965 livery, consisting of a blue hull below the sponsons with a white superstructure and a red funnel with black top, displaying the BR double-arrow insignia in white. *Grimsby Telegraph*

The hovercraft *Mercury* comes alongside Hull's Minerva Pier in 1968. *Grimsby Telegraph*

The hovercraft *Mercury* operating a pleasure trip alongside *Lincoln Castle* in February 1969. *Hull Daily Mail*

'I had just got off and was standing on the steps when I heard a big crack' he said. The café staff took up the story: 'There was a terrific crash and the café shook as the gangway gave way'. A dock official insisted that there was no connection between the dredging work and the collapse. (The café had been opened in 1952. It survived until the 1980s and was demolished in the early 1990s, although there is now a small food outlet with outside seating on the waterfront.)

On 10th July 1963 the pontoon was brought back to the pier. According to the *Hull Daily Mail*,

> The final lift of Hull's collapsed Corporation Pier gangway, to slip the floating pontoon underneath, began this afternoon. The pontoon was brought back from dry dock by three tugs this morning and pushed alongside the pier waiting for the slack tide, so that the tug Yorkshireman could nudge it into place underneath the gangway.

The pier was back in commission by the weekend, with the service back to normal for the first time in three weeks.

By the sixties the two older ferries were beginning to show their age, having been active on the Humber for over thirty years. Considerable re-plating was carried out on *Tattershall Castle* by the Humber Graving Dock and Engineering Company in 1964, details of which are held in the Hull Maritime Museum archive. A new rudder was also fitted by Brigham and Cowan (Hull) in 1965. *Wingfield Castle* also underwent extensive re-plating work between 1965 and 1970. In early 1965 the upper deck of Corporation Pier was demolished, altering forever the Victorian aspect of the structure. The demolition was covered extensively in the *Hull Daily Mail*.

In 1967 British Rail launched an investigation into the future of the Humber ferries. It considered replacing the fleet with new vessels. Bridging the Humber was also a factor to bear in mind. BR stated that the survey 'is not being done with the intention of abandoning the service, nor is it because

we are thinking of replacing the ferries with hovercraft – although this is not to say that such a service might not ultimately be put into operation'.

The cost of new craft was estimated at around £2 million and the major concern was, of course, that they would become obsolete should a bridge be built. Hull Maritime Museum archives holds two BR plans, dated July 1967, for a proposed new vessel. It was of a radically different design, but the proposal was taken no further. However, two hovercraft, *Mercury* and *Minerva*, were given several test runs during 1968 and tried out on a ferry service between Grimsby and Hull, operated by Humber Hovercraft Services Ltd. The experiment was short lived, being discontinued in October that year, although a photograph of *Mercury* on a pleasure trip was published in the *Hull Daily Mail* in February 1969.

On 1st January 1968, the Shipping and International Services Division of BR was formed, taking over control of all ferries and ships from the regions. However, Associated Humber Lines continued to operate the Humber ferries on its behalf. In 1971, with increasing competition and constantly rising costs, AHL ceased trading and the Humber ferries spent their final decade being operated by Sealink. Formed in 1970 as a subsidiary of British Rail, it also operated ferry services across the English Channel and Irish Sea. (Sealink was sold to Sea Containers Ltd in 1984 and is now owned by Stena Line UK.)

On 9th January 1972 the coal miners came out on strike and there was concern locally that, unless the dispute was resolved within days, the Humber ferries would be unable to continue. Indeed, with depleting coal supplies a one-ship service was operated during February by *Tattershall Castle*, whilst both *Wingfield Castle* and *Lincoln Castle* were laid up to conserve stocks. Between 19th February and 5th March 1972 all three ferries were laid up. Although the miners' strike was called off on 28th February a reduced service was provided until 5th March by a small diesel vessel, *Flamborian*, a Bridlington pleasure-boat hired by Sealink. As she was

Watching the world go by in August 1969 as *Lincoln Castle* comes alongside Corporation Pier. *Hull Daily Mail*

only able to carry passengers, vehicles had to make the long journey around via Boothferry Bridge near Goole.

The following month *Tattershall Castle* was permanently withdrawn from service. Her captain's and engine room log books for the winter of 1971–2 are held in the North East Lincolnshire Archives. They show that she made her final crossing on Monday 24th April 1972. The final entry in the captain's log reads: 'Captain's Log on the last day on the Humber Ferry Service of PS *Tattershall Castle* after 38 years. Captain Charles King, Engineer Eric Deans'. *Tattershall Castle* was moored up and out of use on the landward side of the western end of the pier at New Holland. There were plans to use her in the northwest or northeast as a floating restaurant, and she was also offered to Hull Corporation before being towed in July 1973 to Immingham and would later be refitted for use as a floating art gallery on the Thames. This left only two vessels on the Humber, and when each went for maintenance in January and February a one-boat service had to be operated.

Wingfield Castle made her final crossing on Thursday 14th March 1974, with Captain Stan Wright in charge. She was

The diesel-powered Bridlington pleasure boat *Flamborian*, which operated the ferry service during the coal shortage caused by the miners' strike in 1972. *Grimsby Telegraph*

A lifeboat on *Wingfield Castle*. These were easy to swing out over the water, whereas the life rafts, like the one to the left, would take a little longer to launch. *Kirk Martin*

Wingfield Castle heads away from Hull Corporation Pier. *Hull Daily Mail*

The fireman has just pitched the fires on *Wingfield Castle* as she clears Corporation Pier in 1974. *Kirk Martin*

then withdrawn because of problems with her boiler which, like that of *Tattershall Castle*, dated from 1934. Her engine room log book contains the entry: 'Last day in service, 5.30 ex-Hull'. She was sold to a number of owners before moving to Hartlepool, where she is now preserved.

By the middle of March 1974 *Lincoln Castle* was the last of the old Humber paddle steamers still in service. To sustain the two-ship timetable, the diesel-electric paddle vessel *Farringford* had been brought from the Isle of Wight, a plan that had been initiated the previous year. *Farringford* had been built in 1947 by William Denny and Brothers of Dumbarton for the Southern Railway. She entered the service of British Railways, Southern Region, in February 1948, and worked between Lymington, Hampshire and Yarmouth, Isle of Wight. (Her name derives from that of Tennyson's house on that island.) In order to operate on the Humber she needed several modifications, including facilities for the side-loading of vehicles. Details of these, and of her journey north, were reported in Issue Ten of the staff magazine *Sealink News* in 1974:

The timetable of events leading up to her transfer was pretty hectic. After making her last trip to the Isle of Wight last September, she sailed to Southampton where she entered dry dock for an underwater survey. Then it was a much less glamorous journey to [Harwich] Parkeston Quay towed by the tug *Moorcraft* where she underwent modifications to enable her to operate on the Humber.

Deck machinery fore and aft on the vessel was removed to allow space for five extra cars, bringing her car-carrying capacity up to 41. The bow and stern loading doors were also removed and the openings left were plated in. New side-loading doors were fitted on her port and starboard sides. Slight alterations to ladders, signs, lifeboats etc. were also effected and the lower saloon bar converted into a crew mess room.

Farringford then made the journey from Parkeston to Hull again under tow, this time by the tug *Masterman*, where more work was carried out. She entered dry dock to have her paddle floats and an echo-sounder – essential because of her 6ft draught – fitted. The cost of the modifications was £11,000.

Farringford entered service on the Hull to New Holland route in late January 1974, but within months she proved unreliable. In August she spent three weeks at Immingham under repair, leaving *Lincoln Castle* to run a one-boat service. At this time *Wingfield Castle* was languishing in Royal Albert Dock Basin in London.

There was much local interest in *Lincoln Castle* as the last coal-burner operating on the service. The Humber Paddle Steamer Group (HPSG) had been formed in April 1973 and produced its first newsletter, the *Humber Packet*, in July. By September it had chartered *Lincoln Castle* for a cruise and, by the end of the year, had enrolled the 100th member. The South Humberside branch of HPSG met at the Yarborough Arms. People in north east Lincolnshire have always been strong supporters of the ferries, which were registered in the county's town of Grimsby, and on 27th April 1974 the first monthly meeting of the combined Hull and Lincolnshire members was held at the Yarborough Arms (attendees from Hull enjoying the crossing to New Holland by paddle steamer). The secretary reported that Kevin McNamara MP and Ian Holden, Hull's director of industrial development, were in favour of a public appeal to keep *Lincoln Castle* on Humberside.

The HPSG organised a cruise to Grimsby on *Lincoln Castle* on 19th May 1974. The combined newsletter and cruise programme stated its aims as: 'Forming a permanent record of the services and the boats that operated on the Humber', and 'to retain one of the steam paddle boats on Humberside,

Lincoln Castle approaches Hull in 1974, with just a wisp of smoke from her funnel. *Kirk Martin*

in working condition, after the opening of the bridge and use it for leisure activities as well as serving as a reminder of a form of transport which has existed in the estuary for over 150 years'. HPSG secretary Barry Beadle also proposed a museum of the ferry service in the old ferry offices at Corporation Pier, complete with a visitors' café.

In May 1974 *Lincoln Castle* met with an accident while moored at Corporation Pier. She was struck at the bow by the London-registered tanker *Polarisman*, which was being towed into the River Hull, sustaining damage to her forepeak and rails. Her mooring lines parted under the strain and she began to drift into the Humber. Fortunately no one was injured and the damage was described as superficial. She met with another incident while moored at Corporation Pier on 27th February 1975. This time the coaster *Theresa* collided with her in fog, damaging her bridge wing and the starboard sponson, and she had to spend time in dock for repairs.

An article in the *Guardian* in January 1975 described Barry Beadle's proposals for *Lincoln Castle* after the Humber Bridge opened. Life on the vessel was depicted vividly by two photographs, one of Mate Ted Cundell on the bridge at the wheel, the other a fine study of Les Bingham firing in the stokehold. Mr Beadle was realistic in pointing out that the ship's operating costs were in excess of £1,000 a week. This was perhaps the group's best year, with optimism for the future still evident. The final HPSG newsletter appeared at the end of 1976. In the editorial, Barry Beadle explained:

For three years the production of the Humber Packet has been subsidised out of the HPSG cruise fund; when cruising activities were restricted by British Rail we knew we would have to find other sources of income or put up the membership fees…Neither local industry nor councils on Humberside have come to our rescue –

in spite of the tremendous publicity given to us by the Hull Daily Mail, Radio Humberside and Television.

A cruise to Goole in July 1976, organised in conjunction with the Coastal Cruising Association, had resulted in a loss of £200. The CCA made a donation of £75 to the HPSG, indicating the association's belief that the cruise, primarily organised for the Wirral Railway Circle, would be well supported by local people. Barry Beadle and his wife Esther – the group's treasurer – stated that they had not been able to make up the loss, 'due to having to cancel the Grimsby cruise – unfortunately all the advertising and tickets had been done – monies had to be returned to people who had already paid in advance…Then came our bombshell, we could not afford to run further cruises'. The ferry was clearly a cause close to their hearts: they thanked their family, friends and fellow members and admitted that 'This article has been one of the hardest to put together'.

Lincoln Castle was by this time thirty-seven years old. A 1977 report by Geoffrey Reid, held in the North East Lincolnshire Archives and Records Office, recorded some of the problems experienced in operating such an elderly paddle steamer:

On the last run from Hull to New Holland Pier on 9th April 1976, the king arm and driving rod coupling both failed. Radius rods and brackets bent but no floats broken. We worked from midnight to 6am. Changed all the bent gear and the ship was in service at 7.30am. When trying to fit the new king arm it was found that, owing to the feathering eccentric being out of line, it was impossible to couple up to the driving bracket with the connecting bolt owing to the king arm being laid off 4 to 5 inches. To overcome this at such a late hour a 1/8th inch packing was placed in the vicinity of the top bolt in the socket of the feathering eccentric, thus throwing the arm over sufficiently to allow it to be coupled up. On Saturday 8th January 1977, 06.30, Hull, king arm broken off at base and at the top of the socket. Wheel then collapsed, three broken floats, two bent paddle arms, all radius rods bent, some broken, one driving bracket badly bent. All broken floats and radius rods removed whilst at anchor in mid-river, remaining floats lashed in fully feathered position, ship weighed anchor and paddled slowly into deep water then dropped anchor to await tugs. Towed to Brigham & Cowan, Alexandra Dock, Hull for repairs.

By 1977 a new society had been formed: the 'Save the PS Lincoln Castle Campaign'. The Humberside co-ordinator was Andy D'Agorne, whilst Martin Longhurst of Croydon became membership secretary and treasurer. Others involved included Chris Ketchell and Richard Clammer. In April 1977 Humberside County Council agreed 'in principle' to purchase the vessel, and within a short while working parties were negotiating with British Rail, the National Railway Museum and the local authorities.

In February 1978 the *Hull Daily Mail* reported the proposed purchase of *Wingfield Castle* by wealthy Texan Gene Darcy. He intended taking her across the Atlantic and then transporting her overland to San Antonio on a 'massive military transporter'. If he could not get *Wingfield Castle* he said he would consider purchasing *Lincoln Castle,* which was 'due to carry on at least until the opening of the Humber Bridge next year'. However, that same month *Lincoln Castle's* career on the Humber came to an unexpected end.

According to the engine room logs (held at Hull Maritime Museum), on Saturday 11th February 1978 *Lincoln Castle* completed ten return crossings, starting with the 06.30 from Hull and ending with the 21.50 from New Holland. The next day she made three further round trips, leaving Corporation Pier with the 13.30 to New Holland in heavy snow. She stayed at New Holland until 13th February, when her fifteen-minute late departure was attributed to 'awaiting train'. She docked at Corporation Pier at 08.50 but, rather than returning to New Holland, left the pontoon at 09.00 and headed straight for Hull's Alexandra Dock, arriving at the lock entrance at 09.20 and setting off again at 09.55 with the assistance of the tug *Tugsman*, finally arriving at dry-dock No. 2 at 10.30, where she had settled on the chocks by 15.00. *Lincoln Castle* was due for her annual overhaul about that time of year and it seems likely that the recent problems with her boiler had brought this forward.

The *Hull Daily Mail* published a photograph of *Lincoln Castle* in Alexandra Dock, stating that she was having her annual survey and repairs were 'likely to last until next week'. However in mid-March the paper reported that the old boiler had severe structural deterioration and Britain's only remaining coal-burning paddle steamer in daily use had 'made her last trip across the Humber', as BR had decided it was 'not practical' to retain her, especially as she would be withdrawn when the Humber Bridge opened the following year. Furthermore, the new boiler would take nine months to obtain and fit, and would cost £150,000. This decided her fate: she would not return to service. The next issue of the *Hull Daily Mail* stated that BR had been accused by Humberside Labour Councillor Michael Wheaton of taking 'unilateral action' in withdrawing *Lincoln Castle,* and claimed it would cause 'considerable dislocation to the travelling public', adding: 'It is not the first example of such behaviour by British Rail, who should surely have consulted the County Council and other local bodies to see whether there might be a possible solution to this problem'. Councillor Bill Sanderson, chairman of Humberside's Transportation Committee, agreed.

In late March the *Hull Daily Mail* reported that British Rail was 'on an economic knife edge in their quest for a replacement' for *Lincoln Castle*.

They not only have the difficult task of finding a suitable vessel but also the problem of balancing the costs involved against a probable short-term operation. With the Humber Bridge scheduled to be opened in June next year, the acquisition of another ferry to enable the crossing to return to a two-boat service is bound to be a matter of economics.

An emergency meeting of the Save the PS Lincoln Castle Campaign, held in the New Theatre on 27th April, discussed becoming a charitable trust, the name 'Humber Paddle Steamer Trust' having already been used on an earlier poster. Mike Scrimshaw and David Pettingale agreed to look into likely berths for the vessel, Chris Ketchell was to establish a list of volunteers who could assist with restoration and I took on responsibility for publicity, producing a series of leaflets and posters at the university. The *Hull Daily Mail* supported the campaign and reported Cllr Bingham's suggestion that an independent survey of *Lincoln Castle's* boiler be performed. Cllr Bingham accused BR of purposely running the service down, and added: 'Providing the repairs are not too fantastic, let us do the repairs, on condition that at the end of the day we are allowed to buy the vessel for scrap value'. The National Railway Museum was considering taking over the vessel, but insisted that it 'would have to be certain that some public or private organisation would take it on loan from the museum and provide it with a good home'. Peter Semmens, Deputy Curator at the NRM, suggested that, if his museum took her on, it would be happy to lend her to Humberside County Council, thereby allowing her to remain in the area in which she had spent her working life.

BR held a crucial meeting with Humberside County Council on 4th May 1978, at which it was confirmed that *Lincoln Castle* was beyond repair. The Humber Bridge was expected to open in 1979, and until then the ferry service could be maintained by *Farringford* alone. In the event, the bridge was not completed until 1981, and so the one-boat service operated for three years. If *Farringford* broke down, the Bridlington-based, 1947-built *Yorkshire Belle* could be

First mate J. Davies rejoins the stranded *Lincoln Castle* following damage to her paddles. She was towed to Brigham & Cowan, Alexandra Dock, Hull, for repairs. *Hull Daily Mail*

Lincoln Castle in Alexandra No. 2 Dry Dock in February 1978, at the time her boiler failed. *Hull Daily Mail*

The diesel-electric paddle vessel *Farringford* approaching Hull Corporation Pier. Note the gated openings cut out in 1974 to allow side loading on the Humber. During her years on the Solent she had been a drive-through, end-loading ferry. *Kirk Martin*

chartered, but only as a passenger ferry. In October the *Hull Daily Mail* reported that Sealink was considering bringing the Tilbury–Gravesend ferry *Edith* up from the Thames.

Lincoln Castle was again in the news in late May, when the *Hull Times* expressed concern over its fate:

> The historic Humber ferry *Lincoln Castle* is again under siege and fighting to retain its birthright – and perhaps become Hull's biggest tourist attraction. Her future is now in the hands of Hull City Council. The choice facing councillors is whether to allow Francis Daly, the paddle steamer's new owner, to breathe new life into her rusty bones and move her to Prince's Dock to become a floating restaurant and museum piece, or to hasten her removal from Humberside which she has served for nearly forty years.

The Isle of Wight motor vessel *Freshwater*, built by Ailsa Shipbuilding in 1959, was brought north to cover for *Farringford* during her three-week absence for routine winter maintenance in January 1980.

By 1981, as the bridge neared completion, reporters from the *Guardian* visited the ferry and published a feature article

on 3rd June. They interviewed staff on board *Farringford* and at New Holland, where sixty-three-year-old Geoffrey Reid recounted his forty-one years as a fitter maintaining the ferries. He had no time for the unreliable *Farringford,* but recalled with pride the steamers *Killingholme, Brocklesby, Cleethorpes* and the three 'Castles'. Seventy-three-year-old Laurence (Loll) Clayton had started work as a 'chocolate boy' on the pier before working in the yard and eventually on the ferries. John North, a lecturer in geography at Hull University, pointed out that the bridge had been tacked awkwardly onto a motorway system already established on the presumption that the Humber would not be bridged. Captain Charles King was philosophical about the end, but pointed out the difficulty for a man of his age taking up a new post on the Portsmouth ferries, which he had been offered by Sealink.

A vivid description of the final days of the ferry service is provided by Steve Priestly, an enthusiast who visited New Holland several times and witnessed its demise. His first visit was at Easter, on 6th April 1981.

> Everything was still intact, and the weather was, as usual, cold, windy and overcast....Four totems [station

Farringford at Hull Corporation Pier, ready to cross to New Holland. *Kirk Martin*

name boards] were in situ at the Town station, as well as a black and white seat back plate on the platform seat. The large Great Central Railway bell still hung under the New Holland Town signal box name board. At the Pier station the Adlake lamp was on the buffer stops at the end of the line, bearing the name New Holland on a copper plate…The signals on the pier had gone; all that remained were the cut down wooden posts.

He visited again on 19th June:

A two-car Diesel Multiple Unit was in the platform at the Town station and a film crew on the platform. The DMU moved over the crossing and then reversed back into the platform. The signals at the Town box did not appear to be working because the signalman gave the 'right away' with a green flag waved from the box. It was noticeable that the totems had been removed, also the enamel seat back sign and several blue enamel signs. As I walked down the pier I noticed the two blue enamel signal box name boards had gone…The Adlake lamp remained on the buffer stop, which bore the chalked legend 'almost the end'. Whilst on the platform the

DMU came down the pier into the station with the film crew on board, filming from the front window.

His final visit was on 24th June, when the last crossing to Hull was scheduled for 6.15pm.

The Humber Bridge had opened at 11.30am that morning. The weather was cold and windy, as usual, when I arrived at New Holland at 5.15pm. The car park attendant's hut was already closed, the last train had left the station at 12.15pm, and the new station, comprising a platform and bus shelter, was already in operation. Both the bells had gone from the signal box, also the signal box name board…

On the platform a handful of enthusiasts were taking photos and peering through what were now redundant office windows. Members of staff were huddled together in a small office marked 'staff only' talking of better days and the opening of the bridge… At 5.54pm I bought three old LNER tickets from the booking office for 11 pence. By now more people were arriving for the last ferry trip. We walked down the pier, Mr Reeves, the area manager, told us that all the relics were going to the

A 1979 poster announcing the planned closure of the ferries when the Humber Bridge opened. The poster reveals that the bridge was expected to open in 1980. *Rodney Clapson collection*

Lincoln Castle moored in Alexandra Dock, Hull, after withdrawal in 1978. *Kirk Martin*

National Railway Museum at York. We went down the gangway onto the pontoon to wait for the ferry to arrive. She came in at 6.15pm and tied up.

The boat working the last trip was the *Farringford* and she bore a wreath on her bridge saying 'what you leave behind no bridge will ever span'. We went on board and departed for Hull at 6.31pm arriving at 7.14pm. We left the ferry briefly, boarding again at 7.24pm with a large crowd of people. Radio Humberside were also on board making a live broadcast. A man on the deck played an accordion; it created quite a party atmosphere. On the return trip the crew signed autographs, I purchased some postcards and a T shirt. We arrived back at New Holland at 8.05pm. We disembarked and waited on the pontoon for the ferry to leave for Hull.

She went at 8.20pm leaving many sad faces on the pier, including Les Claxton, who had been a crew member on the ferries for 34 years and was now out of a job. He said he would miss meeting people as much as anything, and had many happy memories. We shook hands and he got on his bike and rode off along the pier, not waiting for the ferry to leave. He did say that a party had been arranged on Saturday night aboard the *Farringford*.

Leaving New Holland I drove to the Humber Bridge and crossed it at about the same time as the ferry was to arrive at Hull for the last time. The irony was that I could not return over the bridge because a lorry had an oil spillage and the bridge was closed. I had to return the long way around via Goole, arriving home at 11.30pm; the ferry had had the last laugh!

The final days were so busy that Paul Thomas, a depot relief clerk based at Immingham, was instructed to report for duty in the booking office at New Holland Town station purely to answer the telephone for the ticket clerk, who was inundated by people purchasing tickets for the final crossings. He told me: 'Whilst I was there I noticed in the ticket rack that some of the Edmonson style tickets were printed by the LNER, so I purchased a child ticket for my collection'.

A private cruise was booked for Saturday 27th June. In a letter held in the North East Lincolnshire Archives and Records, Mr E.T. Fisher, ferry manager for Sealink, wrote that 'the D.E.P.V. *Farringford* will remain at Hull Corporation Pier pontoon until all the life saving equipment, barometers, clocks, etc., are removed on Monday 29th June 1981'. Arrangements were made for the vessel to be berthed until disposal. She left Corporation Pier on 29th June bound for Alexandra Dock, and was reported as having been sold in October 1981 to Western Ferries (Argyll) Ltd for the Gourock to Dunoon vehicle ferry. However, she never left the Humber, and was sold in March 1984 to a ship breaker, John Hewitt of Heddon, and broken up in Silcock's Basin in Hull.

A trip across the Humber on 13th June 1981

The Sealink ticket office opposite Hull Corporation Pier. *Steve Clark (Dave Enefer collection)*

The entrance to the connecting bridge, Hull Corporation Pier. *Steve Clark (Dave Enefer collection)*

A trip across the Humber on 13th June 1981

New Holland Pier seen from *Farringford* on the 10am crossing. *Steve Clark (Dave Enefer collection)*

A well-used service. A two-car Cravens DMU from Cleethorpes arrives at New Holland. *Steve Clark (Dave Enefer collection)*

A trip across the Humber on 13th June 1981

Hull Corporation Pier as seen from *Farringford* on the 14.30 crossing from New Holland. *Steve Clark (Dave Enefer collection)*

New Holland Pier station, with the Adlake lamp on the buffer stops and only one track remaining along the pier. Note the tractor and the four-wheeled barrows. *Steve Priestly (Alf Ludlam collection)*

The final day, 24th June 1981

The *Farringford* on the last day of service on 24th June 1981 arrives at New Holland. *Steve Priestly (Alf Ludlam collection)*

The crew of *Farringford* on 24th June 1981, the final day for the Humber ferries. Angie Stephenson's father, George Bone, is holding the RIP sign. *Angie Stephenson*

The final day, 24th June 1981

Farringford on her final day of service, 24th June 1981. The 'Humber ferries RIP' banner and the crowds on board and on the pier say it all. *Grimsby Telegraph*

A letter from ferry manager E.T. (Ernie) Fisher to George Bone, advising him of the termination of his employment on the Humber ferry. *With kind permission of Angie Stephenson*

Sealink ticket issued to George Bone for the last private sailing of *Farringford* on 27th June 1981. *With kind permission of Angie Stephenson*

Sealink UK Limited

Humber Ferry Service,
Corporation Pier,
Hull.

Mr G.C. Bone,
Leading Rating.

y/r
o/r   HF 8/1

Date 23rd June 1981.

<u>Closure – Humber Ferry Service.</u>

The Humber Ferry Service will cease to operate after Saturday 27th June 1981.

In accordance with your reply to my letter of 28th November 1980 you expressed the wish to accept redundancy.

I therefore give you formal notice that your employment with Sealink UK Ltd., will cease on Saturday 4th July 1981.

I would like to express my appreciation for your loyal service, particularly during the last few difficult weeks, when staff shortages were acute. Without your unstinting cooperation it would have been extremely difficult to have continued the normal service.

Thank you once again.

Ferry Manager.

Registered in England No 1402237 Registered office Eversholt House 163/203 Eversholt Street
London NW1 1BG A subsidiary of British Railways Board

BR 25/379

HUMBER FERRY
SEALINK UK LTD.

The Manager of the Humber Ferry Service invites you to a
Last Private Sailing of the D&PV 'Farringford'
on 27th June 1981 at 12.30 hours
from Hull Corporation Pier
to commemorate 150 years of the service between Hull and New Holland

Buffet Lunch

Chapter Eight

WORKING ON THE FERRIES

Over the centuries many people have worked on the Humber ferries, but their stories are largely unknown. The life of one early-nineteenth-century ferryman – John Ellerthorpe – is well-documented because, in a life spanning sixty-one years from 1806 to 1867, he saved at least forty people from drowning. Drawing on two biographies, one published by the Rev. Henry Woodcock in 1880 and the other by Michael G. Free (currently on the Hessle Local History website) Helena Wojtczak compiled the following précis of John's life.

John Ellerthorpe (ferryman 1832–1845)

Despite being an habitual drunkard, John Ellerthorpe's father, also called John, began as a crewman on board the Hessle to Barton ferry in 1816, when young John was ten, and worked on them for forty years. Growing up around the Humber, young John became a strong swimmer, crossing the estuary many times and lending a hand when vessels and passengers were caught in gales. When his father became master of the ferry he sometimes went along to assist, saving his father the shilling he would have to pay a crewman. During one trip his father fell overboard into high waves of freezing water. He was drunk, about fifteen stones in weight and unable to swim. The boy, then fourteen, dived in and pulled him back to the boat, to which he clung until help was obtained. That was to be the first of at least forty lives saved by the 'Hero of the Humber'. He spent about a decade working on ships between London and Quebec, and to the Baltic, during which time he saved at least four more people, although he was – in his own words – a 'drunken blackguard'.

The sixth life John saved, in 1825, was that of Robert Clegg, owner and captain of *Ann Scarborough*. In 1832, when *Magna Charta* began to operate between Hull and New Holland, John joined the crew and was later its master. He saved eight lives between 1832 and 1836, one of whom was a little girl called Mary Ann Day, who fell from the ferry into New Holland harbour one day in 1833.

> I sprang in after her while the paddle-wheels of the steamer were in motion, and brought her ashore, though at a great risk of losing my own life. The noise of the paddle-wheels, the screams of the girl's mother, and the confusion and shouts of the passengers, made this a very exciting scene, but it was very soon over, and the little girl, having got some dry clothes on, her mother brought her to me, and said to her, 'Now what will you give this gentleman for saving your life?' when she held out her little chin and, with a full heart, said, 'A kiss'. She gave me a kiss, and O, what a kiss it was. I felt myself well paid for my trouble.

The following year, whilst acting as watchman on *Magna Charta*, John went on board 'not quite sober' and lay down on the forecastle. He heard a strange noise.

> A plank had been put from the *Ann Scarborough*, into our Taffelrail, and as this plank had fallen down, I thought it was its fall I had heard…I got a boat hook and pulled the plank on board our vessel…on taking a light I saw Crabtree…engineer of the *Ann Scarborough*, stuck in the mud, for the vessels were dry. I put down a ladder and went to help him, but he was so fast in the mud that I could do nothing with him.

John obtained the help of three other men:

> He was dead drunk, but we soon got him ashore, gave him some brandy, and he was very little worse. The case was kept a profound secret at the time, and for this reason – Crabtree was afraid that if his master should get to know of the affair, he would lose his situation, and as we all thought the same, we promised not to tell anyone of it.

In 1835 a fellow crewman called Robert Brown fell overboard during a gale. John leapt in, and Brown almost drowned him in his desperate struggle to stay afloat.

In 1836 John became master of *Ann Scarborough* and worked the Hessle to Barton crossing. To advertise the service, he ordered some special publicity pottery to be manufactured. A jug that survived bears the words: John Elerthorp is my name/A ferryman of noble fame/And when my boats they are afloat/My stock then I begin to boat/Then to Barton I do go/To land my beasts on Lincoln shore/Then when I've landed take my pay/And set my sail and come away.

One day *Ann Scarborough* was drawing a tow boat, attached by a thick rope, carrying 'a great number of fat beasts'. The tow boat capsized, and, John recalled:

[S]ome of the beasts swam one way and some another, while several got entangled in the rails attached to the boat's side, and were every moment in danger of breaking their legs. So seizing an axe I jumped into the water and cut away the rails, and then went in pursuit of the oxen, heading them round in the water and causing them, by shouts and gestures, to swim for the land. Most of them were driven back to Barton and landed safely, others swam across the Humber and were landed at Hessle. I was up to my chest in water and mud for nearly three hours swimming backwards and forwards after the beasts; sometimes I had hold of their tails, and anon had to meet them and turn them towards the shore.

During a gale one night in 1842, John was thrown overboard between Hull and Barton and was 'one moment lost in the trough of the sea, and the next on the crest of the billows, now near the boat and again fifty yards from it'. He eventually got back onto the ferry after half-an-hour in the freezing river. His narrative of the incident is not only hair-raising, it also includes an interesting description of his clothing and possessions:

I had on the following garments, made of very stout pilot-cloth: a pair of trousers, a double-breasted waistcoat, a surtout coat, and a heavy great coat, which came down to my ancles, a thick shawl round my neck, and a new pair of Wellington boots on my feet. I had in my pockets the following sums of money: £25 in bank notes; 25 sovereigns; £4 16s. 6d in silver, and 8d in coppers; also a tobacco-box, a large pocket knife, and a silver watch and guard. I made an attempt to throw off some of my clothes, but the thought of losing another man's money checked me. Besides, the suit of clothes I had on was bran-new, and being a poor man, and only just earning a livelihood, I could not brook the thought of having to get a new 'rigging'. When a wave carried me a great way from the boat, I unbuttoned my coat and prepared to throw it off, that I might more easily swim to land. And when it seemed certain I should have to make this attempt, I felt for my knife, that I might cut off my boots, and I believe I could have done it; but, after a desperate effort, I approached within a few yards of the boat, when I again buttoned my coat. I felt confident I could have reached the shore – a distance of one mile – had I been compelled to make the trial. My Wellington boots had nearly cost me my life, as they were heavy and difficult to swim in, and I never wore a pair after this fearful night.

Two years later, whilst captain of the Winteringham to Brough ferry, he was halfway across when again the tow boat capsized, pitching the livestock into the Humber. This time he spent five hours in the river, and afterwards the crew 'hastened to the public-house at the harbour-side, and got drunk'. John kept his wet clothes on, 'until they dried on my back'.

Having married in 1828, John fathered fourteen children and, in 1846, saved the life of his own young son, who had sunk to the bottom of a bathing pool whilst being taught to swim.

John's life-saving adventures were often undertaken in highly dangerous conditions and with no regard for his own safety. Although he never sought recognition he received many rewards and awards, including a pile of half-crowns raised during a whip-round, a lump sum of £11 and, much later, £133 in cash and a gold watch paid for by public subscription. Among his awards were the Silver Medallion of the Royal Humane Society in 1836 and its Certificate on Vellum in 1861. He was honoured by local townspeople in 1861 and 1864, the Board of Trade struck a specially inscribed silver medal, portraying a group of people on a raft, and Prime Minister Lord Palmerston granted him £20 from the Royal Bounty.

In January 1845 John became foreman at the Humber Dock gates, but the census reveals that, by 1851, he had returned to being a 'Master of a Packet'. After saving yet another life in 1861, he was offered £2 a week to patrol Hull Docks, ready to save anyone who fell into the water, and remained in that job until his retirement.

The following reminiscences were collected from various members of staff who were employed between 1937 and 1981. These derive from personal interviews by the author and by newspaper reporter John Howard, from crew members interviewed for the DVD *Monarchs of the Humber* and articles in the *Hull and Yorkshire Times*, the *Hull Daily Mail* and *Sealink News*. The first is from an item in the 'bygones' section of the *Hull Daily Mail* of 4th February 2004.

Ferryman Jack Coupland (1937–1939)

My wife and I were brought up in New Holland and… were both taken to Hull regularly, as both our fathers were railwaymen and got reduced fares. We travelled on the *Brocklesby*, *Cleethorpes*, *Killingholme* and the three Castles…I started work at 14 at New Holland goods depot, number taking, and did this until 1937, when I moved to the passenger side as a carriage cleaner. I also had to assist on the pier…This was just before the new pontoon was built. There was a traverser on the old pier worked by hydraulic power which also worked the cranes on the dock. On low tides, barrows were put on the traverser and taken down to the boat. This was very heavy work. I was on the afternoon shift when the new pontoon was put in and later when we had a few minutes to spare and the tide was at turning point, Don Wright and Billy Lambert and myself took the small safety boat out on the river and I took a photo of the new pontoon. This picture is now in the Immingham Museum, along with other material which I donated. I worked on the pier from 1937 to 1939 when I moved to Immingham as a loco cleaner, later working as a fireman at Lincoln before returning to Immingham as a driver, retiring in 1984.

Tom Nagy fills the ash bucket, ready for it to be hauled up and tipped into one of the four-wheeled coal barrows for unloading at New Holland. *Eric Wright (Martyn Ashworth collection)*

A wing fire, one of the four fireboxes on *Lincoln Castle*, with its firebox door and ashpan door open. *Eric Wright (Martyn Ashworth collection)*

The paddles are already turning in reverse as the member of the crew on the sponson feeds the rope to the man ashore as the ferry comes alongside Hull Corporation Pier. Note that the lighter rope is thrown first and then the heavier mooring rope is hauled in to drop over the bollard. *Kirk Martin*

Deck Hand and Leading Seaman Ken Edwards (1940–1981). Interviewed by John Howard in 1975

Ken Edwards, of New Holland…served as a crewman, leading seaman, and as a non-certified mate for a time, mainly on the three coal-burning Castles….He told me that he was often at the helm, a task which he enjoyed. His other duties included responsibilities for the deck and lifeboat maintenance. He recalls that sheep and cattle were often carried to and from the Hull market in special pens designed to fit on the deck. The sand spread out for the animals helped to scour the deck of the sump oil drips from the cars when it was brushed off and hosed down. On one memorable occasion, a bullock fell into the crew's quarters, ten feet below, and the crew had great difficulty in getting the animal up the steep and narrow stairway. However, seamen are not easily defeated and they rigged up some tackle to lift it out. During the struggle, the unfortunate animal left the crew with a few reminders of its unexpected visit…

It was hard work in winter, especially in freezing fog. The ferries kept going except in storm winds of force 9–10, or thick fog, pre-1948, when radar was first installed. VHF radio was added in the early 1970s.

The working atmosphere was friendly. Few people left the service, except to retire. The crews belonged to National Union of Railwaymen [NUR] since the ferries were owned by a railway company, but there were no strikes and Mr Edwards only recalls one work to rule in his thirty-five years service…

He also recalls the occasion of the Queen's visit [on 18th May 1957], when the *Wingfield Castle* was used as a pontoon with special stays fixed over the side for the Royal Barge. When the Queen and Prince Philip walked across the deck on their way to the Barge they stopped to have a few words with the crew before embarking for the *Britannia*. The *Lincoln Castle* was used to carry sightseers on a short trip around the *Britannia*.

He also has a clear recollection of the Flixborough Disaster [in 1974]. 'I was at the helm on a passage to Hull when the explosion at Flixborough wharf shook the paddle steamer although it was twenty miles away. I think we would have been involved in the rescue but the tide was on the ebb and even with our shallow draught we would not have been able to land.'

Deck Hand Ken Woodger (1946–1981)

An article about the abolition of the Humber ferries, published in the *Yorkshire Post* on 8th August 1981, featured Ken Woodger, who had joined the service in 1946 after fifteen years in the Royal Navy. Mr Woodger was honoured with a Royal Humane Society Award for rescuing a woman who had attempted suicide by jumping overboard on a winter's night. On another occasion a drunk had 'come dashing up to the pier at Hull under the impression the ferry was just pulling away. He made a leap for the deck, missed, and fell into the river'. The ferry, however, was actually coming in. 'He was dragged out of the water and dumped in the boiler room to sober up,' recalled Mr Woodger. He also remarked

that *Farringford* 'never caught the imagination of the public, although she was quite efficient'. Although, he said, 'the old Castle class steamers had lots of style', there were times when the crews 'cursed them and the rotten Humber weather. But regular passengers became friends and [the ferries] provided an interesting way of life that has now gone forever'.

The following anecdote derives from the DVD *Monarchs of the Humber* narrated by Rob Haywood who interviewed former ferry staff for the production.

Captain Arthur Harvey (1953–1979)

I first went to sea in 1941 in troop ships, tankers and cargo ships travelling worldwide. It was during the war and I was in the Italian campaign, the Pacific and the Battle of the Atlantic. I joined the railway ferries in the south of England in 1946, spending time on the cross-channel Dover service, the Portsmouth service and also the Channel Island service before, in September 1953, moving up to the Humber to take over as a master on the Humber ferries.

Obviously it was a specialised job, so I had to spend a month under another master to learn certain specialised skills. After that I took up my turn on the roster. I spent most time in the early days on the *Tattershall Castle,* but all three ships were on the roster so I had time on all of them. I did not have a favourite ship. The *Wingfield* and the *Tatty* were identical ships but the *Lincoln* was a little different because she had a shallower draught than the other two. When you look at the ferries, and note the size of them, and consider that the draught was only 4ft 6in, they were very obviously prone to winds, more so the *Lincoln* than the *Wingfield* and *Tatty* as there was six inches less in draught so the *Lincoln* was certainly very prone to the winds, like a balloon on water.

Over those years I experienced two collisions; one was when a trawler's bow went into the first class saloon on a day of very dense fog, and the other was due to the tides. I was trying to do a particular manoeuvre and it didn't come off and I ended up with a float wrapped in the paddle, which disabled the ship and meant that we had to be towed back. But they were the only two incidents so the rest was quite satisfactory, I hope!

We got to know our passengers over the years and one or two became very close friends. Yes, we've watched those young girls crossing in the 1950s and we've seen them grow up and start work, as solicitor's clerks and so on, and then have families of their own. They may be grandmothers now. Back in 1953 the traffic was quite different. There were fewer cars. There was the odd time when we had horses, but we were not carrying cattle as they did in the days before the war.

In 1963 there was a bad winter and there was a lot of ice on the river. That was the time when the engineers found that we had a steam jet in the paddle wheel that went to the outer edge of the wheel, what we call the 'banjo'.

I don't think anyone knew about it, as we had not had a severe winter like that since 1947. Getting along-side was a problem because you would pack the ice between the ship and the side, and it took a lot of smashing up before you could get in. Yes, that was an interesting time, but the ice was never thick enough to really create problems or cause damage to the paddles. The bow would part the ice and by the time it got to the paddles it was well broken up. It never stopped us, anyway.

Fog was the biggest problem, of course, especially in the days when we had hundreds of trawlers. A colleague of mine, one of the masters, who was a keen photographer, took a photograph of the radar screen one day and within one mile of us there were thirty-four ships anchored. That did present problems, especially in view of the Humber tides and getting in and out, because the paddles weren't independent, so we could only steer with the rudder and not by operating the two paddles independently, as you could on some steamers.

The *Tattershall Castle* was the first ship on the Humber to have radar, but by the time I started all the ships had radar, of course. Radar had been used during the war, when it was in its infancy, and the operators were as well so we all progressed together. When it broke down, you could use sounds, such as the siren at New Holland, and at Hull we used the bell on Minerva Pier. You could come in by listening to the sound. This was especially so with the siren on the New Holland side – you could come in and bring the ship right round with the sound of the siren. It was very effective – you could actually run right past it and then bring the ship round and bring it in gingerly, so that you just came in right. We could use the sound of our own horn as well and use the echo off buildings and time it. They were the old ways of doing it and I don't suppose they could do that now!

I left the ferry service about eighteen months before the end. I knew I had to start a new career and I decided to make the move. I had served twenty-five years as master and, although many others worked longer on the ferries than me, I understand that I was the longest-serving master in recent years.

On 16th June 1956 the *Hull and Yorkshire Times* published the following article, written by Derek Tyson and illustrated by cameraman Harry Parker. It provides a lively and amusing account of the ferries and the crew of the 1950s.

Riverboat

A chill drizzle cut like whips of ice across the ship's bridge. Captain John C. Hempseed, huddled in black greatcoat, creased his eyes and gave casting-off orders to the barely-visible men on the quayside. Suddenly the vessel became a live thing and with a dip and a roll gently swayed the streaming decks.

The captain's hand went to the engine room signal… 'Slow ahead'. The ship heaved to the sound of threshing water. The voyage was beginning. Captain Hempseed turned to the seaman at the helm. 'Take her straight through, Loll', he said.

Yes, ships' commanders do speak as casually as that to their helmsmen. For this wasn't the Royal Navy, or the merchant navy – it was British Railways' own private little navy of three ships, the ferry boats that link the bustle and commerce of the city of Hull with the quiet fields and farm houses of Lincolnshire.

It's a twenty-minute trip – twenty minutes of mud banks and currents – and Captain Hempseed and his crew know every ripple and sign of trouble. For the Humber is a treacherous stretch of water, with mists and fogs that blot out everything and make the trip three miles of anxious hooting and peering from the bridge.

Not for nothing is radar installed on the ferry boats and not for nothing do British Railways insist that every man aboard their ships is water-wise and every inch a sailor. The casualness among the captain and his men is deceptive for every inch of the way their minds and instincts are all bent on one aim – to get the ferry as safely and quickly as possible to the other side.

Captain Hempseed and his crew were manning the *Wingfield Castle* when we travelled with them and watched them at work. You can imagine it ploughing up the Mississippi in the days of the riverboat gamblers and the show boats; but the *Wingfield Castle*, far from being a pleasure steamer, is a utilitarian vessel, despite its refinements and amenities for passengers.

Captain Hempseed has seen wider waters than the Humber – and less peaceful trips. For the ferry captain was a merchant navy man for years and saw hectic war service. But like the majority of all the ferry crews and captains, he is a married man and being able to get home at night counts for a lot.

At eighteen he was running coal and grain up the river Plate and during the war he served in rescue ships as a 'tail-end Charlie' in convoys. These were the vessels which tagged along at the end of a convoy, picking up survivors from sunk or damaged merchant men. He saw ships sink and he saw men die; he underwent the terror of being bombed at sea and took part in the dicey supply run to North Africa.

Then after the war, he took potatoes to the people he had been fighting – helping to feed the Germans. Then came spells with Associated Humber Lines and then Humber Conservancy Board, looking after the all important Humber buoys and floats. 'And then I came to British Railways,' he told me with a smile, sitting at his desk in the captain's cabin before we set sail. 'Yes this job's OK and as long as I have water under my feet, short trips and a small ship it don't matter so much'.

'Call her the belle of the ferry', said Captain Hempseed, when he introduced us to bar stewardess Jacqueline Thorndyke. Not many heads as attractive as Jacqueline's pop up from behind bars these days.

Nineteen in August, she lives in New Holland, and has been on the ferries only a few months. Previously she was a snack bar assistant. 'Do you like your new job?' we asked. 'Oh yes, it's smashing', was the reply! 'She doesn't like it when she rolls', Captain Hempseed chipped in.

Mrs E. Moore, also of New Holland, is one half of a husband-and-wife railway team. While hubby works as a pier porter, Mrs Moore acts as a summer relief bar stewardess. What made her enter the ferry service? 'It's a nice change from housework, for one thing!'

Bar steward Roland Turner of Healing, near Grimsby, is a widower with an eleven-year-old daughter, Jean. He has had five years on the ferries and is often accompanied by his daughter when the ships go on pleasure cruises down the estuary. Roland was a hall porter at the Yarborough Hotel, Grimsby, but entered the ferry service for health reasons as he found the fresh air did him good.

Mrs Nora Turner of New Holland is kept busy, serving biscuits and tea, as a saloon stewardess. To the rest of this happy family, the ship's company, she's known as Aunty Nora.

Following in his father's footsteps is *Wingfield Castle's* deck hand Laurence (Loll) Clayton, whose father was on the ferries for many years. Laurence has been a ferry man for twenty-seven years. There's a good reason for him wanting a job where he can be with his family every night. For at his Manchester Square home in New Holland he has got a large family.

Doyen of the *Wingfield Castle* crew is sixty-year-old Cecil Forman, who can tie up, cast off and take the helm as well as ever after thirty-six years service. He has also seen trawler service and served in the army during World War One, when he was wounded three times. Cecil of New Holland is now a grandfather. In five years he will reach retiring age and there is real regret in his eyes and a touch of sadness when he says 'I'm nearly at the end of my run now'.

A North Sea minesweeper was the cheerless – and dangerous – sphere of operation for deck hand Kenneth Edwards during the war. And the Fleetwood trawler *Evelyn Rose*, in which he served, survived the minefields only to be sunk on a fishing mission a year ago.

A part time ferry worker is ticket collector Thomas E. Todd of Hull. Mostly he works on Hull Pier, but does two days a week on the ferries, plus two week holiday relief periods during the summer. And his verdict on ferry work? 'It's OK when the weather's good'.

'The *Lincoln Castle's* really our ship. She's the queen of the river', says fifty-four-year-old deck hand George Woods. 'She's the newest and the biggest, but she's in dock for repair'. George, who lives in New Holland and has nine children, served with the ferry throughout the war. The Humber had its war time perils too, and he remembers when the ferries could not sail for thirteen days while mines were being cleared.

Relief engineer Robert Redhead, of Barton, busies himself around the massive leaping cranks. Although he's only fifty-two, Robert has had thirty-seven years of ferry experience. He started when he was a boy of fifteen as a cleaner, became a fireman, sweating and shovelling in front of the open fire-doors, and finally made it to relief engineer.

Chris Braithwaite, a thirty-five-year-old fireman and deck hand, started working on the ferries in 1939 but was called up soon afterwards and saw service with the Royal Army Medical Corps in North Africa. Chris lives in New Holland and has three daughters, and says 'It is a good steady job and I get home every night'.

The following reminiscences of crew members Chris Braithwaite and Martyn Ashworth, maintenance man Maurice Mawer and ferry manager Ted Sangster were collected between 2010 and 2012. I had not seen Chris Braithwaite since working on the ferries in the 1970s, and was able to contact him thanks to his daughter Sandie Braithwaite, who responded to my request for the memories of former crew members.

Deck Hand and Leading Seaman Chris Braithwaite (1939–1981)

I went on the Humber ferry in June 1939 when I was sixteen. A chap off the ferry who was a painter asked if I wanted a job, because there was a vacancy. I had left school at fourteen, and had been a gardener and an office boy. I started as a boy engine cleaner on the *Killingholme*. I had to clean the engines and keep them in tip-top condition, especially all the brasses.

During the war we used a three-boat shuttle service to evacuate mothers and children from Hull. After a short period on the *Killingholme*, I was promoted to fireman on the *Tattershall Castle*. The *Killingholme* was replaced

Chris Braithwaite in 2011. He worked on the Humber ferries from 1939 until 1981 apart from three years' war service. He is looking at an album of my photographs of crew members. *Kirk Martin*

The captain looks ahead
while a leading hand
stands at the wheel on the
bridge of *Wingfield Castle*.
Hartlepool Borough Council

Barrows loaded with fruit and vegetables for Hull Market left to one side, whilst a van and cars are loaded at Corporation Pier. One of the tractors is seen in the background.
Hull Daily Mail

Humber ferry staff at New Holland, 7th June 1960, attending Fred Doughty's retirement presentation. Fred is standing in the centre; Stan Johnson is 2nd left, front row; Chris Braithwaite is 4th from left, back row. Ron 'Ginger' Bell stands in the doorway at the back whilst Les Claxton is behind the man 4th from left in the second row. *Sandie Braithwaite collection*

Sally Braithwaite, far left, with other Humber ferry buffet staff. *Sandie Braithwaite collection*

on the ferry service by the *Lincoln Castle* in 1941 and I fired her on her first crossing.

A black flag was flown at Corporation Pier when mines had been dropped in the river by enemy aircraft. On one occasion we set off just before the flag was raised and there were mines in the river. We were lucky because we went downriver (because it was an ebb tide) and the minesweepers were clearing the mines, but we could have hit a mine if we had been on a flood tide and come in the other way around. One trawler was sunk at that time, so we had a near-miss on that occasion.

I remember during the cold winter of 1941–2, the ferry was coming in and I was waiting on the pontoon at New Holland. The river was full of shoals of ice. We had got one rope off when a big shoal came floating down, pushed the boat away and broke the rope. The ship had to go around and come back in again. That was a very bad winter, but not the only one we had on the Humber.

I was called up in 1942. I entered the Royal Army Medical Corps, because I had been in the St John's Ambulance Brigade. I served in Algiers and Italy, working in the operating theatres. I met my wife, Sally, in North Africa and we were married in Bologna and she settled in England with me when the war was over; she later worked in the buffet on the ferries.

I managed to get my job back on the ferries. The foreman called me into the office because I had had a permanent job before the war. I went back in the workshops before I got a job as a fireman, working on all three ships, but then I decided to go into deck work because it was easier. The engine room staff had to stoke the boilers and clean the fires out and all that sort of thing. We had manual work to do on deck as well, such as cleaning the decks and splicing the ropes, but I did put a bit of weight on, I can tell you. When I came on deck I was the first man ever to transfer from the engine room, and it caused a real row. I started as a deck hand and enjoyed the work. We all took a turn as leading hands in steering. After the war one vessel was sent down to Grimsby to run special cruises to Spurn Head, sometimes doing two or three trips before returning to New Holland.

I remember horse-drawn vehicles and cattle using the ferry. We used to load the cattle at New Holland and put them into individual pens: some for cows and others for sheep. We would take them across to Hull market. Once, on the *Lincoln Castle,* a cow collapsed as we were crossing to Hull. Its legs were spread and it couldn't get up. It had to be slaughtered on the ship by some butchers, who then carted it off to the market. What a mess that caused! In the mid-fifties we lost a man over the side. He was repainting the stern of the *Wingfield Castle* in preparation for a royal visit and went over. They didn't find his body for about a month or more.

When the pontoon was away for repair, we used the crane to load cars on and off at Hull. Later, on the *Farringford,* a chap drove his big Jaguar onto the ferry, but had forgotten to put the hand brake on. As the ferry rolled the car went straight through the railings. Fortunately, she didn't end up in the river, she was lodged on the edge of the deck; but the owner had left his briefcase inside with his money in it, so he had to get that out. We managed to pull the car back onto the deck with the tractor at New Holland, but the skipper had to come around the wrong way alongside because the car was hanging over the side.

Once the Humber Bridge opened, well, that was it for the ferries, of course. We all saw it coming. I did my best for the ferries and the men. I had been the National Union of Railwaymen branch secretary since 1960; I made sure they all got another job. Three of us applied for a job on the Humber Bridge. Me and Terry Hopper were the lucky applicants, and the third, a ticket collector, I think he got a job on Hull Paragon station, so he stayed on the railways, anyway.

I was on the ferries for over forty years – apart from war service. It was a good life and there was a happy atmosphere among the crew. I recall only one day's strike in all that time. I missed the ferries a lot when they finished, but there was no hope of them continuing once the bridge opened. You could say they were the happiest days of my life and that went for most of the people who worked on the ferries.

Charge Hand Engineer Maurice Mawer, Humber Graving Dock (1956–1990)

After leaving school in 1951 Maurice worked in a garage in Lincolnshire, gaining his City & Guilds certificate in motor mechanics. Aged twenty-one he switched jobs to work in Humber Graving Dock because, in his words, 'there was more money in it'. He was to stay for thirty-five years. In 2011 he told me about his work in maintaining the Humber ferries.

I went to the Humber Graving Dock & Engineering Company in Immingham in 1956. When I first started they were just building the larger dry dock, which would be big enough to take the larger ships, including the paddle steamers, which were too wide to go into the older docks. They were brought into the dock and then the gates were closed and the water pumped out. The shipwrights then saw to the shoring up of the ship, both underneath and at the sides. Once secure we could get started. The superintendent would go over the ship and make a list of all the work that needed doing and he would divide it amongst us. Before we could start our work the whole ship was cleaned and dried out thoroughly, as it could be pretty damp and dirty when it first came onto the dry dock, as you can imagine.

After a few years I was made a charge hand engineer, so I was in charge of the team that carried out maintenance on the engines, the boiler valves and sea valves, the condenser and pumps and the capstan and windlass machinery. There was a charge hand for each group of men: the tinners, who did all the sheet metal work from trunking to vents and even tables; the joiners, the electricians, the plumbers, the shipwrights, the boilermakers and the riggers – who looked after all the chains – and even a group of cleaners who got stuck into all the mess in the bilges.

Our work was mainly mechanical, so we would carry out any repairs needed on the engines; for example, attending to the piston rings and the crank bearings. I don't remember any of the major bearings ever needing replacing, it was all so well built. We also had to deal with the condenser if the tubes needed attending to. We would use ferrules to deal with any leaking joints. The condenser turned the used steam from the cylinders back into water which was pumped back into the boiler.

There were all the pumps to attend to as well – bucket pumps, we called them – and the feed pumps for putting water in the boiler. There were the valves as well, the safety valve being the most important one. That would have to be tested with the boiler under pressure. We also had to carry out any repairs needed on the paddles themselves. By the time we had finished she would be ready for a complete repaint and then, once all that was done and dried, she would be floated and be steamed up and made ready for the journey back up to Hull or New Holland, depending on which side she was based.

In my time I worked on all three ferries, the *Wingfield Castle*, the *Tattershall Castle* and the *Lincoln Castle*. The Humber Graving Dock closed in 1990. Although in my late seventies I am still working with ships, running my own ship repair business, Maurice Mawer Engineering Co. Ltd.

The DVD *Monarchs of the Humber* presented the reminiscences of a British Rail employee who travelled on the ferries to check tickets.

Travelling Ticket Collector Bill 'Jock' Burns (c1960s–1970s)

I was a relief man on the railway and one of my jobs was to go to the ferry and do anything required, such as helping on the barrier collecting tickets. Then I applied for the travelling ticket collector's job, which meant travelling back and forth on every trip and inspecting tickets and seeing that everything was all right. It was twenty minutes' sailing time, twenty minutes' loading time and twenty minutes' sailing back within the hour.

We used to charge different fares – it varied, of course – and this was before decimalisation. There was a difference between second class and first class so you could go around and find people in the first class with second class tickets and you had to charge them a shilling even if they went up on deck. One chap asked me how much I charged for a person to have a breath of fresh air! I charged him a shilling for sitting upstairs in the first class saloon!

We didn't have many animals then, but we did have horses and carts; the rag and bone men used to come across with them, and we charged them for the horse and cart. The crew had to pen them in the corner at the back, near the stern of the ship, between the stairs to the crew's quarters and the bulkhead at the back.

It wasn't always easy and I was out in all weathers, of course. There was one bad year when the ropes got twice as heavy with all the ice on them and the water coming over was wetting the ship and freezing. We also had fog at times, and I remember one of the old skippers telling me how they would use the sound of Holy Trinity church to come alongside at Hull, but that was before my time.

We got stranded [on sandbanks] quite often but we used the pole and found the channel. Then a new channel appeared on the Lincolnshire side when they started to build the bridge. There had never been a channel on the Lincolnshire side, but with all the work on the bridge we found that we could go down that side and go around the banks from there. It took forty minutes going around when the tide was out.

I remember one time in very bad weather when we had two ferries out. I was on the *Lincoln* and she was hard to control in the wind, and we had to keep trying to get alongside and we had to go around and try again. The *Tattershall* kept coming back and forth and we were still there trying to get in. There was a lot of fun on the horns then!

I lost one passenger in the water once. I always remember the night. It was when we had the two city teams playing a final and there was this young fisher lad. He wanted to go to the match, but his wife had just had a child and they were going back home with this child. I had been at the barrier at eight o'clock at night and thinking I'm having a right trouble here and they had this newly born child in their arms, like, and so they went on board. It was a quiet night with everybody at the football match, and the people were all waiting for the celebration and this lad wanted to be in the crowd when his team came back.

We got to New Holland, it was one of these rushed jobs, the tide was on the turn and we had so many minutes to get back over the sandbanks. We had just seventeen passengers and three cars, and it was my job to make sure every passenger got off, or we would have taken them back to Hull again. Then this young couple were there and when the man saw me coming he jumped down and caught his foot on the bar and went into the river head first! I shouted out 'Man overboard!' and it was in the dark, as well! I warned the crew what had happened and we were all looking over the side. Luckily the tide was on the turn and there was only about four feet of water. Any later and he could have been swept up stream with the tide. He was a good swimmer and we got him out all right.

Alan Harrod (left) who was on board when *Tattershall Castle* broke loose overnight on 19th to 20th January 1963, with other crew members on Humber ferry. *With kind permission of his son, Alan Harrod*

A crew member stands ready to catch the rope, which will be thrown by one of the men on the sponson, as *Lincoln Castle* comes alongside Hull Corporation Pier on 13th July 1963. This was the first day of operation since the connecting bridge had collapsed some three days earlier, whilst the pontoon was away for repair. *Hull Daily Mail*

Chris Braithwaite splicing ropes on *Lincoln Castle*. *Kirk Martin*

Ron Bell splicing ropes on *Lincoln Castle*. *Kirk Martin*

Blackey on *Lincoln Castle*. *Kirk Martin*

Fireman Jimmy Allison on *Lincoln Castle. Kirk Martin*

Fireman Tom Marrison on *Lincoln Castle. Kirk Martin*

Fireman Ken Rehman and Fitter George Coupland on *Lincoln Castle*. *Kirk Martin*

Ken Rehman and engineer Arthur Mount on *Lincoln Castle* at Hull Corporation Pier. *Kirk Martin*

Leading seaman Ken Edwards and Engineer Pete Moore on *Lincoln Castle*. *Kirk Martin*

Fireman Joe Davies on *Lincoln Castle*. *Kirk Martin*

Ken Rehman in the engine room of *Lincoln Castle*. *Kirk Martin*

Hassan looks on as a fireman pulls clinker from the fire of *Lincoln Castle*. *Kirk Martin*

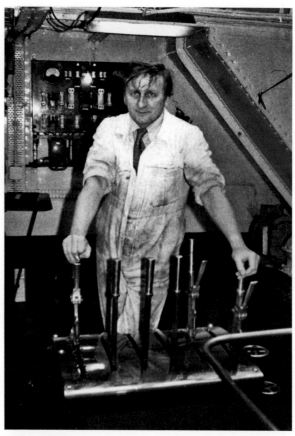

Engineer Pete Moore at the controls on *Lincoln Castle*. *Eric Wright (Martyn Ashworth collection)*

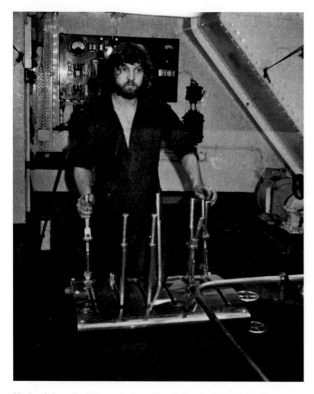

Martyn Ashworth at the controls on *Lincoln Castle*. *Eric Wright (Martyn Ashworth collection)*

Martyn Ashworth oiling the 'motion', or valve gear rods and connecting rods of the engine. *Eric Wright (Martyn Ashworth collection)*

The view ahead from the engineer's position. Note the 'turning gear IN' sign, indicating that a member of staff is in the paddle box, applying grease to the main bearings. *Eric Wright (Martyn Ashworth collection)*

View back towards the cylinder showing one of the expansion links and die blocks, which allowed the engineer to alter the engine from forward to reverse and also vary the admission of steam into the cylinder. *Eric Wright (Martyn Ashworth collection)*

The mechanical lubricators were situated to one side and in clear view of the engineer, which enabled him to ensure that they were providing constant lubrication to the cylinders. *Eric Wright (Martyn Ashworth collection)*

The auxiliary pumps provided pressurised water for cleaning the decks and could also be used for fire-fighting. *Eric Wright (Martyn Ashworth collection)*

Fireman Tom Nagy, a Pole who had also worked on coal burners in the Merchant Navy. *Eric Wright (Martyn Ashworth collection)*

Humber ferry staff on a cruise on *Lincoln Castle* in 1971, including Alan Harrod, Ken Edwards and Les Claxton. Sally Braithwaite is standing centre, with husband Chris behind her and other buffet staff to the right. *Sandie Braithwaite collection*

Sally Braithwaite's retirement party. Sally is standing centre with her husband, Chris, behind her to the left. Also present are Shirley Yare, Ron Turner, Ken Edwards and Les Claxton. *Hull Daily Mail (Sandie Braithwaite collection)*

Engineer Jock Deans on *Farringford* in 1981. *Angie Stephenson*

In 1974 Brian Ashton and Alan Cheek visited the Humber ferry service to research an article for issue twelve of *Sealink News*. I was in the stokehold as fireman, with Ken Rehman as the leading fireman (Ashton uses the terms 'Assistant Engineman and Engine Room Attendant' to describe our jobs). Also on board was Stewardess Sally Braithwaite (wife of Chris). According to this article the bridge was scheduled to open in 1977.

One Day in 1974

Churning the muddy brown waters of the Humber into a white spume, paddle steamer *Lincoln Castle* ploughs her way each day between Hull and New Holland, helping to maintain Sealink's passenger and car-ferry service between the Yorkshire and Lincolnshire banks of this important river. And she is unique in the Sealink fleet in that she is the only coal-fired paddle steamer still in service in the British Isles. She first entered service on the route back in 1941 – the third of three ships to be built around that time.

Such is the rarity of this type of vessel that the other two similar ships – the *Wingfield Castle* and *Tattershall Castle* – recently sold by Sealink, have not gone to the breaker's yard, but have been preserved as monuments of a bygone age. *Tattershall Castle*, now a floating art gallery, is berthed on the Thames, and *Wingfield Castle*,

when fitted out as a floating restaurant, is to rest in Brighton's new marina.

The Humber road bridge, due to be completed in 1977, casts doubts on the future of Sealink's Humber ferry service and already a preservation society has launched an appeal to raise funds to preserve *Lincoln Castle*, if she is sold.

So what makes this ship such a star attraction to so many people? Photographer Alan Cheek and I journeyed to Humberside to find out and also to meet some of the staff who work aboard her. We found that besides being such a unique vessel, so different in construction from other Sealink ships, it was her crew who helped immensely to make her such an attraction. They are friendly, courteous and above all extremely proud of their vessel.

There is also a spot of rivalry among staff working on Humberside because there you are either Yorkshire-born or Lincolnshire-born and each side likes to think it is crewing the best ship in the service. Nowadays with the mixed crews aboard, they go a little further by insisting their ship is the best in the Sealink fleet. They go out of their way to prove this point and it is not unusual to see members of the public being given a guided tour around the engine room or chatting to the stokers as they fire the engines.

The *Lincoln Castle* carries a Master, Mate, Engineer, three Leading Ratings, Assistant Engineman, Engineroom Attendant, Steward and Assistant Steward on normal sailings. Together with the ex-Isle of Wight paddle vessel *Farringford* she operates a service which sees 17 sailings a day from New Holland and 16 sailings from Hull. It is a service that starts early morning and finishes late at night. And, just for a change from normal duties, she also cruises on the Humber. In fact, last year, 25 such cruises were arranged, mostly dance cruises with bands, groups or discotheques in the evenings, but some for enthusiasts or the general public to view Humberside from the water.

Captain on our trips across the Humber was Relief Mate Harry Tarbotton taking a step upwards on the promotion ladder. His service history typifies the fighting spirit that prevails on the Humber because after starting as an Assistant Dock Master at Hull in 1956 he was made redundant in 1972, but bounced back last year to return as Mate aboard the ships.

The Humber is notorious for its shifting sand banks so Captains on our ships have to hold a seagoing Master's 'ticket' and if they go cruising, a river pilot's certificate. 'Sandbanks here are always shifting so you have to have a vast experience of these waters and know exactly where they shift to on any tide,' said Harry. 'The journey across takes 20 minutes, but at very low water it has taken as long as 45 minutes,' he added. The road journey between the two points, a distance of 70 miles through busy and sometimes congested roads, can take

Joe Davies, left, and Pete Moore, right, on *Farringford* in 1981. *Angie Stephenson*

up to 2½ hours, so it's no wonder that most motorists prefer to take their vehicles on the ferry!

The *Lincoln Castle* cast off, the ship's telegraph rang slow ahead and we were away – the ship's paddles threshing through the murky waters of the Humber. The paddles I shall deal with later, but the first thing that struck me was the smoke standing up from the very tall funnel of the ship as she made for midstream – certainly a different sight from say *Horsa*.

We had on board a full complement of cars. *Lincoln Castle* is a side-loading ship and she takes up to 20 average cars and 500 passengers. She must also be the only ship in the Sealink fleet where the Engineer is literally 'behind bars' because walking along her alleyways leading to the saloon, you can actually watch the steam engines at work, the huge pistons driving the paddle wheels with a rhythmic beat while the Engineer keeps a watchful eye on his machinery.   That man was 34-year-old Terry Spragg…who joined us just a year ago after ten years in the Merchant Navy. 'I suppose you get used to being part of a peepshow and besides, it makes the job interesting,' he said. 'This engineroom is certainly different and a rare one these days so I don't mind explaining its functions to passengers. Many are genuinely interested in this machinery,' he said.

The engineroom is also spacious and well set out so if anything did go wrong, Terry could quite easily get in among the machinery. 'Bearing that in mind, I suppose I should add here that you could get the whole lot in the sewage tank of a large container ship,' added Terry. Some thought!

Another plus point for this ship is that a lot of the machinery is still original and even now there is little vibration – a remarkable fact considering her age. Turning away from the engineroom and looking across the alleyway, one can often see father lifting his youngsters up to look through the porthole at the huge orange paddles threshing continuously at the water.

A little farther along the alleyways you come across the door leading to a dark hot place in the depths of the vessel. It is the stoke hold where the necessary diet of coal is continuously fed into the four huge fires that provide power for the engines. Stokers Ken Rehman and Kirk Martin were on duty when I called. A heart breaking job? Not according to Kirk, who has been a Porter, Signalbox lad and a Loco Fireman before giving up his rail career to become a student studying social history. 'It's a summer job for me,' he said. 'Sure the work is a bit heavy, but this is good for me because it gives me an entirely different slant on life from what I am used to now'. Said Ken 'Sure it's hot, but when the steam gauge allows it, we do get a breather on the top deck'. The ship uses between six and seven tons of coal a day and to make certain stocks do not run too low, reserve supplies are kept at New Holland. The coal arrives by train, is then shovelled into coal barrows, tractored aboard ship and released into bunkers.

During voyages Leading Ratings also take turns at the wheel. Les Claxton was doing the job when I arrived on the bridge. He's seen a few ships on the Humber Ferry service in his 28 years with BR but *Lincoln Castle* is the one he likes the most. 'She was always based on the Lincolnshire side of the river so simply was the best,' he said. Stan Johnson, a man with a similar service record, also echoed those thoughts. 'This is the ship on which I learnt the job. I remember carrying cattle across in the old days and one animal in particular breaking loose and sprinting down the alleyway towards the Saloon Bar – it must have had a terrific thirst,' he said. Sadly, the cattle and sheep trade is no more, but the *Lincoln Castle* still carries fresh fruit and vegetables across the river each day, destined for local markets…

'Want a cuppa,' called Stewardesses Sally Braithwaite and Joyce Claxton, when I called in the saloon which was once part of the first-class section of the ship. 'I suppose we can class you as a BR employee so you can have it on the crew,' they said. It really was a good 'cuppa', so I just had to chat to the pair, whose husbands also work aboard the ferries. 'Not that they get any preferential treatment – to us, during working hours, they are just part of the crew,' they said. Bad luck, lads! One thing that caught my eye, was a number of pen sketches of the ship which are on sale behind the bar. 'They are popular with the passengers, even more so now this ship is the last remaining coal fired paddle steamer in service,' they said. The girls also sell several hundred postcards of the ship every month.

Mate Bob Currie has spent 28 years on the ship and he was relaxing in the crew's quarters with Senior Rating Ken Edwards when I caught up with him. Speaking about the ship, he said, 'She's a good ship and I suppose the only fault I can find with her is the fact that she can be a bit sluggish in a strong wind'. Ken Edwards agreed, but said, 'She's really our baby though and we all take pride in keeping her clean. Some may not agree, but I suppose that's Lincolnshire pride'.

It's that pride, whether Lincolnshire or Yorkshire, that has kept our Humber ferry service in the forefront around Humberside. *Lincoln Castle* is certainly a ship with a separate identity, but would she have been just another ship if that pride had been missing from her crew?

Fireman Martyn Ashworth (1976–1977)

Martyn took my place when I left the ferries. He worked on *Lincoln Castle* through the winter of 1976 and into the following year, as both an ordinary and a leading fireman.

In the summer of 1976 Tony Walton and I were volunteering on the Keighley & Worth Valley Railway at Haworth. We fancied a break and headed off to Hull for a day on the Humber ferries. It was a great trip; we were allowed to go below and help the fireman in the stokehold. We found all the crew very friendly and taking a great pride in their work.

As I was on holiday from university, I asked at the ferry office if there were any summer jobs available. They had a relief fireman, Kirk, employed for the summer, but took my details. A few days later the phone rang: Kirk had left to do some travelling. Could I start at 6am Monday? I did not have to be asked twice! I was soon in Hull, had found an empty student flat and started work. I already knew how to fire a steam locomotive, but this was very different. Fortunately the old hands showed me the ropes and I soon picked it up and could even reach the end of the fireboxes with a number ten shovel full of coal. It helped being just twenty – and fit! I soon joined the NUR and wore my badge with pride.

There were five chief engineers, all passed to work on both vessels, and all very different characters with a huge amount of experience between them. It was fascinating to sit and listen to them as they told tales of their Second World War exploits in the Merchant Navy or the Royal Navy, all told in a very matter-of-fact way. They remembered bringing convoys across the Atlantic in force nine gales, where a German U boat might appear at any time. There were two Somali fireman; one called Osman, known to us as 'Ozzie', and Hassan, who had several times been on ships which had been sunk and on one occasion was the sole survivor when his ship was torpedoed from under him.

Taking the firemen as a whole, there were three leading hands at Hull for the *Lincoln Castle* and two at New Holland to work on the *Farringford*. There were also three ordinary stokers based at Hull of whom I was one. The two firemen at New Holland were Terry Hopper and Geoff Staves; Geoff had previously been a fireman on the railway at Immingham shed. There were two coal men at New Holland: George Coupland and Harry Holmes, both senior men who could help out on the *Farringford* if required, or even act as firemen on the *Lincoln Castle* if it was short of crew. Although approaching retirement age, both were as fit as the younger men; they got rid of the ashes and brought in the coal. To watch them fire the *Lincoln Castle* was to see poetry in motion. They also did much of the running maintenance on the engines and pumps on the *Lincoln Castle*, and I learnt a great deal from them about all three paddle steamers.

The chief engineers I worked under the most were Arthur Mount, Peter Moore, Jock Brown and Jock Deans. There was also an old man called Henry, who did an occasional turn as chief engineer. He filled in at weekends when he could get someone to look after his son, who was disabled. Jock Deans worked mainly on the diesel vessel *Farringford,* so I did not know him very well. Peter

Moore was frequently on duty with me and was always happy to let me have a go at the engine room controls, under his supervision, of course. My main memory of Arthur Mount was that he liked to 'go for it', so we used to get more coal on the fires as he and the skipper tried to beat the fast-moving currents on the Humber and skim us over the sandbanks to avoid having to go the long way round, which took twice as long as the usual twenty-minute crossing. However, it was not easy to keep her quiet after putting a good fire on.

My favourite chief was Jock Brown. We always got on very well and he taught me a lot. Jock started his working life as a cabin boy on a Clyde 'puffer'. He was my hero immediately, and my interest increased when I learnt he had done a full apprenticeship at Ayr shed on the London Midland & Scottish Railway and spent several years on the railways. He was called up in the war and went into the Royal Navy, where he worked his way up the ranks to become chief engineer. In peacetime he worked mostly on steam vessels, both reciprocating and turbine, and sailed the world many times. One Friday we went off duty at 14.00 and I said, 'see you Monday', as I was off for the weekend. Jock was due to work on the late turn on the Saturday and was then due to go on late shift with me the next week. He went to a party on the Friday night and went to work on Saturday afternoon, but his liver packed up and he died very suddenly, there in the ship's engine room. This was, perhaps, a fitting end for a great steam man.

The other leading firemen at Hull were Joe Davies and George Hambley. Joe came from a Merchant Navy background, but George had been a fireman on the railways; he always wore a pork pie hat and had a short Woodbine cigarette in one corner of his mouth, which was occasionally lit. When one of the leading hands, Harry Baker, went off on long-term sick leave, we had to cover his duties by working twelve-hour shifts. I didn't mind. I was young and fit and single and earning my first wages at a job I thoroughly enjoyed.

I also did the occasional turn on the diesel paddle ship *Farringford*, but I was not so keen on this. As I ate my sandwiches one day there was a huge flash and a bang and a cloud of smoke filled the engine room. I looked across at the chief, who was not at all concerned. It had an oil-fired steam heat boiler in one corner, and this was one of its party tricks. It would have been nice to have been warned!

There were times when I filled in as leading fireman in the engine room. This meant I had a new range of duties, which included climbing out of a small hatch onto the middle of the paddle wheels to fill up the grease cups. This was quite an experience with the winter swell on the Humber and the ship swaying. I also used to oil and grease the main engines and keep them clean. The engine room was always spotless and towards the end I helped when we gave it a full repaint in our own time,

and that included lining out the cylinder covers.

The deck hands had great skill in fitting all twenty cars onto the rear deck. Before the bridge opened this was the only practical way for cars to cross and the ferry was kept busy. I got on well with the deck hands, and they let us use their cabin under the rear deck to brew our tea. As I used my railway tea-can, I soon got the nickname 'the Billycan Kid'. One deck hand I recall was called Ken Woodger, a cockney who came to work on a 50cc motorbike.

The bars and café had to be staffed as well, and they did a roaring trade. Many of the regulars caught the same ferry every day and would sit on the long benches with their backs to the engine room, where it was warm, and read papers and drink their tea.

My diary shows that I worked over Christmas and New Year. On the week commencing 27th December 1976, I worked every day until my rest day on 3rd January. The *Farringford* went into Alexandra Dock at Grimsby for some work and the *Lincoln Castle* carried on alone until 8th January, when they swapped over. This was the time of year of her boiler work, so I was laid off until 21st February, when I was back on early shift again. Later I note from my diary that I was on a late shift, working 14.00 till gone midnight on one of the famous jazz cruises, and then booked on again at 06.15 that morning. That would not be allowed nowadays! The spring and summer was a busy time with several cruises in the evening after running the service trips. One of these in July was for the Paddle Steamer Preservation Society.

We had a new fireman at Hull, a Pole called Tom Nagy who sang all the time in Polish and, as a result of him joining the crew, I got more leading fireman turns as, although an experienced man, he was junior to me in the service. In fact, on one day we were so short-handed on the late turn that I worked single-handed after 18.45 as the early shift leading hand had already been on duty since 06.15.

The summer was passing by and I had a problem: I loved the life, but had already taken time out from university and the new term started on 26th September. With a heavy heart I handed in my notice to Ted Sangster, the unflappable general manager. My last turn of duty was on Thursday 22nd September, when I worked 06.00 to 14.00. I moved back to Keighley the next day and started at college on the Monday. My diary contains the entry 'said goodbye to all my dear friends', but I knew that I was saying goodbye to a whole way of life.

Ferry Manager Ted Sangster (1975–1976)

Ted took over from David Wise, who was the manager in 1974 when I first worked on *Lincoln Castle*.

I was appointed to the role of ferry manager on 3rd March 1975. Up until then I had been working at York, running passenger market research for the Eastern Region of British Rail. I spent a week at Sealink's headquarters in London, meeting the chief ports' manager and various other people, and then went to Hull, starting work on 10th March. I remember feeling quite strange: nervous, excited, apprehensive, as I walked into the parcels office, introduced myself and asked where my office was.

On the first day I walked straight into something that was going to become very familiar. One of our two vessels, the *Lincoln Castle*, was out of service and undergoing repairs following a collision she had had with a vessel called *Theresa*. Anyway, she came back into service that afternoon and I was able to go on board, meet the crew and look around my new responsibility. That day also brought about another regular theme – that of dealing with the press, as the local paper was on the doorstep wanting an interview.

My first few weeks were spent getting to know people, including officials and regulators, one of the first being a visit from the local fire brigade chief regarding the extinguishers on board the vessels. I also had an early discussion with Sealink's civil engineer based in London HQ, Clive Pougher, about the problems we were having at Corporation Pier with siltation alongside and underneath the pontoon, causing it to ground. There was lots of discussion about ways in which that could be overcome, and the answer suggested by my senior master, Capt. Stan Wright, was a system of underwater pumps which jetted water to move the sand silted up against the pontoon. After many trials of different pumps, and times of use, it did work, but was expensive in terms of the hire of equipment and, of course, in staff time deploying the pumps.

As a young manager, fresh to shipping and ports, I had a lot to learn, but luckily there were several very experienced and competent people who took me under their wing and from whom I learned a great deal. One of these was Stan Wright, the senior master on the Humber ferry service, and another was Eric Tinney, one of the marine superintendents at Sealink headquarters. Eric was new to the shipping division and enthusiastic about what he did.

The *Lincoln Castle* also required frequent boiler scaling and in May we called in the Hull Boiler Scaling Co. for a three-day period, and they cleared the boiler and also cleaned and flushed the sewage and freshwater tanks. I remember being amazed at how dirty they could get and yet stay cheerful.

In June *Lincoln Castle* suffered damage from a pilot boat when at Corporation Pier, an incident that had me calling Capt. Collier, the chief marine superintendent, and resulted in a joint survey a couple of days later and some subsequent acrimonious (albeit, on the face of it, politely worded) correspondence. There was also the annual maintenance to consider. The specifications would be drawn up by the local team working with the superintendent engineers at Harwich (the senior being Peter Frost; others included Henry Perry). They had retained Hull-based Dick Coward, a semi-retired superintendent engineer, to work on their behalf locally, and he was available on call if there were any issues that went beyond the on-board team. The allocated marine superintendent, Capt. Eric Tinney, was also involved in this process. They had to decide whether to use the local facilities at Alexandra Dock, Hull or the Humber Graving Dock & Engineering Company down at Immingham. This would depend on tender price, dock availability and any requirement for specialist work which may be required.

There were early intimations of another theme during my period: the Humber Bridge, and its inevitable effect on the ferry service. I was asked about this in almost every contact I had with the media, including on my first day. We even hosted a visit from the York branch of the Institute of Transport, who were coming to look at the Humber Bridge, and I showed them around and took them across on the *Lincoln Castle,* in the shadow of the growing bridge that was to bring about its demise.

As manager I gained my first real experience of dealing with the unions. I had been on all the management courses and knew what it should be all about, but it was different to experience it 'on the ground', as it were. Some lessons were learnt here, including my first visit from the district organiser of the NUR, who was responding to concerns expressed by one of our captains (one of his members) regarding lieu days. All the other captains were members of the Transport Salaried Staffs' Association and felt that he was taking unfair advantage and therefore not co-operating with duty rosters.

Service disruption was more likely to result from the ever-changing bed of the river. For example, on 7th August the *Farringford* got stuck on a sandbank and missed the 15.15 sailing and 16.00 return crossing. She also went aground off New Holland on 14th September at around 16.20. This was a regular occurrence, because sandbanks were constantly moving. Tracking these changes was a speciality of Stan Wright, who would take soundings and come into the office with his recommended plan for timetable changes to meet the new configuration of passages at spring tides. The normal timetable also allowed for catch-up times in the event of longer passages, which happened frequently.

The ferries, particularly the *Lincoln Castle*, were so attractive and historic that they were often used for filming, for which we charged a facility fee of a few hundred pounds, depending how long the filming was going to last. On 28th October a Japanese TV crew spent the morning on the *Lincoln Castle,* and came to see me in my office afterwards. Not speaking any Japanese and them not speaking much English, it wasn't easy to communicate; but they were very friendly and seemed to be very pleased by the experience.

We also ran cruises in the summer. They were a useful and well-received addition to our normal service, although to be frank were never very profitable. I have a record of some of the prices we charged. For example on a Friday in July 1976, we ran a cruise to and from Grimsby one way by ferry, and the other by rail. The tickets were £1.60 adult return and 85 pence child, not bad prices as we see them today! My note on 8th August shows that coal for the *Lincoln Castle* was costing us £27.30 per ton and a further £2.44 per ton for BR to transport it for us.

On one occasion a passenger on one of our cruises had got his timetable planning wrong, and only realised when he was on the cruise that the scheduled arrival time back would be too late for him to catch his last train back to Leeds. On hearing this, Capt. Wright made a quick diversion to Corporation Pier to let the passenger off to catch his train home. I also remember our ferries being used for ceremonies such as a naval memorial service off Spurn, and of course fairly regular requests for scattering of ashes. We would often do these on a regular crossing, slowing down for the dispersal of the remains and whatever solemnity was required.

On 7th October 1976 the chief traffic manager, Derek Roberts asked if I would be interested in being put forward for a new job as a lecturer at British Rail's management training college at The Grove in Watford, which was a promotion and move into a new area of experience. My application was successful, and as a result I finished as ferry manager at Hull on 12th November, with some sadness but, of course, excitement about moving to my new job. My chief clerk at Hull, Ernie Fisher, was appointed as my successor as ferry manager, and he saw the service out until the opening of the Humber Bridge in 1981.

A 1976 view of *Lincoln Castle* approaching Hull Corporation Pier with an early evening service from New Holland. *Kirk Martin*

Chapter Nine

PASSENGERS' MEMORIES

A very positive response was received to an appeal I placed in local newspapers and on Radio Humberside for people to send me their memories of the ferries. The first quote, however, is from the *Lincolnshire & Humberside Transport Review* of November/December 1988. Mr N.J. Drewery recollected using the ferries from 1934, when he was not much more than a toddler. His family lived in Grimsby, but after his aunt moved to Hull he was taken by ferry to visit her, sailing on the steamers *Cleethorpes*, *Brocklesby* and *Killingholme* as well as the three 'Castles'.

We had a routine on embarking. Firstly we would watch the loading of the vessel. Not many cars used them in those days, but quite a lot of goods were transferred from the railway by hand trolley; also livestock was sometimes ferried across. Pens were erected on the vehicle deck. I remember once some bullocks stampeded down the ramp and charged into the boat, causing it to rock at its moorings. Fortunately, there were no casualties, either human or bovine. After loading we would hasten to the saloon, where I would sit with my hands over my ears to deafen the noise of the siren which was sounded on departure. As soon as we heard it we would hurry on deck to avoid paying the saloon supplement.

In the mid-1930s my aunt moved back to Grimsby, so my visits to Hull became less frequent, and with the coming of the war you did not visit Hull without good cause…

In the immediate post-war period I made numerous trips to Hull, the journey was an interesting one from a

Mrs Ethel Rogers and her daughter Kathleen on board either *Brocklesby* or *Killingholme*, alongside Corporation Pier in 1929. *Ashley Howard*

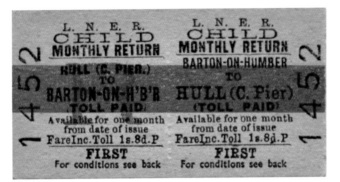

LNER child monthly return. *Brian Peeps collection*

Third class single from Barnetby to Hull Corporation Pier via the ferry. *Brian Peeps collection*

LNER military service ticket Hull to Barton. *Brian Peeps collection*

Tri-car and accompanying passenger ticket New Holland to Hull and return. *Brian Peeps collection*

A day return from Hull to Grimsby or Cleethorpes, dated 16th June, owned by Angie Stephenson.

A Single motor car ticket dated 19th June 1981, owned by Angie Stephenson.

Two single tickets dated 4th August 1954 belonging to Kathleen and Dave Parry.

transport enthusiast's point of view. The railway rolling stock had a Great Central flavour about it. The ferry at this time was usually met by a Kingston upon Hull City Transport AEC Regent with a Gardner 5LW engine and a Massey body. On one visit I was just in time to have a final ride on the Hull trams just before their withdrawal.

My crossings between New Holland and Hull were mostly made in calm weather. However, my grandmother related a story of a crossing in very bad weather. It was so rough, she said, that in the saloon passengers were praying for deliverance. On reaching New Holland the crew had great difficulty in mooring the vessel.

I made a final trip across the Humber by the *Farringford* shortly before the bridge opened. A gentleman was collecting signatures on a petition to have the ferry retained after the bridge opened. I could certainly see his point of view.

Pat Watts also used the ferries in the 1930s. She told me:

My father was a commercial traveller and I would frequently accompany him on his trips over to Lincolnshire on business. He would take the car over on Monday and bring it back on Friday, using the ferry as a foot passenger in between…My mother was an artist and painted several pictures of the ferries and these were displayed in local pubs. I wish I knew what became of them all!

As teenagers in the 1950s Dave Hunter and his friends would take their bikes on the ferry when crossing from Hull to see motorcycle events at Cadwell Park in Lincolnshire:

On one occasion, returning later than usual, we missed the last ferry back. We were very worried and had no idea what we were going to do. Going down to the pier at New Holland in the dark we found the ferry moored up for the night. However, the night watchman took sympathy on us and let us on board to sleep in the saloon so that we could cross over on the early morning ferry to Hull.

John Miller, who was born and raised in Grimsby, took many trips across the Humber to visit his uncle's family in Hull.

It was a great adventure for a small child in the early 1950s to travel by train from Grimsby to New Holland Pier and then to walk down the ramps to the waiting ferry. Once aboard, it was down to the side gangways alongside the engine room, and stand on the wooden slat seats there to watch the engines in motion. It was fascinating to watch them and of course on the other side of the gangway you could actually look through a small porthole and see the paddle wheel going round and round and splashing through the water.

By 1960 I had left school and invested in a motorbike, but the quickest way to get to Hull from Grimsby was still to use the ferry. I moved away from Grimsby in the late 1960s so I never used the ferries across the river again.

John was, however, to board a Humber ferry once more. In 1990, when *Lincoln Castle* was moored in Alexandra Dock in Grimsby, he chose her as 'the ideal venue' for his silver wedding celebration.

On their wedding day on 4th August 1954 Kathleen and Dave Parry from Cleethorpes took a trip on the ferry and kept the tickets as a souvenir. During the war, Kathleen's mother had been on a ferry that became stuck on a sandbank during an air raid, which she recalled as 'a harrowing experience'.

However, in peacetime the sandbanks were not always a disadvantage to the passengers. In the 1950s Beryl Chamberlain's father was on a ferry that was delayed from being stuck on one, but 'on this occasion nobody complained as the bar stayed open the whole time and they all enjoyed some late drinking'.

As a child in the 1960s Dave Carrick lived in Hull. He recalled his many trips across the Humber to see his great grandmother in Grimsby.

We would have a cup of tea in the café near the pier, before purchasing tickets from the British Rail ticket office. We walked across the road to the sloping walkway down to the pontoon, where you could see the river getting deeper through the boards, and onto the waiting ferry. I enjoyed looking through the brass bars into the engine room to see the movement of the engines, and once my mum spoke to Pete, the engineer. I was then allowed into the engine room to see things first hand! At New Holland the ramps were lowered for the cars and vans to leave the ship and us passengers to walk up the ramp and board the train for Grimsby. Coming back around tea time we were hurriedly moved from the platform down the pontoon when the train was late and the tide was turning. I have a memory of my nana allowing me to sit in the first class lounge with her as a treat.

Ken Knox was a trawler captain working out of Hull between 1951 and 1973.

A Hull trawler man will remember the ferries with mixed feelings. This is because using the ferries meant our trawler had received orders to land the fish at Grimsby. With only a couple of days off, it meant less time with our families. But the ferries and the train service provided us with a splendid link. Many Hull fishermen got to know the crews of the ferries; our engineers were

A woman sits on one of the seats formed of a life raft, on the upper deck of *Wingfield Castle* on a windy day in 1973. *Kirk Martin*

The former first class saloon on *Lincoln Castle*. An illustration of the real Lincoln Castle is to the left of the small bar. *Kirk Martin*

often invited into the engine room to have a close look at the magnificent and exceptionally clean engines. The brass work was just brilliant. We would often have a case of beer with us and we would share this with the crew. I well remember on one occasion getting onto the small two-coach train to take us from New Holland to Grimsby one evening. We were not sailing until about 2am so we had time on our hands and asked the guard and driver if there was a pub we could stop at by one of the stations along the way, so that we could catch the last train of the night later on.

They suggested a pub, the Green Man in Stallingborough, more or less alongside one of the stations. We jumped off and visited the pub, which is still there today. We had a whale of a time with the locals, playing darts and dominoes, the publican thinking he was in heaven with the cost of the rounds we were buying. Time was forgotten and the frivolity went on and on.

Suddenly the pub door opened and there stood the same train driver shouting, 'come on, I can't hold the train up any longer'. What a scramble! He had come looking for us and for the rest of the trip we all sat in the front of the train along with guard and driver having a good old sing-song. There were no other passengers on board and they took us all the way to Grimsby Docks. All hands had a collection of what we called 'oddments', all our left-over money, as a huge thanks to them both.

John Beasley lived in Grimsby from 1946 (when he was two) until 1960.

My uncle Harold Sellers had helped during the rebuilding of the New Holland Pier. I used to say that I hoped that he was a good workman as the train eased out along the slender structure. Usually, my mother and I would go in the first class lounge, even though she had to pay more. This was much nicer than the third class one downstairs, which was free. During the Festival of Britain in 1951 my mother took me across to Hull so that we could visit an aircraft carrier that was moored there. On one occasion the pontoon in Hull was out of use and when I walked down the old pier I turned left instead of right and I nearly walked off the end and into the Humber.

When I was ten or eleven I was considered old enough to cycle with a friend to New Holland and take our bikes across on the ferry to explore the East Riding and the coast to Spurn Head and up to Scarborough. On another occasion we joined one of the cruises down to Spurn Head. I still have very fond memories of the Humber ferries although I now live in south east London many miles away.

Guiding cars off the ferry at Hull Corporation Pier. *Hull Daily Mail*

In the mid-1970s Henry Irving, a former lecturer at Hull University, took a visiting architectural professor from Rome, Giorgio Ceccerelli, for a trip on his century-old Paull shrimper, *Venture*. Unfortunately, the visitor had broken his leg and it was in a plaster cast.

We sailed to Barton as planned, but the exertion in mooring and climbing up the quay walls set him back and gave him considerable pain. To get him back to Hull we hired a taxi and took him to New Holland and right along the pier for the ferry. The difficulty now was to get him onto the steamer. However, the crew were ever resourceful and put him onto one of the coal trucks used to take coal on board and we wheeled him down the slope and onto the *Lincoln Castle*. It was an undignified but memorable journey for a visiting professor to make.

In 1981 Henry Irving was to join Francis Daly on *Lincoln Castle*'s final trip, when she was towed up the Humber to her new berth on the foreshore at Hessle.

Chapter Ten

CRUISES

For as long as ferry boats have traversed the Humber there must have been a desire to travel further than the simple crossing from one side to the other. Cruising on the Humber certainly has a long tradition and, by the 1930s, was an established part of the railway ferry service. Even after the bridge was opened and the ferries were discontinued, the Sprotbrough-based *Wyre Lady* operated some cruises on the Humber. By looking through a variety of contemporary literature and speaking to people who went on cruises, the atmosphere on board can be appreciated through the eyes of those who experienced them.

The July 1933 issue of the *LNER Magazine* featured this article on a cruise upstream:

The popularity of river cruises, like those overseas, seems to be an ever increasing one. The season on the River Humber began on Whit Sunday, with an afternoon trip from New Holland and Hull to Burton Stather, a journey of about 20 miles. The weather was in keeping with the event, and about 400 passengers from Grimsby, Hull and district participated in the first of these attractive cruises of the season.

The journey was made by the LNER paddle steamer Brocklesby, which was suitably decorated with bunting, and provided ample accommodation for the comfort of those taking part. The provision of music on board the

steamer by members of the LNER Orchestral Society (Grimsby) was an added attraction this year, and the catering facilities also proved highly popular.

Following the south channel of the Humber, the principal places passed included Barton and Ferriby, where the northern part of the Lincolnshire Wolds terminates, and round Read's Island, which is occupied by a single farm. Passing Brough and Whitton Point, the vessel soon came to the Trent Falls, where the rivers Ouse and Trent join the Humber, and after turning a short way up the Trent, the destination was reached at Burton Stather.

The country hereabout is hilly and wooded, and the fields run steeply down to the river, providing an ideal place for picnicking. The village of Burton Stather is a typical old-world place consisting of only 100 or so people and, being cut off from the railway and main roads, seems to be one of the few retreats remaining unaffected by the speed and progress of the present age. After an enjoyable stay of about 2 hours, the party re-embarked on the Brocklesby for the return journey of about 1½ hours in the evening. In addition to the Burton Stather cruises, other equally popular trips are being run by the Humber Ferry steamers under the management of the Port Master at Grimsby, including excursions up and down the river every Sunday evening and occasional afternoon cruises down the Humber to the vicinity of Cleethorpes and Spurn Point.

After the war cruising was resumed and British Railways continued the tradition of the LNER and earlier railway companies. An unusual and exciting event was recalled by Jean Robinson, whose school organised a trip down the Humber on *Tattershall Castle* in June 1957.

We all met at Mersey Street Junior School, East Hull, where buses were ready to take us to Corporation Pier to catch the ferry. Excitement was rife and it was a particularly lovely day. We all boarded the ferry, disappearing to all parts of the ship as she sailed down the River Humber to Spurn Point.

Later, everyone was gathered on the deck to witness a 'Crossing the Line Ceremony', which was to take place on crossing the imaginary 'Equator'. Well, the weather was certainly playing its part in creating the illusion. Then seemingly from the sea, up the side of the ferry, came the figure of Neptune, actually our headmaster

Killingholme with bunting flying, passing New Holland Pier on a pleasure cruise.
Alf Ludlam collection

Ticket for a one-hour cruise from Hull Corporation Pier. *Brian Peeps collection.*

Ticket for a combined rail tour and river cruise from Manchester. *Brian Peeps collection*

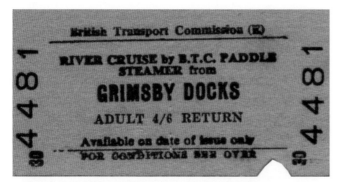

Ticket for a river cruise from Grimsby Docks. *Brian Peeps collection*

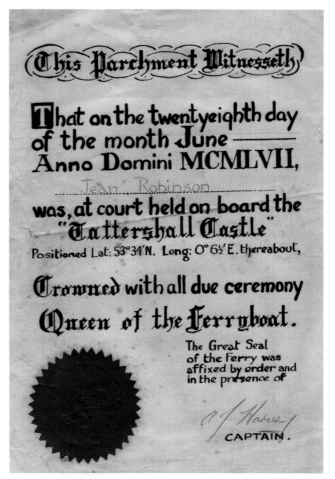

'Crossing the line' certificate awarded to Jean Robinson during a special school trip in 1957. *Jean Robinson*

Mr Canham in disguise. Once on board he went over to another part of the deck where there was a container of water, and each of the members of staff present was 'forced' into a ducking and a 'shave' by Neptune.

Then, from below decks, came the announcement of the arrival of the King and Queen. None of my friends knew I was to be the Queen. I was wearing a long apricot dress with a royal blue satin cape around my shoulders and the King, actually Richard Garbutt, was dressed in a knickerbocker suit. We were duly crowned King and Queen by Captain Harvey and each of us was presented with a certificate, which I still have. This was a great honour and the memory of a lovely day has remained with me ever since. The ferry then turned for home calling in at Grimsby for tea, which was fish and chips. On arrival at Corporation Pier in Hull, we were taken back to school by bus. A day I shall never forget although it was over fifty years ago.

In 1958 there were Sunday cruises from Hull to Grimsby between May and September, departing from Corporation Pier at 11am and arriving at Grimsby Royal Dock Basin at 12.30. The return trip left at 6.30pm and arrived back at Hull at 7.30pm. The return fare was six shillings for adults and three for children under fourteen. There were also shorter, one-hour cruises 'down river with a view of the docks' on Sundays from April to September, departing at 3pm with a return at 4pm, for a fare of just two shillings.

Two years later cruises were being offered from Grimsby to Spurn on Sundays between June and September and on weekdays between July and September at a fare of four shillings and sixpence, although 'Landing facilities will not be afforded at Spurn'. There were also Sunday afternoon cruises between June and September from New Holland and Hull downriver to view the docks, the fare from New Holland being three shillings and ninepence, or four shillings and ninepence to include the fare for the train. 1960 was a busy year with additional cruises, incorporating rail journeys, running on Saturdays between July and September from Grimsby to Hull, New Holland and Cleethorpes, with the steamer leaving Grimsby at 10am and travelling to Hull

Wingfield Castle in LNER livery, with a black hull as carried from 1937 to 1948, flying bunting during a cruise. *Hartlepool Borough Council*

Wingfield Castle in Associated Humber Lines livery during a cruise in 1960. *Hartlepool Borough Council*

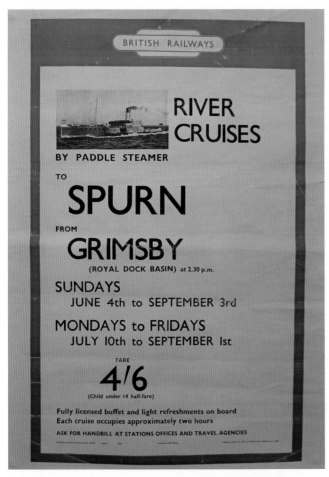

Poster advertising cruises from Grimsby to Spurn. *Peter Hough collection*

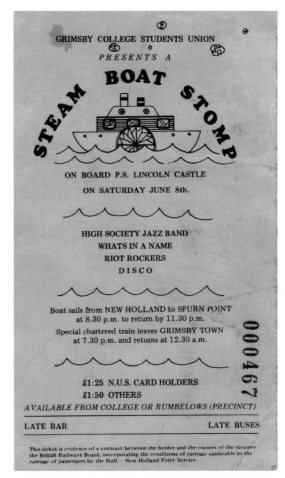

Steam Boat Stomp ticket 000467 for Grimsby College Student Union
from New Holland to Spurn Point and back. *Alf Ludlam collection*

Corporation Pier with passengers returning to New Holland by ferry for the train back to Grimsby and Cleethorpes – where, no doubt, some people will have commenced their journeys. The return fare was six shillings and sixpence. Posters advertising these cruises can be seen in the National Railway Museum archives.

The Paddle Steamer Preservation Society (PSPS) produced a leaflet advertising an afternoon cruise on Sunday 15th August 1971, departing New Holland at 14.05 and Hull at 14.35 and returning to New Holland at 17.45 and Hull at 18.05, at a cost of eighty new pence for adults and children half fare. As well as a connecting train from Cleethorpes and Grimsby there was a special bus linking Hull Paragon station and Corporation Pier. The leaflet provides the information that 'This trip will take passengers down the River Humber, passing Hull Docks and the variety of waterside industry, towards Spurn Head where the Estuary widens and meets the North Sea. This cruise recalls the regular excursion sailings which were made up to 1967 and is the only Sunday afternoon cruise of 1971 in which the general public are invited to take part. Escape from the usual Sunday routine and come aboard for a breath of sea air'.

Bertram Thorpe was involved in providing entertainment on many cruises in the 1960s and 1970s. Now in his late eighties, he recalls organising onboard discos. His business partner, the late Alan Watson, was asked to run a disco on the car deck while a jazz band was playing in the restaurant.

I was on the first Riverboat Romp and the last one as well. The loudspeakers were tied on with ropes on the car deck and we had our gear on the seats by the gents' toilets. It was a great success and we went on to organise many discos over the years. Later on, Alan made a mobile unit which wheeled on the deck and had a seat for the DJ and space for all the records.

On one occasion all the dancers were dancing around to the 'March of the Mods' and the captain came down and said 'For God's sake, stop that' because one side of the boat was lifting out of the water. One night Alan ran a small strobe light in the gangway and the pilot boat came alongside and told Alan to stop that as it could be mistaken for a beacon.

Years later I went on the *Lincoln Castle* when she was moored in Grimsby and there was a poster on display advertising the Riverboat Romp with the High Society Jazz Band and the Ultrasonic Disco – that was us!

It may seem unusual that a cruise should run with a disco as well as a jazz band. However, Alf Ludlam, who was in a 1950s-style rock band called the Riot Rockers, recalls playing

HPSG Newsletter, May 1974, advertising a cruise to Grimsby on 19th May. *Author's collection*

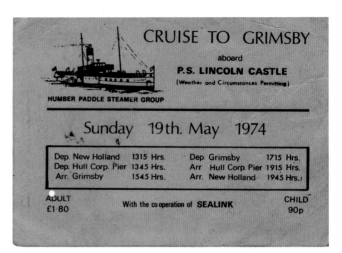

Ticket and landing card with bus ticket for HPSG cruise from New Holland and Hull to Grimsby on Sunday 19th May 1974, belonging to the author. *Author's collection*

on a cruise on *Lincoln Castle* in the early 1970s, organised for Grimsby College Student Union, in which two bands alternated sets in the main saloon, whilst a traditional jazz band performed down in the small bar. In addition, there was a disco on the rear deck. A special train left Grimsby at 7.30pm bound for New Holland, where the cruise started, returning to Grimsby at half-past midnight. There was a late bar, open well after the normal drinking-up time in force in those days, and late buses were provided from Grimsby to take the revellers home.

> The boat was very full and the people would move from area to area and focus on their favourite band or style of music. Between sets we could get a drink ourselves and mingle with the crowd and move around listening to the other bands. The boat was packed with people and the whole night was a great success. It's hard to imagine a river cruise featuring such a variety of entertainment running today.

The PSPS members' magazine *Paddle Wheels* published several accounts of cruises. In the winter 1973 issue William Blakeney described the arrival of *Lincoln Castle* as witnessed from the shore at Goole:

> Goole had not been visited by a Humber paddle ferry for many years until 10th June, when…no landing was practicable. Undaunted by this…the Humber Paddle Steamer Group…chartered the PS *Lincoln*

Castle on Sunday 23rd September, for another sailing to Goole, and this time everyone who wished could land…Eventually *Lincoln Castle* came into sight across the cornfields. That's what's special about Goole, the sailing through the fields close enough to wave and shout to those ashore. Anchor aweigh, and then what I had come to see: a fully laden passenger ship bucking about in the midst of that filthy brown water, listing with the wind pushing her round, held fast (or nearly fast) by a length of chain. Then slowly the anchor is allowed to drag as the *Lincoln Castle* edges stern first upstream from the mouth of the Ocean Lock to the Victoria Pier, the anchor being allowed to drag and so steady the vessel for this distance, perhaps nearly a quarter of a mile.

Then at last ropes came ashore, one at my feet. I felt honoured, did the necessary and then encountered the proper chap, who said I was depriving him of his job. Next the passengers began to disembark…John and I were allowed to board to see the poster competition display and of course to pause for a chat at the engine room…Soon *Lincoln Castle* was ready to leave. Again I had a rope at my feet inviting attention. This time the proper chap didn't come. The vessel was soon away into slack water and within ten minutes was no more than a pair of masts and a funnel belching forth smoke from the midst of a corn field.

The same edition carried an article about another PSPS cruise on *Lincoln Castle* on Sunday 26th August 1973.

A trip across the Humber by PS *Wingfield Castle* on the 12.00 ferry sailing from Hull…found a group of PSPS stalwarts already assembled at New Holland for the Society's second charter of PS *Lincoln Castle*, on this occasion bound downriver to Spurn Head. After awaiting the delayed train connection, on which there was only one passenger for the charter sailing, *Lincoln Castle* cast off at 14.15, having already embarked some cars for Hull to aid *Wingfield Castle* in moving Bank Holiday traffic.

There was a large crowd waiting to embark at Hull's Corporation Pier, where the approaching steamer made a fine sight with the PSPS flag at the foremast and bunting flying from the main mast. Unloading the cars and embarking passengers caused a further delay, so it was some 20 minutes late, at 14.40, when *Lincoln Castle* set sail down the Humber with over 450 passengers aboard, among whom we welcomed the ferry manager, Mr David Wise, and his charming wife.

Under the command of Captain Stanley Wright, now the only Humber ferry skipper to hold a down-river Humber pilot's ticket, *Lincoln Castle* followed the northern shore at first, but soon crossed over to the southern side, passing a variety of waterside industry and shipping at Immingham. Some of the crew of a moored Russian tanker were following our progress through binoculars…nearing Grimsby with its familiar clock tower well in evidence, we turned back up-river, now sailing with the tide and the slight south easterly breeze. The weather throughout the cruise was rather overcast but warm and dry…By this time Captain Wright was holding 'open house' on the bridge, while a visit below found assistant stokers, in the shape of Scottish PSPS branch members Douglas McGowan and John Beveridge, hard at work in the stokehold as *Lincoln Castle*'s engines made a steady 40 revolutions per minute. The PSPS bookstall in the forward saloon was doing good business…some members caught a fleeting glimpse of *Tattershall Castle*'s funnel as we passed Immingham Docks and all too soon we were passing Hull's Corporation Pier, where *Wingfield Castle* was now moored awaiting departure with the 18.05 ferry service. At 18.10 we tied up at New Holland Pier, where many passengers disembarked, and we again loaded a complement of cars, as a relief to the 18.40 sailing to Hull.

Lincoln Castle with bunting flying in the wind during a cruise. *Grimsby, June 1974. Grimsby Telegraph*

In *Paddle Wheels* of autumn 1975, Russell Plummer reported a trip on *Lincoln Castle* to the River Trent.

PSPS Humber charters are invariably attended by clear blue skies and favourable tides and Sunday August 3rd was no exception…*Lincoln Castle*…paddling off fully laden to add to the growing selection of 'firsts' achieved while flying the PSPS flag. After previous successful cruises towards Spurn Head and twice to Goole, this year saw the *Lincoln Castle* penetrate the River Trent's navigable limits for a vessel her size.

After collecting passengers at New Holland and Hull, the ferry headed upstream. The apparent lack of progress on the construction of the Humber Bridge suggested that the paddler's twilight career may be a long one, the bridge completion estimate of 1977 being unrealistic. After the bridge works, Captain Charles King took the boat close to the south shore and inside Read's Island, before following the twisting channel around Whitton Ness and Whitton Sands to Trent Falls.

There the wheel went over to port and the *Lincoln Castle* swung into the Trent. The old ferry point at Burton Stather was soon passed and the light hearted atmosphere of the steamer contrasted with the desolation of the Flixborough site, devastated in last year's explosion. With Hull pilot William Smedley at

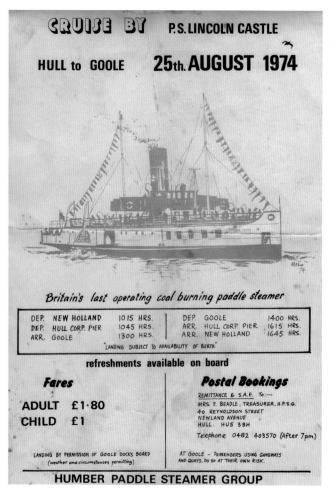

Poster for Humber Paddle Steamer Group cruise to Goole on 25th August 1974. The fare was £1.80 (children £1) and landing at Goole was 'subject to availability of berth'. *Author's collection*

A poster advertising the Humber Paddle Steamer Trust (the new name of the Save the PS Lincoln Castle Campaign) on one of the publicity items we produced at the university. *Author's collection*

the helm, *Lincoln Castle* passed by half a dozen coasters from as many countries and then across the fields ahead was the box girder structure of Keadby Bridge. Moving slowly past Keadby village until the black hulk of the bridge was only half a mile away, the *Lincoln Castle* was turned just below the entrance to the Sheffield & South Yorkshire Navigation.

With an audience of several hundred on the bank, Mr Smedley's handling of the steamer was immaculate, *Lincoln Castle* being allowed to drift round to starboard with the minimum of steerage way before the anchor was let go and the engine put astern. Although the Trent at this point is only about 260 feet wide and the *Lincoln Castle* measures just three inches under 200 feet, the manoeuvre was completed with the minimum of fuss. Once back on the Humber, Engineer Peter Moore opened up and the *Lincoln Castle* ploughed homeward at well over 12 knots.

Many onlookers are welcoming the *Lincoln Castle* when she ties up at Goole on 25th August 1974 on a cruise organised by Humber Paddle Steamer Group. Note the damaged bow caused by the tanker *Polarisman* colliding with her at Hull in May that year. *Kirk Martin*

Chapter Eleven

THE HUMBER BRIDGE

There had been several schemes to build a bridge over – or a tunnel under – the Humber during the late nineteenth and early twentieth centuries. In 1872 the Hull Chamber of Commerce was becoming increasingly concerned about the stranglehold that the NER had as the only railway company operating a line into and out of Hull, and one which had strong links with ports further north on the east coast such as Hartlepool. One solution involved building a new railway, which would run in a tunnel under the Humber to join the Manchester, Sheffield & Lincolnshire lines to the Midlands and via the Great Northern Railway and the Midland Railway lines to the south.

The prospectus of the proposed scheme, known as the Hull and South West Junction Railway, mentioned the intolerable situation: the traffic 'overwhelmed the powers of the railway company; orders for the supplies of goods could not be executed; vessels could not receive or discharge cargoes and the general trade of the port was paralysed'. The engineer would be John Fowler, who estimated that a tunnel of about 1½ miles in length between Hessle and Barton would cost £375,000, and the cost of the entire scheme £960,000. The plan involved two tunnels, ten feet below the bed of the river, with dimensions of 18ft by 15ft 6in, with ventilation provided by the passage of trains through the tunnels.

Despite NER opposition the Bill passed the House of Commons, but by the time it reached the Lords, the Manchester, Sheffield & Lincolnshire Railway and the Lancashire & Yorkshire Railway, both of which had initially supported the proposal, had been induced by the NER to oppose it. The NER offered the two other companies rights it had previously withheld, and the proposers reconsidered their position and decided not to proceed with the Bill.

The railway bottleneck in Hull was finally eased by the construction of the Hull, Barnsley & West Riding Junction Railway and Dock Company, which opened – along with its own new dock – in 1885. This new facility, Alexandra Dock, was reached

The Humber Bridge seen from Barton-on-Humber, looking toward Hessle and following the same course as the early ferries. *Kirk Martin*

via a high level line which crossed waterways, railways and main roads on a series of bridges. The company also had a new terminus at Cannon Street station in central Hull. From 1905 it became the Hull and Barnsley Railway and, by the time of the railway grouping in 1923, had already amalgamated with its former rival the NER.

Another proposal for crossing the Humber, devised in 1908, was for a railway from Nottingham to Hull, again via a tunnel under the Humber. This was deferred in 1914 and, ultimately, abandoned. In 1923 the Hull Chamber of Commerce once again became interested in a fixed crossing, passing a resolution in favour of a tunnel, which was considered 'extremely desirable both in the local and national interests' and would also help to alleviate unemployment. It called for a meeting of relevant authorities and railway companies to consider whether the tunnel should carry railway, road or combined traffic. In that year the railway grouping also took place, uniting the railway companies on the south and north banks of the Humber as the LNER. Due to the clearance required for sailing ships, any crossing, other than a tunnel, would have to be at a considerable height above high water level.

Sir Ralph Freeman planned a multi-span road bridge in 1927, and in 1935 he suggested a suspension bridge. However, in May 1929 Hull City Council proposed to convene a conference to decide between a tunnel and a bridge. The conference was presided over by the Lord Mayor of Hull (Alderman Benno Pearlman) and attendees included sixteen local authorities and representatives from the LNER. By November a tangible proposal was put forward for a bridge, the plans being drawn up by Sir Douglas Fox & Partners, who stated: 'The engineers understand that the railway company do not regard as a commercial proposition worth considering, the funding of the capital required for their share of the crossing and that, in our opinion, no case for the construction of a railway crossing can be established'.

It was decided that the best site for the crossing was between Hessle on the north bank and the outskirts of Barton-on-Humber on the south. Comparative estimates were given for the road and rail tunnels, as well as a road or combined road and rail bridge:

Two railway tunnels of 18ft diameter:	£4,600,000
Two road tunnels each with 27ft diameter:	£7,200,000
Road only bridge:	£1,725,000
Combined rail and road bridge:	£4,000,000

The length of the proposed bridge, including the approach roads, was estimated at 3½ miles. The resulting Bill passed the House of Commons committee stage and went before the House. However, due to the prevailing national financial situation, the government withdrew its promised grant. Despite efforts to find alternative finance, the Bill was withdrawn in 1933.

The *Hull Times* quoted Hull Councillor Banham in December 1936 saying that it was a 'crying shame that the Government had made the admission that the piling up of arms was of more importance than an essential national development'. He referred to the minutes of the Parliamentary Sub-Committee meeting of 19th November, which mentioned a letter from the Ministry of Transport. This stated that the government had come to the conclusion that there was no justification in embarking upon the execution of such public works as new bridges over the Rivers Humber, Severn and Forth. In 1937 further plans for a single-span bridge were announced but, owing to the worsening political situation in Europe, the scheme made no further progress and was shelved for the duration of the Second World War, during which the ferries continued to maintain their essential link across the Humber Estuary.

In March 1956 *The Times* reported that,

Hull Corporation are to seek talks with Government departments about their proposal to link Lincolnshire to Yorkshire by a suspension bridge across the river Humber between Barton and Hessle Cliff…A report by a London firm of consulting engineers has been sent to the Ministry of Transport, and members of the corporation will next month meet local M.P.s. It is expected that a deputation to the Ministry will then be arranged. The report was prepared by Messrs. Freeman, Fox and Partners, of Victoria Street, S.W. who designed the Sydney Harbour bridge. The Humber bridge, which could be completed in about five years, would have two side spans of 1,395ft. The main span of 4,500ft would provide clear headroom of 85ft above high water for the full width of 4,450ft between tower piers of braced steel at approximately low water mark on each side of the river…It is estimated that traffic in the first year of operation would include 2,400,000 vehicles, and that the volume would be doubled in 10 years.

Approval for the construction of a bridge was finally granted in 1959 with the passing of the Humber Bridge Act, and the setting up of a Humber Bridge Board; but it was not until 1969 that the government agreed that the bridge could go ahead. It used the route favoured by several earlier schemes for both bridge and tunnel, namely, between Hessle and Barton. The structure spanned the last major estuary in the British Isles to be without a bridge and would be the longest suspension bridge in the world.

The government agreed the finance by advancing a loan in May 1971 and work began on the approach road on the south side in July 1972. The consulting engineers were Freeman Fox & Partners. Considerable expense was saved by the use of a shallower and lighter road section, first used on the Severn Bridge, as advocated by the engineer Sir Gilbert Robert, who died in 1978 before the bridge was completed.

John Howard & Co. began work on the sub-structure of the Humber Bridge in March 1973, and in April British Bridge Builders began work on the superstructure. The main span measured 1,410 metres. The north tower, which stood on the shore line, was finished in May 1974, just over two years before the south tower, which was completed in July 1976 and stood 500 yards from the southern shore in shallow water. Cable spinning began in September 1977 and was completed by July 1979; the box sections of the bridge were constructed between October 1979 and July 1980. Throughout this time crews and passengers on the ferries had a clear view of the bridge works being carried out several miles upstream.

The bridge was opened to traffic on 24th June 1981, but was officially opened by Her Majesty the Queen on 17th July.

The decision to abolish the ferry service was not an easy one. It involved public consultation among users on both the Yorkshire and Lincolnshire sides of the Humber. According to the Transport Users' Consultative Committee (Yorkshire Area) report on the closure of the ferries and the connecting railway link to New Holland Pier station, during the six-week consultation period a total of forty-eight written objections were received, along with two petitions bearing 196 and 2,940 signatures respectively. Public hearings were held in Grimsby and Hull in September 1980. Despite local unease, only a small number of people turned up, although there were several written submissions by those unable to attend.

At one hearing Sealink accepted that the construction of the Humber Bridge was in the overall public interest. However, its management had been consistent in its view that, once the bridge was completed and opened to traffic, it would transform the local pattern of travel, as had been the case with the bridges crossing the Tay, Forth and Severn. The bridge would undoubtedly affect the viability of the ferry. Unlike passenger trains, there was no provision for shipping services to be subsidised by central government. Sealink was left with no alternative than to put forward a proposal to abolish the ferry. This led to British Rail's decision to close both New Holland Pier station and its Town station. This placed Humberside Council in a position to underwrite an improvement to the rail service to Barton, and the construction of a new station at New Holland. This would operate in conjunction with an hourly bus service over the bridge and an hourly train service from Barton-on-Humber.

An alternative view was presented by Mr M. Walters, assistant solicitor for Cleethorpes Borough Council, who pointed out that the existing ferry provided the most direct route for the people of Lincolnshire to reach the centre of Hull and that, with sufficient car parking facilities, it would also lead to greater use of public transport than by using the Humber Bridge. The rail and ferry services were well co-ordinated at that time and provided a better public transport link than the suggested rail and bus services via the bridge.

Other people spoke in favour of the retention of a passenger-only ferry as an alternative to the lengthy and expensive journey by train and bus. It was also pointed out that buses would terminate at Ferensway bus station rather than the Old Town, and that this would have a detrimental effect on that area. South Humberside Rail Users' Group added its voice to the call for the ferry to be maintained for a period of time after the bridge was opened, on the grounds that the alternatives were untried. Others suggested that it be retained until the effect of high winds upon the bridge was known.

More objections came from a local councillor at Kirmington & Croxton, supporting a submission by Glandford Borough Council. He had particular concerns about the additional cost to foot passengers (who currently used the ferry) of having to use the rail and bus link via the bridge. Several speakers voiced similar concerns. Mr Richman quoted an increase of as much as 77% for a weekly ticket and 127% for a monthly. Mr Brown said he had used the ferries for sixty-two years and was worried about the loss of employment in the area. Mr Smith advocated a small passenger ferry that could cross in about twelve minutes as an alternative to the rail and bus link. Chris Braithwaite, crew member and secretary of the New Holland branch of the National Union of Railwaymen, endorsed the views of the previous speakers and said that his members were also concerned about the loss of jobs for people currently commuting across to Hull by the ferry.

An architect from New Holland, Mr Oldfield, pointed out that the bridge would mean a round trip by car of some twenty-six miles, whereas the ferry took him straight into the centre of Hull, where much of his business was. He was also concerned at the loss of the direct parcels service that the ferry offered (he usually handed over his parcels at New Holland to be collected by the addressee at the Hull Pier office). He pointed out that abolishing the ferry would also lead to an increase in car use in the area.

Many of these points were answered by representatives of Sealink, British Rail and Humberside Council, who stated that the Barton interchange would be improved by the addition of a shelter (but added that there were no plans for a café as there was one nearby). It was confirmed that the fare would be higher than the present ferry, to reflect the additional mileage involved. They felt that continuing the ferry service would result in an inferior rail and bus link via the bridge.

There were also representations from the Humber Bridge Board and the local bus companies, which addressed the issue of tolls and fares for using the bridge. It was pointed out that there could be a limited parcel service by the bus, but this would not include heavy packages; and also that there would be an increased frequency of service via the bridge compared with the ferry, although it was admitted that there was no way of confirming the projected twenty-five minute journey time until the bridge was completed.

In conclusion, the committee members said they had listened with interest to all the arguments. No private operator was offering to run a ferry after Sealink withdrew its service. The committee looked at journey times, and at the destination of the bus link at Ferensway bus station, and felt that neither would have a serious impact on users. Regarding fares, they said that some people – especially those living in and around New Holland – would pay more to cross the Humber, but others – at Barton, for instance – would pay less, because their journey would be shorter via the bridge.

The Humber Bridge during construction, seen from the north bank. *Kirk Martin*

The northern anchorage point of the cables for the Humber Bridge seen in 1977. *Kirk Martin*

Members felt, however, that to maintain a ferry service for more than a few weeks would have a detrimental impact on the alternative route via the bridge.

From 1981, when the ferry was discontinued, New Holland Pier was no longer used by connecting trains. However, in early 1983 a Dutch-based company, New Holland Bulk Services, built a terminal on New Holland Pier to handle the import and export of bulk cargoes such as grain, animal feeds and coal. The length of the pier enabled larger ships to load and discharge their cargo in deep water. The terminal was fully operational by late 1984. There is also freight traffic from the New Holland Dock, adjacent to the pier. There was a rail connection which was active for a few years, but the nature of the cargoes dealt with did not make this a viable proposition.

Although exceeded in length in 1998, the Humber Bridge remains among the longest suspension bridges in the world, ranking fifth in 2013. It is still a toll bridge and many locals object to the charge. After thirty-two years the tolls have still not enabled the Humber Bridge Board to pay off the initial cost of the project. In 2011 the government agreed to reduce the debt by £150m and the remaining debt has now been underwritten by the local authorities, in order to allow the toll to be reduced. (It is currently £1.50 for cars and £4 or £12 for goods vehicles.) The journey time from Hull to New Holland, via Barton by bus and train, is 55 minutes – nearly three times the former normal sailing time by ferry.

A view of New Holland pier from the air as it is today with ships unloading for New Holland Bulk Services. *David Lee Photography Ltd*

Chapter Twelve

THE FATE OF THE FERRIES

The *Tattershall Castle* made her final crossing on 24th April 1972 and languished at New Holland for many months. She was towed to Immingham in July 1973 for refurbishment and by 1974 she was in the ownership or Mr Harry Childs, Chairman of Stainless Steel Equipment Co. Ltd. of Enfield. After being overhauled at the Humber Graving Dock and Engineering Company at Immingham, ownership was transferred to the Tattershall Castle Company Limited, a charitable trust, and in 1975 she was towed to London by the tug *Lady Alma* and berthed at King's Reach, between Hungerford and Westminster Bridges on the north bank of the River Thames. Whilst in London she was maintained for many years by Terry Prudames, who ensured – amongst his other responsibilities – that her triple-expansion steam engine was kept in good order.

Although wishing to ensure the preservation of one of the few surviving paddle steamers, the main aim of the Tattershall Castle Company was to turn the ship into an art gallery, using her three interior saloons as display areas. To this end, on 24th February 1976 she was opened by the Lord

Mayor of Westminster, Councillor Roger Meredith Dawe, as London's first floating art gallery and conference centre. Former crew members Captain Stan Wright and Engineer Arthur Evans attended, and the souvenir programme listed a large number of exhibitors; the Wapping Group of Artists displaying their work in the forward lower saloon, with students from Middlesex Polytechnic using the aft saloon.

Sadly, the venture did not succeed. According to Mr Childs this was due to a lack of support from the government. By late 1980 he had decided to give up. *Tattershall Castle* was bought at auction in January 1981 by the Chef & Brewer group. She was refurbished at Acorn's Shipyard, Rochester, on the River Medway, and re-opened as a bar and restaurant on the Thames in July 1982, with her aft-deck enclosed to form a function room with additional seating area above. Her journey back to London was marred by two accidents, one of which, involving one of the tugs, damaged her paddle sufficiently for her to be moved into dry dock at Blackwall for repairs.

Nine years later *Tattershall Castle* went down to Rochester again, in 1991, this time to Crescent Marine Services, where

Tattershall Castle, withdrawn from service, is tied up alongside the western arm of New Holland Pier. It is clear from this view that the funnel on the Gray-built steamers was well to the aft, whereas that on Inglis-built *Lincoln Castle* was ahead of the paddles. Kirk Martin

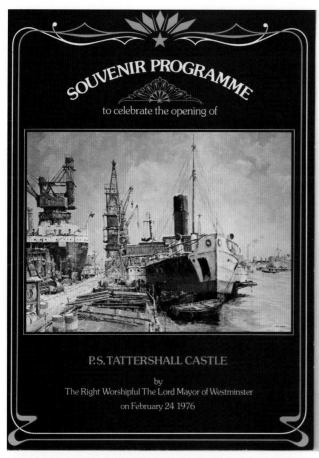

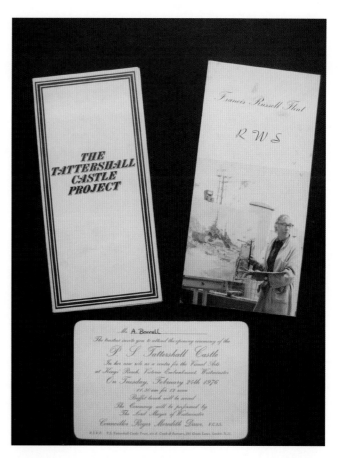

Souvenir programme for the opening of *Tattershall Castle* as an art gallery on 24th February 1976. The cover painting is by Francis Russell Flint, an apprentice at the Shaw, Savill and Albion Steamship Company before serving as an official war artist. *Author's collection*

Invitation and leaflets for the opening day of *Tattershall Castle* as an art gallery on 24th February 1976. *Author's collection*

Tattershall Castle moored on the Thames in 1976, in use as an art gallery. *Hull Daily Mail*

THE AIMS OF THE PROJECT

To preserve and display the P.S. Tattershall Castle one of the few surviving paddle steamers.

To moor her upon the Thames close to the Houses of Parliament and Charing Cross where she will be open to the public.

To utilise the spacious interior saloons as display and exhibition areas to encourage the visual arts, and to provide accommodation for the meetings of societies and cultural associations.

The philosophy behind the arts side of the project is to liaise with arts bodies, with colleges of art and design, and with local education authorities to offer display and exhibition facilities, in particular to aspiring but unknown young artists. The project will also give an opportunity for the public to view original and interesting works of art by eminent artists.

Harry Childs with *Tattershall Castle* in London whilst she was an art gallery. *Hull Daily Mail*

Tattershall Castle being towed under Waterloo Bridge on her return from refurbishment work on the Medway in 1981. Note that her funnel had been removed to pass under the bridges. *Grimsby Telegraph*

Tattershall Castle is a now very successful bar and restaurant moored on the Thames Embankment alongside Hungerford Bridge and opposite the London Eye. Comparing this illustration with that on page 137 clearly shows the alterations which have been made to this vessel including a new bridge, covered stern deck and removed paddles. *Kirk Martin*

she underwent repairs to her sponsons, re-plating, re-wiring and repainting; returning to her mooring on the Thames in November 1991. Since then she has undergone major refurbishment at George Prior's yard at Great Yarmouth in 2003. Graham Hand points out that, having just refurbished the *Waverley*, 'they were well versed in paddle steamer matters'. Unfortunately, commercial interests superseded her historical significance and her original bridge was replaced by the present structure, which accommodates another function room, whilst her two paddles were removed to give room for seating and other facilities below decks. Luckily her engine room was retained and is still visible though windows aft of the main bar. *Tattershall Castle* is currently owned by the Tattershall Castle Group (TCG UK), and is a very successful and popular venue, offering meals as well as drinks in a bar overlooking the Thames.

Wingfield Castle made her final Humber crossing on 14th March 1974 under Captain Stan Wright. She was sold by British Rail to the Brighton Marina Company for £30,000 and she was towed to London for an £80,000 refit. However, East Sussex County Council refused permission to use her as a clubhouse and restaurant in Brighton Marina so the refit was not carried out. She then lay in Royal Albert Dock for some time. In 1978 Gene Darcy proposed to dismantle her and take

her to the USA, intending to display her in San Antonio, Texas, but this fell through. She later lay in King George V Dock in east London, where she was used in the 1980 film *The Elephant Man*, disguised as an 1824 cross-channel paddle steamer. Sadly, many of her brass and copper fittings were stolen during this time. She was at one point moored near Tower Bridge in London, where I was able to photograph her. In 1982, after some further changes of ownership, Thomas Whitbread bought her for use as a floating restaurant in Swansea, but this plan was later abandoned because she was too wide for the marina dock gates.

In 1986, after languishing at Swansea for several years, she was purchased by Hartlepool Borough Council and towed in a dilapidated state by the tug *Towing Wizard* to Jackson Dock in Hartlepool, to be renovated before taking her place in the town's Maritime Heritage Centre. Thus she was finally returned to her birthplace after what must have been – for a half-century-old steamer – a gruelling voyage around the coast. Thankfully she was restored as far as possible to her original condition. Eleven thousand gallons of water were pumped out of her hull, which had been sealed with concrete to prevent leaks during her years of neglect. Damaged and rusted hull plates were removed and replacements fitted. The original Oregon pine decking was removed and much was reused in the saloon. New Douglas fir

Wingfield Castle moored close to Tower Bridge in London in the early 1980s. *Kirk Martin*

Wingfield Castle restored to original condition, although not in working order, and moored at Hartlepool's Maritime Heritage Centre. In the background is the 1817-built HMS *Trincomalee*. *Kirk Martin*

The Museum Café in *Wingfield Castle*'s former first class saloon at Hartlepool's Maritime Heritage Centre. *Kenny White*

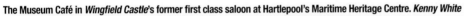

Lincoln Castle moored in Alexandra Dock, Hull, after withdrawal in 1978. *Kirk Martin*

A view of the former First Class saloon when *Lincoln Castle* was moored in Alexandra Dock in 1978. *Kirk Martin*

A view down the side passageway looking towards the rear car deck. Note coal barrows on the car deck and the cast iron bunker lid, on the bottom right of the picture. In the ceiling above the lid is a shackle to which the pulley was attached to winch up the coal barrows when filling the bunker. *Kirk Martin*

planking was laid over the main decks and she became once more both watertight and presentable. Internally, her engines have been overhauled and can be turned by an electric motor. The restoration was completed by 1995.

Wingfield Castle is now a centrepiece of Hartlepool's Maritime Experience, which covers part of the site of William Gray's yard, where she was built in 1934. Her engine room and stokehold are once more an attraction, with life-size model figures giving a realistic impression of her in service, complete with a fireman, who stands with his shovel raised in the glare of a fire. Brass fittings have been carefully recreated by local apprentices, including those on the bridge, which is also open to public view. The rest of the Maritime Experience is also of great interest, and a café is situated in *Wingfield Castle's* former first class saloon, providing a welcome spot to rest after a visit.

The *Lincoln Castle* was withdrawn after her final crossing on Monday 13th February 1978. Her boiler had been declared a failure, and she was laid up for some time in Alexandra Dock, Hull. Some interest in purchasing her had been shown by Humberside County Council, and the National Railway Museum was investigating possible locations for her if it acquired her under the terms of the 1968 Transport Act as an important aspect of railway history.

Despite a 5,000-strong petition, organised by the Save the PS Lincoln Castle Campaign, in favour of the council and other bodies preserving the vessel in working order on

Humberside, in the end neither the council nor the NRM felt able to take on the vessel. She was sold in April 1979 to Francis Daly of Hull who, in 1981, formed the PS Lincoln Castle Ltd in order to operate her as a business on the foreshore in Hessle. Mr Daly paid £20,000 for the vessel after she had failed her boiler test owing to a continuous crack along the rivets in the boiler. He initially wanted to moor her in Prince's Dock, but this was not possible as the council would not grant him planning permission.

Beverley Borough Council offered Mr Daly a berth on the foreshore at Hessle, close to the Humber Bridge. He prepared the area, but could not move her there until the highest spring tide. In early March the *Hull Daily Mail* reported that *Lincoln Castle* was 'preparing for what may be her last voyage…Riding on tomorrow's early morning tide, she will be shepherded out of Hull's Albert Dock soon after dawn'. The journey was made on Sunday 8th March and was described in an illustrated article in the *Hull Daily Mail* the next morning:

It was soon after dawn yesterday when she was nosed out of Albert Dock and taken in tow by her escort of three tugs…In just over a month her owner, Francis Daly, hopes to open her as a floating bar and restaurant. But her last trip was marked with style and affection. 'There were hundreds of people lining the banks as we came past the Hessle shipyard' said a tired but triumphant Mr Daly last night.

PS *Lincoln Castle* newly arrived at Hessle foreshore with ropes attached ready to be hauled to her new mooring at the highest tide. *Hull Daily Mail*

Lincoln Castle on the foreshore at Hessle after being towed from Hull on 8th March 1981. *Hull Daily Mail*

Dr Henry Irving with Francis Daly and Angela Wilson on board *Lincoln Castle* after the move to Hessle. *Hull Daily Mail*

View of Lincoln Castle at Hessle taken from the Humber Bridge. *Tom Baxter*

As Francis Daly explained when I met him in 2011, when one of Dave Cook's tugs arrived and took up the tow, 'chugging' noises were heard coming from the engine room. With the hair standing up on the backs of their necks, he and his team rushed over to see the engines apparently working. Fortunately, he had fixed the steam valves open during maintenance so that the engines did not come under compression, and this allowed them to turn as the pressure of the river water turned the paddles. He confessed that the noises and the air hissing through the steam valves had made it seem as though she had come back to life.

The voyage down to Hessle, in darkness, was a very nostalgic one, with the engines still turning all the way. Upon her arrival the tide was not quite high enough, and she had to sit between the tide-lines until the high tide at night allowed her to settle in her new berth. She was then moored up and secured in position behind a wall of heavy concrete blocks left over from the construction of the Humber Bridge. Francis Daly, who had recently developed the Waterfront Club by Prince's Dock in Hull, and his renovation team wanted the engines turning as an attraction. He engaged Fenners, a Hull company who made gearboxes, to provide an electric motor to achieve this, via the worm drive on the timing gear, which would have been used during maintenance. This meant the feathering paddles turned as well, which was a safety issue, so they had to make sure that no daredevil children were anywhere near the paddles when the engines were turning.

The fully refurbished *Lincoln Castle* was opened for business as a bar and restaurant on 11th April 1981 and soon became a popular venue, although Francis confessed that much potential profit was lost because people who used to be regular passengers on the Humber ferries loved to recreate the atmosphere by bringing their own sandwiches on board to eat while sitting on the deck rather than patronise his bar and restaurant.

Cleethorpes café proprietor Colin Johnson and his mother became regular visitors to *Lincoln Castle*. Mr Johnson had long dreamed of owning the vessel; Francis Daly was aware of this but was reluctant to sell her. Mr Johnson obtained the backing of Grimsby Borough Council to site *Lincoln Castle* in Alexandra Dock, alongside the planned new National Fishing Heritage Centre, and they also agreed to assist in the move. After some discussion, Francis Daly agreed to the sale in the spring of 1987. *Paddle Wheels* reported in its summer issue that 'Hundreds of people crowded Hessle foreshore close to the Humber Bridge on the evening of Tuesday 31st March to see the PS *Lincoln Castle* floated out of the berth it has occupied for the past four years following purchase by the Cleethorpes café proprietor. The coal burner, built in 1940…was taken to Riverside Quay in Hull and then to Immingham for repairs, and will open later in the year as a carvery and public bar in Grimsby'.

Lincoln Castle was reopened to the public in 1989. It proved a great success and soon earned a reputation for

Lincoln Castle, stripped of her bridge and funnel and with reduced sponsons, being towed under the road bridge into Alexandra Dock, Grimsby, in May 1987. *Grimsby Telegraph*

hosting weddings as well as being a popular venue for meetings of Grimsby Folk Club. Martyn Ashworth, who had fired her in the 1970s, visited her in 1995 and spoke to Russell Hollowood, curator of the National Fishing Heritage Centre.

He asked me to open up the engine room for the day, with lunch provided by the fine restaurant on board. At the same time, the National Railway Museum's replica of *Rocket* was steaming on a short stretch of track alongside with a good friend, Ray Towell, at the regulator. We had a lot of visitors, who showed a great deal of interest in the engine room, and many recalled travelling on the ferries. The engines were turned by an electric motor, but the stokehold had gone and was now the kitchen, so it was still the hottest place on the ship.

The success of the restaurant declined and eventually it closed. *Lincoln Castle* was in a poor condition and her hull was prone to leaks, which Mr Johnson did his best to seal with concrete. With declining business he eventually advertised her for sale at £20,000 through the ship brokerage firm Norse Shore. He also offered her free of charge to the PSPS, and in the autumn 2009 issue of *Paddle Wheels*, PSPS chairwoman Myra Allen announced that the society had commenced discussions with him 'with a view to securing a long term future' for the vessel. Six months later Ms Allen reported that the *Lincoln Castle* had been offered to the PSPS, but it was undertaking a survey to assess her condition, because 'before agreeing to take her on

we must ensure that we have a robust and ongoing business plan to ensure that she does not jeopardise the future of our two operational paddle steamers'. Graham R. Hand was involved in the PSPS project group which considered taking on the *Lincoln Castle*. He pointed out that the owners were assisting the group by 'putting back the scrapping deadline'. Meanwhile, local enthusiasts were also trying to save the vessel. Foremost among them was the newly formed Lincoln Castle Preservation Society (LCPS), whose members worked tirelessly to raise both awareness and funds.

The summer issue of *Paddle Wheels* revealed the results of a survey of members. The majority were in favour of taking on *Lincoln Castle,* but only if it did not affect the operation of the ships the society already supported. After consideration, the PSPS Council of Management meeting 'reluctantly concluded that ownership was not possible due to the potential costs needed in the relatively short term to renovate the ship's hull'. The report continued:

It is to be hoped that *Lincoln Castle* will now have a secure future and not be yet another British paddler over the years that is scrapped or languishing in various states of decay. We most certainly will remain in contact and keep an eye out for what is happening. The PSPS council appointed a *Lincoln Castle* project team…led by our Vice Chairman, David Haddleton, and I must record my heartfelt thanks for the enormous amount of work he did, negotiating with the owner, several councils, a broker, surveyors and various other parties interested in the ship.

Lincoln Castle **in Alexandra Dock, Grimsby, after the construction of the National Fishing Heritage Centre and the Heritage House and craft units, also showing the trawler** *Ross Tiger* **and the fishing smack Esther.** *Geoff Byman*

The circumstances were ever changing, and I saw David go from delight to despair on many occasions…

The *Grimsby Telegraph* reported in June 2010 that Stephen Sharpe, chairman of the LCPS, remained hopeful of saving the ship from the scrapheap: 'We have worked so hard over the last 21 days and I think we have made magnificent steps forward… we are going to continue fundraising while the PSPS negotiates with the Johnson family'. However, by then contractors were dismantling the boat, and Colin Johnson's brother Peter remarked that 'attempts to save the ferry…were a lost cause'.

The *Grimsby Telegraph* revealed that attempts to save the engine were being considered. It quoted Peter Johnson saying that demolition firm H. Cope & Sons had investigated the possibility of 'salvaging the coal-fired steam engine after calls from organisations who want to see it preserved and put on display'. The Johnsons hoped that the preservation group would raise the £20,000 needed 'to save the heart of the Humber ferry', which endeavour would involve hiring a crane to lift the engines clear of the vessel. The article concluded by saying that 'many people will be sad to see the vessel go'.

Having been alerted to the imminent destruction of *Lincoln Castle* by an article in *Steam Railway* magazine, I travelled to Grimsby on 26th July 2010 and met Preston Fox and Stephen Sharpe of the LCPS. I managed to obtain permission to board and take some photographs. Although areas of the vessel were being dismantled, the engine room was untouched and the engine itself looked to be in good condition – there was even a layer of greased paper coating the handrails to prevent rust. Despite the poor condition of the hull I was confident that she could be saved and that the next meeting of the group would be held on board.

I returned to London and, through a friend, the railway historian and author John Scott-Morgan, I met William Palin of Save Britain's Heritage (SAVE) and also contacted Martyn Heighton of National Historic Ships UK. SAVE was very concerned and, following a meeting, Mr Palin sent me a letter, dated 2nd August 2010, to pass on to the LCPS. It stated:

SAVE writes in support of your courageous and important campaign to prevent the destruction of *Lincoln Castle*, a vessel of international interest and importance which, until her withdrawal from service,

Lincoln Castle in Alexandra Dock in 2010. *Kirk Martin*

The engine room of *Lincoln Castle* in Alexandra Dock in 2010. Only the front of the boiler survived as the rest had been cut away to make room for a kitchen. *Kirk Martin*

was the last coal burning paddle steamer in regular use in Britain. SAVE was dismayed to learn that this unique vessel, with its magnificent three-cylinder triple-expansion diagonal steam engine still installed and in working order, is in the process of being broken up by its owner in Grimsby's Alexandra Dock. It seems tragic that this elegant and well-maintained vessel should be consigned to such an ignominious end. Sadly, although it is listed on the Historic Ships' Register, this does not in itself confer any statutory protection. SAVE hopes that your campaign, so nobly supported by Steam Railway magazine, will help raise, as quickly as possible, sufficient funds to purchase the vessel – thus halting its destruction. We have no doubt that should this happen, with the support of so many friends and enthusiasts *Lincoln Castle* could be repaired, restored and put back into use.

In response to an email I sent to Martyn Heighton, of National Historic Ships UK, I received the following reply, which I have been granted permission to quote:

I share both your dismay and frustration that PS *Lincoln Castle* is being scrapped when she was in relatively good condition and with potential buyers on the sidelines. I have had some dealings with the local authority and the Environment Agency over the provision of a licence to scrap her where she lies but, unlike other cases in which I have been involved, there was no willingness to delay the agreement to demolish…I have no legislative powers to stop the scrapping of any vessel on the National Register, and can only fall back on cooperation by owners, agencies and local authorities. In this instance the owner has shown no willingness to respond to overtures from prospective buyers, presumably preferring the certainty of the scrap value over what might prove to be protracted negotiations.

The autumn 2010 issue of *Paddle Wheels* confirmed that 'the decision of PSPS Council not to proceed with the acquisition of PS *Lincoln Castle*…was a heartbreaking decision, but our heads had to rule our hearts and it was the right one'. It continued:

Since then, we have been working behind the scenes to assist potential buyers for the ship and a lot of good things have happened. National Historic Ships and a local council have both confirmed they would give a grant, but in the end the owner has refused to sell or give the ship to another body. Even when at one point it seemed a sale of the ship was going ahead, the owner insisted that the bottom plates of the ship could not be sold, which of course makes a rescue attempt for the complete vessel impossible.

On the last day of July the *Grimsby Telegraph* reported the tragic news that, although 'campaigners are desperate to save the stricken vessel from the scrapheap' the owners 'have ruled out any chance of transferring the vessel' to the LCPS. Moreover, the exterior of the boat 'will be cut up'. Peter Johnson said 'It is beyond repair. It is too far gone. The amount of money they have doesn't matter – it is too late'. He pointed out that the vessel was 'so seriously damaged that it is not a question of thousands or even hundreds of thousands of pounds. It would cost millions, but I don't think it could ever be done. It can't be moved to be dismantled and has a rotten bottom'. Printed alongside the article was a letter in which I appealed for people to come forward in a last-minute effort to save her.

The *Hull Daily Mail* of 14th August reported a fresh attempt to preserve at least part of *Lincoln Castle*. Her owners, it stated, were 'pushing on with plans to dismantle the historic paddle steamer despite a last minute £50,000 donation towards the campaign to save it'. The LCPS was 'waiting on tenterhooks for confirmation of the gift but that still hasn't been enough to sway owner Colin Johnson'. It continued: 'The crushing blow has left campaigners devastated'. The LCPS 'vowed to buy as much of the vessel as possible and rebuild it'. However, Colin Johnson still would not sell because the family wanted 'to clear their liability'. The LCPS replied that it was 'very frustrating and there will be some very sad people'. Peter Johnson continued to insist that the vessel was beyond repair, but 'anyone can negotiate a deal to take parts'.

The *Grimsby Telegraph* of 15th September displayed a harrowing photograph of the *Lincoln Castle* with her sides torn away, leaving a gaping metallic gash and ending all hopes of saving her. Despite all the efforts made by national and local organisations and enthusiasts, the last coal-burning paddle steamer to operate in regular service in Britain was demolished by breakers H. Cope & Sons in Alexandra Dock and, tragically, not even her triple-expansion steam engine was saved. As a private company, Cope was carrying out the instructions of its client and could not afford to be sentimental. Cope's website contains a number of images of the demolition.

It is a great shame that *Lincoln Castle* did not find a home, if not on the Humber, then alongside her birthplace in Glasgow. The site of A. & J. Inglis's yard, at the point where the River Kelvin enters the Clyde, is now covered by Riverside Museum – Scotland's museum of transport and travel. What a fine feature she would have made as a representative of a Clyde-built paddle steamer, even if only statically preserved, as with *Wingfield Castle* in Hartlepool. *Wingfield Castle* is therefore now the only surviving Humber paddle steamer in its original condition. *Tattershall Castle*, though certainly worth seeing, is very much altered from her original condition and without her paddles.

Crossings of the Humber had started out with crude wooden craft in prehistoric times, had been an important link to the Romans, had thrived in various forms throughout the Early Middle Ages, had been authorised and regulated by the monarch in the early fourteenth century, had seen the first paddle steamer arrive in 1814 and had been operated between New Holland and Hull by a succession of railway companies from the 1840s to the 1980s, culminating in the final crossing by *Farringford* on 24th June 1981. The last ferry has long gone, but you can still stand on the stump of the old Corporation Pier in Hull, or upon the wide river bank at New Holland, look out across the water and, using your mind's eye, see the ferries plying back and forth on their mundane but essential duty, maintaining the link across the wide estuary as they did for centuries.

The engines of *Lincoln Castle* whilst she was being scrapped in Alexandra Dock, Grimsby, in 2010. *Kenny White*

Lincoln Castle during scrapping by H. Cope and Sons in Alexandra Dock, Grimsby, in 2010. *Kenny White*

How it could have been for *Lincoln Castle*. Passengers admire the triple-expansion steam engine on *Waverley* during a cruise on the Thames on Saturday 12th October 2013. *Kirk Martin*

PS *Waverley* on a cruise down the Thames from Tower Pier to Southend on 24th September 2011. From her base in Scotland she operates cruises during the autumn at various places down the west and south coasts of Britain and as far as Clacton on the east coast. If *Waverley* ventured further north she could recreate one of the cruises operated by the Humber ferries from Grimsby up to Hull and New Holland. *Kirk Martin*

SAILING TIMES AND TICKET PRICES 1948, 1961, 1974 AND 1980

Sailing times and ticket prices 1948, 1961, 1974 and 1980 taken from posters and leaflets in the National Railway Museum 'Search Engine' archive:

In 1948 there were thirteen departures from Hull between 7.35am and 8.30pm and thirteen from New Holland between 7.20am and 9.25pm. On Sundays there were eight departures from Hull between 7.30am and 7.05pm and eight from New Holland between 8.25am and 7.40pm allowing for a one-boat service. Fares were complicated as they varied depending on class. The saloon fare was one shilling and fivepence single and two shillings and tenpence return, whilst the fare on deck was tenpence halfpenny single and one shilling and ninepence return. There was a cheap return at one shilling and fivepence in the saloon and elevenpence on the deck for commercial travellers, and there were also reduced fares for children, scouts and military personnel. Annual tickets were £13.19 for the saloon and £9.19 for the deck. Motor car fares ranged from five shillings and sixpence to ten shillings and sevenpence, depending on the engine size; tickets for cattle were two shillings and fivepence, for donkeys one shilling and twopence, and for sheep and pigs threepence. A two-wheeled carriage was charged at seven shillings and threepence, whilst the fare for one with four wheels was ten shillings and a penny.

In 1961 on weekdays there were seventeen departures from Hull between 07.30am and 10.5pm and seventeen from New Holland between 7.20am and 10.30pm. On Sundays there were nine departures from Hull between 7.55am and 8.10pm and nine from New Holland between 8.35am and 8.45pm, allowing a one boat service, although there was an additional departure from Hull at 9.55am on certain dates. Fares were: adult saloon two shillings and fivepence single and four shillings and tenpence return, whilst the fare on deck was one shilling and ninepence single and three shillings and sixpence return, with cheaper fares for juveniles.

Motor cars cost from fourteen to twenty-four shillings single – depending on length – and from twenty-six to forty-four shillings return, whilst horses and cattle were nine shillings each way. Cycles were a shilling for a single crossing (tandems were two shillings and tenpence) although there were higher charges for cycles and tandems with an 'auto-wheel' or motor attached.

In 1974 there were sixteen departures from Hull on weekdays between 06.30 and 21.15 and seventeen departures from New Holland between 07.00 and 21.50. On Sundays there were nine departures from Hull between 07.55 and 19.45 and nine from New Holland between 08.35 and 20.20, thus enabling a one boat service to operate. Decimalisation abolished the shilling and old penny, and fares were 24p ('new pence') for an adult single and 48p return, with season tickets available at £1.70 for a week, £5.70 a month and £54.20 for a year. A cycle or tandem was by this time 12p single and 24p return, and a motor cycle 48p single and 96p return. Cars and caravans up to 10ft in length were charged £1.10; up to 13ft 6in were £1.40; those exceeding 13ft 6in cost £1.65 single, and double for a return journey. Commercial vehicles were charged £1.80 up to one ton unladen and £3.05 from one to two tons unladen, and double for a return journey.

By 1980, with a one-boat service, there were ten departures on weekdays from Hull between 06.30 and 21.15 and ten from New Holland between 07.00 and 21.50. On Sundays there were nine from Hull between 07.55 and 19.40 and nine from New Holland between 08.30 and 20.20. Fares had risen to 67p adult single and £1.34 return, with season tickets priced at £5.35 weekly, £17.00 monthly and £147 annually. Cars ranged from £2.65 to £4 single, the return being double; cycles, prams, wheelchairs and dogs paid 34p single and 67p return; motorcycles £1.34 single and double for the return. Commercial vehicles were £4.40 up to one ton unladen and £7.30 one to two tons unladen with the return costing double the single.

Appendix II

DETAILED INFORMATION ABOUT NINE STEAMBOATS, INCLUDING THE NAMES OF THEIR MASTERS

Detailed information about nine steamboats, including the names of their masters (or captains) as well as the destinations and sailing times, from the 1823 *History, Directory & Gazetteer of Yorkshire*.

The *Caledonia*, John Thompson, master, and the *Aire*, Benjamin Matthewman, master, daily in rotation to Selby, communicating with the same places as the *Favourite* and *Leeds*. The *Rockingham*, John Jackling, master, and the *John Bull*, Wm. Colbridge, master, convey passengers and goods to Thorne, daily, in rotation, and communicating with Witton, Blacktoft, Whitgift, Swinefleet, Goole Bridge and New Bridge. On the arrival of the Packets at Thorne, a coach proceeds with the passengers for Doncaster, Rotherham and Sheffield. The *Waterloo* Steam Hoy, Wm. Good, master, proceeds from the New Ferry Boat Dock, end of Queen Street, every morning at 7 o'clock, and every afternoon at 4, with the mail, passengers & goods for Barton, (forwarded to Brigg & Lincoln). Returns to Hull at 11 morn. And ½ p. 7 evening. The contractor for Barton Ferry are Messrs Boyce, Chaplin & Co., Grace Church Street, London. The *Albion* Steam Packet, John Cook, master, to Gainsborough with passengers and goods every Mon. Wed. & Fri. returning to Hull on the following days. The *British Queen*, William Waterland, master, to Gainsborough every Tue. Thur. and Sat. And returns to Hull the following days (Sundays excepted). The *Favourite*, Frank Potter, master, and the *Leeds*, John Popplewell, master, with passengers and goods daily, in rotation to Selby, communicating on the passage with Witton, Blacktoft, Whitgift, Swinefleet, Howden Dyke, Booth Ferry and Long Drax. On arrival of the Packets at Selby, coaches leave for the following destinations, Leeds, Wakefield, York, Harrogate by Knaresboro'.

As well as a log book the *Tattershall Castle* for 31st July 1967 to 20th April 1968, I have several loose papers dating from 1972 amongst which is one complete weekly crew roster, dated Sunday 16th April, which names the staff on duty that week:

Salaried Staff

Captain	H.D. Bolderson
Captain	A.J.C.W. Harvey
Captain	A.S. Wright
Captain	C.E. King
Mate	H. Kowalski
Mate	A. Burrell
Mate	J.G. Jones
Mate	G.H. Richardson
Engineer	E.W. Deans
Engineer	P. Moore
Engineer	H. Miller
Engineer	H.W. Rowell

Conciliation staff

Leading Seaman	R. Currer
Leading Seaman	K. Woodger
Leading Seaman	K. Edwards
Deck Hand	S. Ayres
Deck Hand	J. Hager
Deck Hand	A. Harrod
Deck Hand	J .W. Hourston
Deck Hand	G.R. Olsen
Deck Hand	E. O'Grady
Deck Hand	F. Guilliatt
Deck Hand	S. Johnson
Deck Hand	W.C. Braithwaite
Deck Hand	L. Clayton
Deck Hand	B. McWilliam
Leading Fireman	G. Daniels
Leading Fireman	J. Davies
Leading Fireman	H. Baker
Leading Fireman	W. Burnett
Leading Fireman	L.S. Bingham
Fireman	J. Allison
Fireman	G. Hambley
Fireman	L. Brown
Fireman	T. Marrison
Fireman	T. Hopper
Fireman	S. Staves

PADDLE STEAMERS AND OTHER FERRIES OF THE HUMBER ESTUARY 1814–1981

The table lists eighty-seven paddle steamers operating ferries on the Humber Estuary from 1814, when *Caledonia* arrived, until 1978, when *Lincoln Castle* was withdrawn. A few non-paddle steamers are included where appropriate (for example, the diesel-electric paddle-vessel *Farringford*). Further research may add to this list.

Information derives mainly from local directories, registers and newspapers, Mercantile Navy Lists and Lloyd's Registers. Entries in pre-1839 Lloyd's Registers are insufficiently detailed to be of use. Mercantile Navy Lists from 1865 to 1870 fail to distinguish between paddle and screw steamers and, therefore, have not been used. After 1871 MNL do not always state if a vessel is a tug, nor if it operated on local waters only.

Statistics for each ship vary between sources; those shown are from the most recent. Where known, the registered number of a vessel is given in brackets.

Main Sources:

AAD–Alun A. D'Orley (1968) *Humber Ferries*

D&L1–C. Duckworth & G. Langmuir (1948) *Railway & Other Steamers*

D&L2–C. Duckworth & G. Langmuir (1937) *Clyde River and Other Steamers*

DOW–George Dow (1959–1965) *The Great Central Railway*

EP–Edward Parsons (1835) *The Tourist's Companion*

FHP–F.H. Pearson (1896) *The Early History of Hull Steam Shipping*

HAND–Graham R. Hand (2012) *A Tale of Three Castles*

HAWS–Duncan Haws (1993) *Merchant Fleets*

HPB–Humber Packet Boats website by Peter Wilde <www.humberpacketboats.co.uk>

JJS–J.J. Sheahan (1864) *History of Hull*

LD–Local directories (with year)

LR–Lloyd's Register 1839/40–1949/50

MNL–Mercantile Navy List 1857–1940 and 1947–1949

NP–Newspaper or advertisement (see main text for details)

RC–Rodney Clapson (2005) *Barton and the River Humber*

NAME (and registered number)	DATE BUILT	BUILDER	ENGINE	HULL, DIMENSIONS	OWNER	ROUTE(S)	SOURCES
PS Caledonia	c1814	Stuart, Dundee	Robertson & Co.	Wooden hull Tonnage 80		Hull to Grimsby, Selby, Gainsboro', Goole	NP1814, LD1817, 1822, 1826, NP1828, AAD, HPB
PS British Queen	1815	J. & H. Smith & Sons, Gainsboro'	Brunton, Birmingham	Tonnage 75	Gainsboro' United Steam Packet Co.	Hull to Gainsboro'	LD1817, 1822, 1826, NP1832, AAD, HPB
PS Albion	1815	J. & H. Smith & Sons, Gainsboro'	Horsly Co.	Tonnage 75	Gainsboro' United Steam Packet Co.	Hull to Gainsboro', Brigg	LD1817, 1822, 1826, NP1832, LD1848, AAD, HPB
PS Waterloo	c1815			Hull 76ft x 21 ½ ft		Hull to Selby, Barton	NP1816, LD1817, 1822, 1826, AAD, HPB
PS John Bull (I)	1815			Wooden hull	Darley & Co.	Hull to Thorne, 1836 replaced by vessel of same name	LD1817, 1822, 1826, AAD–1832, HPB
PS Humber	c1815	Stuart, Dundee	Robertson & Co.	Wooden hull Tonnage 80		Hull to Selby	NP1815, LD1817, 1822, AAD, HPB
PS Maria	c1815					1817 Hull to Gainsboro'	LD1817, 1826, AAD
PS Nottingham						1822 Hull to Gainsboro'	LD1822, HPB
PS Aire (renamed PS Public Opinion, 1831)					Furley & Co., Gainsboro'. 1831 hired by Acland and renamed.	Hull to Selby, 1831 Hull to Barton	LD1822, 1826, NP1828, RC
PS Leeds		Fenton & Co.		Wooden hull Tonnage 87		Hull to Selby, Goole	LD1822, 1826, 1848, HPB
PS Favourite	1817	J. & H. Smith & Sons, Gainsboro'	Horsly Co.	Tonnage 117		Hull to Selby	LD1822, 1826, NP1828, HPB
PS Selby	1818	Foster, Selby	Overton & Co.	Tonnage 80		Hull to Barton	HPB
PS Rockingham	1820	Pearson & Co., Thorne				Hull to Thorne	LD1822, 1826, AAD, HPB
PS Eagle (4908)	1824	Aire & Calder Co.	B. Hawthorne & Co.	Tonnage 85 gross		Hull to Gainsboro', Goole. 1862 MNL shows her operating from Liverpool	LD1826, NP1826, EP1835, LD1848, MNL1857–1861, AAD, HPB
PS Mercury	1825	J. & H. Smith & Sons, Gainsboro'			Gainsboro' United Steam Packet Co.	Hull to Gainsboro'	LD1826, NP1826, AAD, HPB
PS Graham	1825	Hull	Overton & Smith, Hull. Suffered boiler explosion in 1826	Length 85ft 7in, beam 18.1ft, depth 7.9ft. Tonnage 88		Hull to Grimsby, Selby, also Hull Yarmouth, Scarborough and Norwich	LD1826, NP1826, FHP, HPB

Name	Year	Builder	Hull	Engineer	Owner / Notes	Route	References
PS Royal Charter	1826	J. & H. Smith & Sons, Gainsboro'	Wooden hull			Hull to Barton until 1845	LD1826, NP1826, 1831, AAD, RC, HPB
PS Dart	1826	J. & H. Smith & Sons, Gainsboro'	Wooden hull Tonnage 75 gross	Overton & Smith, Hull	Gainsboro' United Steam Packet Co.	Hull to Gainsboro'	LD1826, NP1826, 1832, MNL1857, AAD, HPB, HPB
PS Hero						Hull to Goole. 1829 Gainsboro'	LD1826, HPB
PS Trent						Hull to Gainsboro'	LD1826, HPB
PS Calder		R Pearson & Co., Thorne	Wooden hull Tonnage 75	Fenton & Jackson, Leeds	Aire & Calder Navigation Co.	Hull to Selby, Goole	LD1826, EP1835, LD1848, HPB
PS Duke of Wellington						Hull to Selby, Goole	LD1826, LD1848
PS Victory Renamed PS Public Opinion, 1831	1827				Furley & Co. Gainsboro'. 1831 hired by Acland and renamed.	Hull to Gainsboro'. 1831 Hull to Barton	NP1831, AAD, HPB, RC
PS Elizabeth						Hull to Glandford Bridge and Brigg	LD1826, AAD, HPB
PS Pelham (17757)	1828	J. & H. Smith & Sons, Gainsboro'	Wooden hull. Tonnage 60 gross	James Overton, Hull		Hull to Grimsby	NP1832, LD1848, MNL1857–1858, AAD, HPB
PS Atlas	1828	Furley & Co. Gainsboro'	Wooden hull. Tonnage 49	Butterley & Co.		Hull to Gainsboro'	LD1848, HPB
PS Kingston	1829		Wooden hull Length 76.6ft, beam 17.9ft. depth 9.0ft. Tonnage 60 gross			1832 Hull to Grimsby, 1846 registered in Cork	ROS, AAD, HPB
PS Coronation						Hull to Barton	NP1832, HPB
PS Adelaide					Hull & Selby Steam Packet Co.	1832 Hull to Selby	NP1832, AAD, HPB
PS Trafalgar						1832 Hull to York	AAD
PS Lion						1835 Hull to Goole	EP1835
PS Magna Charta	1832		Wooden hull. Tonnage 62 gross		1845 acquired by Great Grimsby & Sheffield Jct Ry 1846 Manchester Sheffield & Lincolnshire Railway	Hull to New Holland. 1849 used as luggage boat. c1873 Withdrawn	NP1832, 1833, LD1848 MNL1857–1864, D&L1, AAD, HAWS, HPB
PS Echo						Hull to Goole	EP1835, LD1848, HPB
PS Eclipse	1833		Length 87ft. 0in. Beam 23ft. 6in.			Hull to Goole	NP1832, EP1835, HPB
PS Sovereign					Hull & Selby Steam Packet Co.	1835 Hull to Selby. 1837 Hull to Grimsby	NP1832, NP1837, AAD

NAME (and registered number)	DATE BUILT	BUILDER	ENGINE	HULL, DIMENSIONS	OWNER	ROUTE(S)	SOURCES
PS Ormrod	1833					Selby, Goole, Hull, Yarmouth.	HPB
PS Arrow	1834	John Linton, Selby		Iron hull		Hull to York	LD1848, HPB
PS Railway	1835	Samuel Gutteridge, Selby		Iron hull	Audus & Co.	Hull to Boston, Selby	LD1848, LR 1852/3–1855, HPB
PS Laurel	1835	Jeremiah Wandly, York	Jeremiah Wandly, York	Wooden hull		1836 Hull to Barton and Hessle	NP1836, HPB
PS John Bull (II)	1836	R Pearson & Co. Thorne	Aydon & Co. Wakefield	Wooden hull Tonnage 30		Hull to Thorne, replaced John Bull (I). Later to Hamburg	LD1848, HPB
PS Falcon	1836			Wooden hull Tonnage 57 gross	1845 acquired by Great Grimsby & Sheffield Jct Ry 1846 Manchester Sheffield & Lincolnshire Railway	Hull to New Holland. 1849 used as luggage boat. 1873 out of service	LD1848, MNL1858–1864, D&L1, DOW, AAD, HAWS
PS Economy						Humber ferry	D&L1
PS Thrifty						Humber ferry	D&L1
PS Union	1836	Henry Smith & Sons, Gainsboro'			Gainsboro' Steam Packet Co.	Hull to Gainsboro'. 1837 involved in a boiler explosion at Hull	JJS, HPB
PS Ann Scarborough						1836 Hull to Barton. 1841 Hessle and Barton	NP1836, AAD
PS Don				Tonnage 36		Hull, Goole and Thorne	LD1848, MNL1857, HPB
PS Lindsey	1836			Tonnage 48	Gainsboro' United Steam Co.	Hull to Gainsboro'	LD1848, HPB
PS Iris	1838	Henry Smith & Sons, Gainsboro'	Brownlow & Co., Hull	Wooden hull. Length 115ft. Beam 18ft. 8in. Tonnage 97		1852/3 Hull to Goole. Described as a 'coaster' in LR	LR 1839/40–1857, HPB
PS City of York		John Linton, Selby	John Linton, Selby	Iron hull Tonnage 65		Hull to York	LD1848, MNL1857–1858, HPB
PS Ebor (I)				Wooden hull.			HPB
PS Ebor (II)		Henry Smith & Sons, Gainsboro'	Aydon & Read. Two cylinders	Wooden hull. Tonnage 62		Hull to York, Goole	LD1848, MNL1857, HPB
PS Duncannon	1841					1845 Barton to Hull	RC
PS Queen	1842	Ditchburn & Mare, Blackwall	Ditchburn & Mare. Single cylinder	Iron hull. Length 99.5ft, beam 13.8ft, depth 7.5ft. Tonnage 52.4 gross	1848 acquired by Manchester Sheffield & Lincolnshire Ry	Hull to New Holland. 1853 cargo-only (passenger certificate not renewed). 1857 withdrawn	DOW, AAD, HAWS, HPB

Ship	Year	Builder	Engine	Dimensions	Owner/Operator	Service	References
PS Prince of Wales	1843	Ditchburn & Mare, Blackwall	Single cylinder	Iron hull. Length 99.5ft, beam 13.8ft, depth 7.5ft. Tonnage 52.4	1848 acquired by Manchester Sheffield & Lincolnshire Ry	Hull and New Holland service. In 1853, passenger certificate not renewed. 1855 scrapped	DOW, AAD, HAWS, HPB
PS Columbine (17413)	1848	Henry Smith & Sons, Gainsboro'	Penn & Sons, Greenwich	Iron hull. Length 115.6ft, beam 15.1ft, depth 7.6ft. Tonnage 44 net, 84 gross	Gainsboro' United Steam Packet Co. 1905 East Coast Passenger Service.	Hull to Gainsboro'. c1908 scrapped	LD1848, MNL1857–1907, AAD, HPB
PS Harlequin (17412)	1848	Henry Smith & Sons, Gainsboro'	Penn & Sons, Greenwich	Length 121.8ft, beam 15ft, depth 7.7ft. Tonnage 48 net, 74 gross	Gainsboro' United Steam Packet Co.	1857 operating out of Gainsboro'	MNL 1857–1879, HPB
PS Sheffield (I) Renamed Old Sheffield in 1855 (7564)	1848	Henry Smith & Sons, Gainsboro'	J. & G. Rennie, London	Iron hull. Length 160.8ft. Tonnage 161 gross	Manchester Sheffield & Lincolnshire Ry 1863 sold to owner in Kingston-upon-Thames.	Hull to New Holland. 1883 scrapped	MNL1857–1861, D&L1, DOW, AAD, HAWS, HPB
PS Manchester (I) (7563) Renamed Old Manchester in 1855	1849	Robinson & Russell, Millwall	2 x 48in x 53in stroke oscillating cylinders	Iron hull. Length 164.9ft, beam 22.4ft, depth 9.6ft. Double ended with two rudders. Tonnage 174 net, 291 gross	Manchester Sheffield & Lincolnshire Ry	Hull to New Holland. 1858 transferred to Mersey. Returned to Humber. 1864 sold. Withdrawn by 1878	MNL1857–1861, LR 1874/5–1876/7, D&L1, DOW, AAD, HAWS
PS Petrel					Watermans Co. Hired by Manchester Sheffield & Lincolnshire Ry	1850 Hull to New Holland	DOW, AAD
PS Atalanta (17411)	1851	Henry Smith & Son, Gainsboro'	J. Penn & Sons, Greenwich. Two-cylinder 27in–30in	Iron hull. Length 135.6ft, beam 15.2 ft, depth 7.7ft. Tonnage 60 net, 108 gross	Gainsboro' United Steam Packet Co. 1905 East Coast Passenger Service. 1919 W. E. Lowery.	Hull to Burton Stather, Ferriby and Grimsby, excursions etc. 1927 scrapped	MNL 1857–1927, LR 1886/7–1927/28, AAD, HPB
PS Chesapeake (10170)	1853	Thornton & Havant, North Shields	Hepple & Sandells	Tonnage 41		Operating out of Hull. From 1863 operating from Newcastle	MNL 1857–1862, HPB
PS Manchester (II)	1854	Martin Samuelson & Co., Hull. Sister ship of PS Sheffield II	Twin cylinder oscillating engines	Iron hull. Length 160ft. Tonnage 175 gross.	Samuelson. 1855 sold to Manchester Sheffield & Lincolnshire Ry.	Hull to Burton Stather. Hull to Ferriby, Hull to Grimsby, excursions etc. 1875 grounded, broke her back and scrapped	MNL 1860–1871, D&L1, DOW, AAD, HAWS

NAME (and registered number)	DATE BUILT	BUILDER	ENGINE	HULL DIMENSIONS	OWNER	ROUTE(S)	SOURCES
PS Sheffield (II) (7564)	1854	Martin Samuelson & Co., Hull. Sister ship of PS Manchester II	Twin cylinder oscillating engines	Iron hull. Tonnage 148 gross.	Samuelson. 1855 sold to Manchester Sheffield & Lincolnshire Ry.	Hull to Burton Stather, Ferriby and Grimsby, excursions etc. 1861 ceased working on Humber, 1865 scrapped	MNL 1857–1864, D&L1, DOW, AAD, HAWS
PS Royal Albion	1855	Martin Samuelson & Co., Hull	Re-boilered 1863	Iron hull. Length 159.6ft. Tonnage 36 gross	Manchester Sheffield & Lincolnshire Ry	General purpose boat, Humber ferry and tug. 1888 scrapped	MNL 1857, AAD
PS Liverpool (77473)	1855	Martin Samuelson & Co., Hull. Sister ship of PS Doncaster	Engine 1) Martin Samuelson & Co., Hull. Engine 2) 1874 Laird Brothers, two-cylinder simple oscillating, 36in–36in. 1883 new boiler by T. Charlton, Grimsby	Iron hull. Length 159.6ft, beam 18.7ft, depth 8.4ft. Tonnage 164 net, 220 gross	Manchester Sheffield & Lincolnshire Ry. 1897 Great Central Ry	Hull to New Holland. 1905 dismantled (LR)	MNL 1863–1905, LR 1884/5–1905/06, D&L1, DOW, AAD, HAWS
PS Doncaster (75359)	1856	Martin Samuelson & Co., Hull. Sister ship of PS Liverpool	Engine 1) Martin Samuelson & Co., Hull. Engine 2) 1875, Laird Brothers, two-cylinder simple oscillating, 36in–36in. New boilers 1880 and 1892	Iron hull. Length 160.5ft, beam 18.7ft, depth 8.4ft. Tonnage 165 net, 216 gross	Manchester Sheffield & Lincolnshire Ry. 1897 Great Central Ry	Hull to New Holland. 1913 withdrawn after 57 years. Longest serving Humber ferry	MNL 1862–1913, LR 1884/5–1912/13, D&L1, DOW, AAD, HAWS
PS Empress (I) (18064)	1856	Charles & Langley, Rotherhithe	Miller & Ravenhill	Iron hull. Length 114.1ft, beam 12.9ft, depth 5.9ft. Tonnage 43 net, 68 gross.	1870 Goole & Hull Steam Packet Co.	Hull to Goole. 1879 scrapped	NP1856, MNL1857–1879, AAD, HPB
PS Lady Elizabeth (18151)	1856			Iron hull. Length 98.3ft, beam 13.9ft, depth 6.5ft. Tonnage 37 net, 59 gross	1858 registered in Southampton 1860 reg. in Ipswich. 1871 William Fisher West and others, Hull. 1891 sold to Goole & Hull Steam Packet Co.	1891 Hull to South Ferriby. Later crossed the Atlantic under sail and steam and used on the Amazon River	MNL 1858–1900, AAD, HPB
PS Wave	1857	Martin Samuelson, Hull.	Martin Samuelson, Hull.	Tonnage 59		1858 operating out of Hull	MNL 1858–1864, HPB
PS Isle of Axholme (17431)	1860			Iron hull. Length 130ft, beam 16.1ft, depth 7.0ft. Tonnage 48 net, 91 gross	1905 Gainsboro' United Steam Packet Co. 1912 East Coast Passenger Service. Sold to Goole & Hull Steam Packet Co.	Hull to Burton Stather and Grimsby, excursions etc. c1920 scrapped in Scarborough	MNL 1861–1920, AAD, HPB

Name	Year	Builder	Engine	Dimensions	Owner	Route / Fate	Registration
PS Her Majesty (44026)	1860			Length 129.1ft, beam 12.3ft, depth 6.3ft. Tonnage 66 net, 82 gross	Goole & Hull Steam Packet Co.	1861 Hull to Goole. 1913 scrapped	MNL 1861–1913, AAD, HPB
PS Magna Charta (II) (75372)	1873	T. Charlton, Grimsby	T. Charlton, Hull, single-cylinder side-lever engine 23½in–48in. Re-boilered 1885	Iron hull. Length 98.2ft, beam 18.1ft, depth 8.3ft. Tonnage 62 net, 116 gross	Manchester Sheffield & Lincolnshire Ry. 1897 Great Central Ry 1923 London & North Eastern Ry	Grimsby to Hull and New Holland, and excursions. 1924 scrapped	MNL 1885–1923, LR 1884/5–1923/24, D&L1, DOW, AAD, HAWS
PS Manchester (III) (75357)	1876	Goole Engineering & Shipbuilding Co. Ltd.	Laird Brothers, simple two-cylinder oscillating 36in–36in. New boiler 1887	Iron hull. Length 159.7ft, beam 18.9ft, depth 8.4ft. Tonnage 168 net, 221 gross	Manchester Sheffield & Lincolnshire Ry. 1897 Great Central Ry	Hull to New Holland. 1914 scrapped	MNL 1885–1913, LR 1884/5–1912/13, D&L1, DOW, AAD, HAWS
PS Princess (67819)	1876	Goole Engineering & Shipbuilding Co. Ltd.	Two cylinders 24 ½' x 28'	Steel hull. Length 130.7ft, beam 14.7ft, depth 6.7ft. Tonnage 59 net, 100 gross	1879 Goole & Hull Steam Packet Co. Later Hugh Sprotson, London	Goole to Hull	MNL 1877–1879, LR 1878/9, HPB
PS Grimsby (II) (98719)	1888	Earle's Shipbuilding & Engineering Co. Ltd. Hull. (The MS&LR's Grimsby I was a screw steamer)	Two-cylinder compound diagonal 35in–60in x 48in	Steel hull (the first on New Holland route). Length 180ft, beam 25.4ft, depth 7.4ft. Tonnage 161 net, 351 gross	Manchester Sheffield & Lincolnshire Ry. 1897 Great Central Ry 1923 London & North Eastern Ry	Hull to New Holland. 1924 scrapped	MNL 1896–1923, LR 1889/90–1923/24, D&L1, DOW, AAD, HAWS, HPB
PS Lady Rowena (98651)	1891	S. McKnight & Co., Ayr	Diagonal single-cylinder 50in x 72in	Steel hull, length 200.5ft, beam 21.1ft, depth 6.7ft. Tonnage 131 net, 332 gross	North British Steam Packet Co. 1904/5 in Italy. 1908/09 various owners in UK. 1919 Goole & Hull Steam Packet Co.	1923 scrapped (in The Netherlands)	MNL 1892–1922, LR 1892/93–1922/3, D&L2
PS Mermaid	1891				Goole & Hull Steam Packet Co.	Goole to Hull. During First World War, Hull to New Holland	AAD

NAME (and registered number)	DATE BUILT	BUILDER	ENGINE	HULL, DIMENSIONS	OWNER	ROUTE(S)	SOURCES
PS Empress (II) (98395)	1893	J. Reid & Co., Glasgow	Three-cylinder	Steel hull. Length 140.2ft, beam 17.1ft, depth 7.3ft. Tonnage 79 net, 156 gross	Goole & Hull Steam Packet Co. 1917 Tay Steam Boat Co., Dundee. 1918 in Cork. 1923 renamed Sanlucar and in France	Goole to Hull	MNL 1895–1922, LR 1894/95–1921/22
PS Frodingham (104626) (Formerly PS Dandie Dinmont to 1928)	1895	A. & J. Inglis, Pointhouse, Glasgow	Simple single-cylinder diagonal 48in x 66in.	Steel hull. Length 195.2ft (1912 lengthened to 209.6ft), beam 22.1ft, depth 7.2ft. Tonnage 63 net, 218 gross, from 1912 173 net 318 gross.	North British Steam Packet Co. 1902 North British Ry (on Craigendoram and Dunoon / Holy Loch routes) 1923 London & North Eastern Ry	1926–27 Laid up. 1928 Hull to New Holland as PS Frodingham. Forward saloon removed to create open deck for cars. 1936 scrapped (in Belgium)	MNL 1896–1936, LR 1895/96–1935/36, D&L1, D&L2, HAWS
PS Essex (105420)	1896	Earle's Shipbuilding & Engineering Co. Ltd., Hull	Engine two-cylinder compound 24in–48in x 42in	Steel hull. Length 175.5ft, beam 23.1ft, depth 7.2ft. Tonnage 126 net, 297 gross	Great Eastern Ry Co. 1913/4 various owners. 1916 Goole & Hull Steam Packet Co.	Later years of First World War, Hull to New Holland	LR1897/98–1918/19, AAD, HPB
PS Cleopatra (108320)	1898			Steel hull. Length 120.1ft, beam 17.1ft, depth 7.2ft. Tonnage 70 net, 111 gross	1898 Thames Steamboat Co. 1916 Goole & Hull Steam Packet Co., 1919 Tay Steamboat Co., Dundee		MNL1899–1919
PS Cleethorpes (118787) 1934 renamed Cruising Queen	1903	Gourlay Brothers, Dundee	Two-cylinder compound diagonal 25in, 48in x 45in stroke.	Steel hull. Length 190.1ft, beam 25.5ft, depth 7.9ft. Tonnage 67 net, 302 gross, from 1913/14 116 net, 273 gross	Great Central Ry. 1923 London & North Eastern Ry. 1934 sold to Redcliffe Shipping Co.	Hull to New Holland. 1916–1919 requisitioned as patrol vessel FY0109 and sent to eastern Mediterranean. 1934 sent to Scotland to operate cruises from Leith. 1936 disposed	MNL1905–1934, LR 1904/05–1934/35, D&L1, AAD, HAWS, HPB
PS Brocklesby (132124) 1935 renamed Highland Queen	1912	Earle's Shipbuilding & Engineering Co. Ltd., Hull. Sister ship of PS Killingholme	Two-cylinder compound diagonal 25in, 48in x 45in.	Steel hull. Length 195ft, beam 31.1ft, depth 8.7ft moulded, 4ft 0in actual. Double ended. Tonnage 217 net, 508 gross	Great Central Ry. 1923 London & North Eastern Ry. 1935 Redcliffe Shipping Co.	Hull to New Holland. First World War, used as seaplane carrier. 1934 left Humber. Renamed and succeeded Cruising Queen, used for cruises on the Forth from Leith. December 1936 scrapped (in Germany)	MNL1913–1935, LR 1912/13–1934/35, D&L1, DOW, AAD, HAWS, HPB

Ship	Year	Builder	Engine	Hull	Owner	History	References
PS Killingholme (132130)	1912	Earle's Shipbuilding & Engineering Co. Ltd., Hull. Sister ship of PS Brocklesby	Two-cylinder compound diagonal 25in, 48in x 45in.	Steel hull. Length 195ft, beam 31.1ft, depth 8.7ft moulded, draught 4ft. Double ended. Tonnage 217 net, 508 gross.	Great Central Ry. 1923 London & North Eastern Ry	Hull to New Holland. First World War, used as seaplane carrier. 1934 replaced by Wingfield Castle but kept as spare ferry and for excursions. 1940 used as barrage balloon command ship in the Humber. 1945 scrapped at Paull	MNL 1913–1940 last edition of war, LR 1912/13–1945/46, D&L1, AAD, HAWS, HPB
PS Tattershall Castle (162888)	1934	William Gray & Co., West Hartlepool. Sister ship of PS Wingfield Castle	Central Marine Engine Works Hartlepool triple expansion diagonal cylinders 18in, 28½in, 46in x 51in stroke	Steel hull. Length 199.9ft, beam 33.1ft (excluding sponsons), depth 7ft 7in, draught 4ft 7in. Tonnage 321 net, 550 gross	London & North Eastern Ry, 1948 British Railways. 1971 Sealink	Hull to New Holland until 1972	MNL 1935–1949, LR 1935/36–1949/50, D&L1, AAD, HAWS, HPB
PS Wingfield Castle (162889)	1934	William Gray & Co., West Hartlepool. Sister ship of PS Tattershall Castle	Central Marine Engine Works, Hartlepool triple expansion diagonal cylinders 18in, 28½in, 46in x 51in stroke	Steel hull. Length 199.9ft, beam 33.1ft (excluding sponsons), depth 7ft 7in, draught 4ft 7in. Tonnage 550 gross	London & North Eastern Ry, 1948 British Railways. 1971 Sealink	Hull to New Holland until 1974	MNL 1936–1949, LR 1935/36–1949/50, D&L1, AAD, HAWS, HPB
PS Lincoln Castle (166637)	1940	A. & J. Inglis Ltd, Pointhouse, Glasgow	Ailsa Shipbuilding Co. Triple expansion diagonal cylinders 16½in, 26in, 41in x 51in stroke	Steel hull. Length 199.7ft, beam 33.1ft (56ft – with sponsons), depth 8.8ft, draught 4ft. Tonnage 320 net, 598 gross	London & North Eastern Ry, 1948 British Railways. 1971 Sealink	Hull to New Holland until 1978, when boiler failed during overhaul. 2010 scrapped (in Grimsby)	MNL 1947 first post war edition–1949, LR 1941/42–1949/50, D&L1, AAD, HAWS, HPB

Other craft used on the Hull New Holland service:

NAME (and registered number)	DATE BUILT	BUILDER	ENGINE	HULL, DIMENSIONS	OWNER	ROUTE(S)	SOURCES
DEPV Farringford	1947	William Denny & Bros, Dumbarton	Crossley diesels 2 x six-cylinder 4SCSA type 6 SKM 420 bhp @ 650 rpm driving two General Electric paddle motors	Length 178 ft, beam 54.25 ft. Tonnage 489 gross	Southern Ry. 1948 British Railways. 1971 Sealink	1947–1973 Lymington to Yarmouth IOW. 1974–1981 Hull to New Holland. 1984 scrapped (in Hull)	HAWS
Mercury					Humber Hovercraft Services Ltd, operating as 'Hoverlink'	February to October 1968, between Hull and Grimsby docks	NP1968
Minerva					Humber Hovercraft Services Ltd, operating as 'Hoverlink'	February to October 1968, between Hull and Grimsby docks	NP1968
Flamborian (originally Boys' Own)	1938	Cook, Welton & Gemmel, Beverley	Kelvin diesel engines			A Bridlington pleasure boat used on Hull to New Holland passenger ferry 19th February to 5th March 1972, during the miners' strike	LN, HAWS
Freshwater	1959	Ailsa Shipbuilding Co.	Crossley Bros, Manchester 2 x M8cy. 640bhp			1980 Hull to New Holland ferry service to cover for *Farringford* during annual maintenance	NP1980, HAND
Yorkshire Belle	1947	Cook, Welton & Gemmel, Beverley	Two Gardner eight-cylinder engines			Bridlington pleasure boat, 1978–1981, used on Hull to New Holland passenger ferry to cover for *Farringford* when out of service	HAND

BIBLIOGRAPHY

Books

The illustrated journeys of Celia Fiennes 1685–1712, by Celia Fiennes, edited by Christopher Morris. Macdonald & Co., 1982.

A tour through the whole island of Great Britain, by Daniel Defoe. Penguin, 1971.

The history of the town and county of Kingston upon Hull: from its foundation in the reign of Edward the First to the present time, by the Rev. John Tickell, 1798.

The Trent and Humber Picturesque Steam-packet companion, by John Greenwood, Gainsborough, 1833.

The Tourist's Companion, or, the History of the Scenes and Places on the Route by the Rail-road and Steam-Packet from Leeds and Selby to Hull, by Edward Parsons. Whittaker & Co., 1835.

Biography of William Symington, civil engineer: inventor of steam locomotion by sea and land. Also, a brief history of steam navigation, by J. & W.H. Rankine. A Johnston, Falkirk, 1862.

General and concise history and description of the Town and Port of Kingston-upon-Hull, by James Joseph Sheahan. Simpkin, Marshall & Co., 1864.

The early history of Hull Steam Shipping, by F.H. Pearson. 1896. Facsimile edition, Mr Pye, 1984.

Clyde River and Other Steamers by Christian Leslie Dyce Duckworth and Graham Easton Langmuir. Shipping Histories Ltd, 1937.

Railway & Other Steamers, by Christian Leslie Dyce Duckworth and Graham Easton Langmuir. Shipping Histories Ltd, 1948.

Steamers of the Thames and Medway, by Frank Burtt. Richard Tilling, 1949.

Great Central, Vols. 1, 2 & 3, by George Dow, 1959-1965. Ian Allan, 1985.

The Humber Ferries by Alun A. D'Orley. Nidd Valley Narrow Gauge Railways Ltd, 1968.

The Victoria History of the County of York East Riding, Vol. 1: The City of Kingston upon Hull. Editor K.J.Allison, OUP, 1969.

Ferries & Ferrymen, by G. Bernard Wood. Cassell, 1969.

A history of Grimsby, by Edward Gillett. OUP, 1970.

Decline of the Paddle Steamer, by Richard H. Coton. Paddle Steamer Preservation Society, 1971.

The Humber Crossing, by Hull Junior Chamber of Commerce and Shipping, 1974.

Paddle Steamers in the 1970s, by Russell Plummer, Anglia County, 1975.

A history of Kingston upon Hull, by Hugh Calvert. Phillimore, 1978.

A history of Hull by Edward Gillett and Kenneth A. MacMahon. Hull University Press, 1980.

Song of the Clyde: a history of Clyde shipbuilding, by Fred M. Walker. Patrick Stephens, 1984; John Donald, 2001.

Shipbuilders of the Hartlepools, by Bert Spaldin. Hartlepool Borough Council, 1986.

P.S.S. Wingfield Castle, Hartlepool Borough Council, 1991.

Merchant Fleets: Britain's Railway Steamers, by Duncan Haws. TCL, 1993.

Paddle Steamers at War 1939–1945, by Russell Plummer, GMS Enterprises, 1995.

Railways to New Holland and the Humber Ferries by A.J. Ludlam. Oakwood, 1996.

Passage of Humber, by Geoffrey B. Mann. Lockington, 1983.

Paddle Steamer Machinery: A Layman's Guide, by R.J. Ramsay. Paddle Steamer Preservation Society, 1998.

Barton and the River Humber 1086–1900, by Rodney Clapson. WEA Barton-on-Humber, 2005.

The Building of a Port City, A history and celebration of Hull, by David and Susan Neave. Published by Hull City Council in association with English Heritage, 2012.

A Tale of Three Castles: The Untold Story of the Humber Ferries, by Graham R. Hand. Paddle Steamer Preservation Society, 2012.

Newspapers

Bury and Norwich Post, 19th April 1820

Grimsby Telegraph, 31st July 1981; 15th September 1981; 5th June 2010

Guardian, 11th January 1975

Hull Packet and Original Weekly Commercial, 8th August 1826

Hull Advertiser and Exchange Gazette, 24th September 1814; December 1821; 10th November 1826; 14th November 1826; 23rd November 1826; 10th August 1832; 17th August 1832; 14th December 1832; 19th December 1834

Hull Daily Mail, (called the *Daily Mail* from 1896 to 1986, when it reverted to its old title, which I use throughout to avoid confusion with the national newspaper) 14th January 1895; 27th March 1896; 6th May 1926; 12th May 1926; 18th November 1933; 29th October 1946; 28th

February 1948; 30th October 1950; 21st January 1963; 26th June 1963; 10th July 1963; 9th February 1969; 22nd February 1978; 17th March 1978; 18th March 1978; 30th March 1978; 27th April, 1981; 28th April 1978; 11th January 1980; 7th March, 1981; 9th March, 1981; 30th March 1981; 14th August, 1981; 5th October 1981

Hull Packet and East Riding Times, 24th May 1814; 5th July 1833; 27th June 1834; 26th September 1834; 10th October 1834; 7th August 1835; 5th February 1836; 17th June 1836; 22nd April 1836; 9th June 1843; 5th December 1845; 18th February 1848; 14th July 1848; 7th December 1849; 1st October 1875; 28th February 1879

Hull Packet and Humber Mercury, 29th April 1828; 3rd April 1832; 13th September 1831; 1st November 1831

Hull Times, 1st September 1910; 1st May 1926; 18th November 1933; 5th December, 1936; 5th June 1937; 29th April 1939; 25th May 1979

Illustrated London News, 15th April 1848

Morning Post, 21st September 1816; 24th November 1845

Northern Daily Mail, 24th September 1934

Rockingham and Hull Weekly Advertiser, 3rd September 1814; 13th May 1815

Sheffield & Rotherham Independent, 18th January 1845; 16th May 1845; 15th September 1849

The Times, 12th December 1938; 8th April 1939; 24th March 1956

York Herald, 9th March 1875; 4th December 1882

Journals, magazines, directories

Battle's New Directory, 1822

Dalesman, March 1961

East Midlands Geographer. Department of Geography, University of Nottingham

History, Directory & Gazetteer of Yorkshire, Vol. II: East & North Ridings, published in 1823

Hull & District Directories, various years from 1803

Humber Light, the Journal of the Hull & District Branch of the World Ship Society

Lincolnshire & Humberside Transport Review

Lloyd's Registers 1884–1950

LNER Magazine

Mercantile Navy Lists

Paddle Wheels, the journal of the Paddle Steamer Preservation Society

Railway Chronicle

Sealink News 1971–1981

Sea Breezes, January 1966

Ships Monthly

A full account of John Ellerthorpe's life can be found at Hessle Local History Society's website https://sites.google.com/site/johnellerthorpeheroofthehumber/home

The book *Hero of the Humber,* by the Rev. Henry Woodcock, can be read online at www.gutenberg.org

Website

A detailed survey of craft operating on the Humber can be found on the website: www.humberpacketboats.co.uk

The author would be pleased to receive further details, corrections or additional information regarding the Humber ferries. He can be contacted via the publisher.